UNREPRESSED UNCONSCIOUS, IMPLICIT MEMORY, AND CLINICAL WORK

UNREPRESSED UNCONSCIOUS, IMPLICIT MEMORY, AND CLINICAL WORK

edited by

Giuseppe Craparo and Clara Mucci

KARNAC

First published in 2017 by
Karnac Books Ltd
118 Finchley Road, London NW3 5HT

British Library Cataloguing in Publication Data

A C.I.P. for this book is available from the British Library

  ISBN 978 1 78220 248 6

Edited, designed and produced by The Studio Publishing Services Ltd
www.publishingservicesuk.co.uk
email: studio@publishingservicesuk.co.uk

Printed in Great Britain

www.karnacbooks.com

CONTENTS

Giuseppe Craparo, PhD, is a psychologist and psychoanalytically orientated psychotherapist practising in Enna and Catania, Italy. He is Assistant Professor of Psychology at the Kore University of Enna, and a member of the following associations: the American Psychological Association, the Italian Psychological Association, the Associazione di Studi Psicoanalitici (Member Society of the International Federation of Psychoanalytic Societies), and the Italian Society of Psychological Assessment. He is the author of several articles and chapters on psychoanalysis, psychopathology, and trauma. Among his books are: *Trauma e psicopatologia. Un approccio evolutivo-relazionale* (with Vincenzo Caretti, Astrolabio, 2008), *Memorie traumatiche e mentalizzazione* (with Vincenzo Caretti and Adriano Schimmenti, Astrolabio, 2013), *Il disturbo post-traumatico da stress* (Carocci, 2013), *Inconsci, coscienza e desiderio. L'incertezza in psicoanalisi* (Carocci, 2015).

Peter Fonagy, PhD, FBA, FMedSci, OBE, is Freud Memorial Professor of Psychoanalysis and Head of the Research Department of Clinical, Educational and Health Psychology at UCL, Chief Executive of the Anna Freud National Centre for Children and Families, Consultant to the Child and Family Program at the Menninger Department of Psychiatry and Behavioral Sciences at Baylor College of Medicine, and holds visiting professorships at Yale and Harvard Medical Schools. His clinical and research interests centre on issues of early attachment relationships, social cognition, borderline personality disorder, and violence. A major focus of his contribution has been an innovative research-based dynamic therapeutic approach, called Mentalization-Based Treatment, which was developed in collaboration with a number of clinical sites in both the UK and the USA. Professor Fonagy has published over 450 papers, 250 chapters, and has authored or co-authored 18 books. He has received honours and awards from around the world for his contributions to the fields of psychology and psychoanalysis.

Howard Levine is a member of the Contemporary Freudian Society and the Psychoanalytic Institute of New England, East (PINE), a former member of the Board of Directors of the IPA, the editorial Board of the IJP and Psychoanalytic Inquiry, and in private practice in Brookline, Massachusetts. He has authored many articles, book chapters, and reviews on psychoanalytic process and technique, intersubjectivity, the treatment of primitive personality disorders, and the consequences and treatment of early trauma and childhood sexual abuse. He is the editor of *Adult Analysis and Childhood Sexual Abuse* (Analytic Press, 1990), co-editor of *Growth and Turbulence in the Container/Contained* (with Lawrence Brown, Routledge, 2013), *Unrepresented States and the Construction of Meaning* (with Gail Reed and Dominique Scarfone, Karnac, 2013), *Responses to Freud's Screen Memories Paper* (with Gail Reed, Karnac, 2014), *The Wilfred Bion Tradition* (with Giuseppe Civitarese, Karnac, 2015), and *Bion in Brazil* (with Jose Junqueira de Mattos and Gisele Brito, Karnac, forthcoming).

Giovanni Liotti, MD, is a psychiatrist and psychotherapist, and currently teaches in the APC Post-graduate School of Psychotherapy, Rome, and in the Post-graduate School of Psychotherapy of the Salesian University, Rome. His interest in the clinical applications of attachment theory, first expressed in a book co-authored with V. F. Guidano, (*Cognitive Processes and Emotional Disorders*, Guilford Press, 1983), focused on the links between trauma, dissociation, and attachment disorganisation in the past thirty years. For his contributions on this theme, Dr Liotti received the Pierre Janet Writing Award (The International Society for the Study of Trauma and Dissociation, 2005) and the International Mind and Brain Award (University of Turin, 2006).

Mauro Mancia was Professor Emeritus of Neurophysiology at the University of Milan and a training analyst of the Italian Psychoanalytic Society. His major interests were in the link between neuroscientific knowledge and psychoanalytic theories of mind. He has written extensively on the subjects of narcissism (Narcisismo, Boringhieri, 2010), on dreams, sleep, memory, and the unconscious. Among his books is: *Feeling the Words. Neuropsychoanalytic Understanding of Memory and the Unconscious* (Routledge, 2007).

Clara Mucci is a psychoanalytically orientated psychotherapist (SIPP, Italian Society of Psychoanalytic Psychotherapy) practising in Milan and Pescara. She is Full Professor of Clinical Psychology at the University of Chieti, where she has also been Full Professor of English Literature and English Renaissance Drama (Shakespeare). She received a PhD from Emory University on literature and psycho-analysis, a Doctorate on English Studies from the University of Genoa, and then retrained in clinical psychology, specialising in borderline disorders, as a Fellow at the Personality Disorders Institute, New York, directed by Otto Kernberg. She is the author of several monographs on Shakespeare, psychoanalysis, and literary theory, and most recently she has published on trauma, psychoanalysis, intergenerational trans-mission, and the Shoah (*Il dolore estremo*, Borla, 2008; *Beyond Individual and Collective Trauma*, Karnac, 2013; *Trauma e perdono*, Cortina, 2014).

Allan N. Schore is on the clinical faculty of the Department of Psychiatry and Biobehavioral Sciences, UCLA David Geffen School of Medicine. He is author of four seminal volumes, *Affect Regulation and the Origin of the Self*, *Affect Dysregulation and Disorders of the Self*, *Affect Regulation and the Repair of the Self*, and *The Science of the Art of Psychotherapy*, as well as co-author of *Evolution, Early Experience, and Human Development* and numerous articles and chapters in multiple disciplines, including developmental neuroscience, psychiatry, psy-choanalysis, developmental psychology, attachment theory, trauma studies, behavioural biology, clinical psychology, and clinical social work. His Regulation Theory, grounded in developmental neuro-science and developmental psychoanalysis, focuses on the origin, psychopathogenesis, and psychotherapeutic treatment of the early forming subjective implicit self. He is past Editor of the acclaimed *Norton Series on Interpersonal Neurobiology*, and a reviewer on the editorial staff of more than 45 journals across a number of scientific and clinical disciplines. He is a member of the Society of Neuro-science, and of the American Psychological Association's Divisions of Neuropsychology and of Psychoanalysis. He has received a number of honours for his work, including an Award for Outstanding Contributions to Practice in Trauma Psychology from the Division of Trauma Psychology and the Scientific Award from the Division of Psychoanalysis of the American Psychological Association, Honorary Membership by the American Psychoanalytic Association, and the Reiss-Davis Child Study Center Award for outstanding contributions to Child and Adolescent Mental Health.

Mark Solms is Director of Neuropsychology at the University of Cape Town and Groote Schuur Hospital. He is a member of the British Psychoanalytical Society, President of the South African Psycho-analytical Association, Director of the Science Department of the American Psychoanalytic Association, and Research Chair of the International Psychoanalytical Association. He has co-chaired the International Neuropsychoanalysis Society (with Jaak Panksepp) since 2000. He was awarded Honorary Membership of the New York Psychoanalytic Society in 1998, elected member of the Academy of Science of South Africa in 2013, and made Honorary Fellow of the American College of Psychiatrists in 2016. Other awards include the George Sarton Medal of the Rijksuniversiteit Gent, Belgium (1996), the Arnold Pfeffer Prize of the New York Psychoanalytic Institute (2008), and the Sigourney Prize (2011). He was Founding Editor of the journal *Neuropsychoanalysis* and is on the editorial boards of many other journals. He has published widely in both neuroscientific and psychoanalytic journals, including *Cortex, Neuropsychologia, Trends in Cognitive Science,* and *Behavioral & Brain Sciences.* He is also frequently published in general interest journals such as *Scientific American.* He has published more than 350 articles and chapters, and six books. *The Neuropsychology of Drea*ms (1997) was a landmark contribution to the field and his book with Oliver Turnbull, *The Brain and the Inner World* (2002), was a best-seller and was translated into twelve languages. His selected works were published in 2015 under the title *The Feeling Brain.* He is the authorised editor and translator of the forthcoming *Revised Standard Edition of the Complete Psychological Works of Sigmund Freud* (24 volumes) and the *Complete Neuroscientific Works of Sigmund Freud* (4 volumes).

Consciousness, mentalization, and attachment

Peter Fonagy

The notion of the unrepressed unconscious has been a major psycho-analytic puzzle since the inception of the discipline. Psychoanalytic thinking about the nature of consciousness has always implicitly distinguished between a non-conscious and a dynamically uncon-scious mental content, whether marked by distinctions such as repressed *vs.* unrepressed, preconscious *vs.* unconscious or, using Sandler's three-box model, past *vs.* present unconscious. Where the line is drawn, how the distinctions are made, might depend more on the subject matter on which the scholar is focused, which in turn calls for particular metapsychological models.

This excellent book attempts to map this somewhat controversial field and addresses the dichotomy from six distinct perspectives that share the wish to integrate contemporary neuroscience with psycho-analytic perspectives, using the clinical setting as the primary con-straint on theory-building. In this Foreword to a unique and outstand-ing contribution by the major scholars in this field, I can do no more than set out the distinction between the Freudian and current approaches to the dichotomy and introduce our own rather limited perspective (Fonagy & Allison, 2016), which has the advantage of drawing on the past work of many of the contributors to this volume.

Like the neuroscientists and attachment theorists contributing to this work, I would favour a psychoanalytically informed reconsideration of the nature of consciousness, which could shed light on the distinction between an "unconscious part of the mind" (the base of the Freudian "iceberg", which, as this book amply illustrates, is not only accepted but entirely endorsed by modern neuroscience) and the unconscious with which psychoanalysis tends to concern itself—the thoughts and feelings generally referred to as being "dynamically unconscious". Mark Solms (1997) provided a comprehensive review of Freud's struggle with the concept and nature of what is available to phenomenal scrutiny and what is hidden from, or inaccessible to, it. The focus of Freud's interest was always the unconscious. Freud, time and again, assures us that consciousness is a given. In *An Outline of Psycho-Analysis*, Freud (1940a) writes,

> We know two kinds of things about what we call our psyche (or mental life): firstly, its bodily organ and scene of action, the brain (or nervous system) and, on the other hand, our acts of consciousness, which are immediate data and cannot be further explained by any sort of description. (p. 144);

". . . if anyone speaks of consciousness we know immediately and from our most personal experience what is meant by it" (p. 157); and "There is no need to characterize what we call 'conscious': it is the same as the consciousness of philosophers and of everyday opinion" (p. 159). In the *New Introductory Lectures on Psycho-Analysis* (Freud, 1933a), he says, "There is no need to discuss what is to be called conscious: it is removed from all doubt" (p. 70).

Freud explored present preoccupations, memories, current or recent physical sensations, descriptions and physical manifestations of emotions, and more in pursuit of associative networks that hint at the mental states that consciousness hides and disguises. Historically, this approach to consciousness has characterised the psychoanalytic discipline. However, the chapters in this volume suggest that seeing consciousness merely as a route to concerns outside awareness underestimates its role in the dynamics of mind and clinical psychoanalysis.

In his *Outline*, Freud (1940a) did acknowledge the mysteriousness of consciousness, stating that "The starting-point for this investigation is provided by a fact without parallel, which defies all explanation or description – the fact of consciousness" (p. 157). Clearly, the unconscious mind cannot be explicated without reference to consciousness. In "The resistances to psycho-analysis", Freud (1925e) wrote,

> what is mental is in itself unconscious and . . . being conscious is only a quality, which may or may not accrue to a particular mental act and the withholding of which may perhaps alter that act in no other respect. (p. 216)

Freud thought that mental processes were "only made conscious by the functioning of special organs" (Freud, 1924f, p. 198). The association of consciousness with perception leads Freud to combine them most of the time in a single system (Pcpt.–Cs.). (See also Freud, 1900a, p. 574; 1915e, p. 171; 1917a, p. 143; 1923b, p. 18; 1925e, p. 216; 1939a, p. 97; 1940b, pp. 283, 286.)

It has been suggested that Freud failed to elaborate his theory of self-awareness (Fonagy & Allison, 2016; Solms, 1997). Consciousness for Freud is consciousness of self, for this feature was its distinguishing characteristic:

> . . . a consciousness of which its own possessor knows nothing is something very different from a consciousness belonging to another person, and it is questionable whether such a consciousness, lacking, as it does, its most important characteristic, deserves any discussion at all. (Freud, 1915e, p. 170)

The Freudian view is that mental activity is unconscious in itself, and that consciousness is not a proportion of mental activity but, rather, a reflection or perception of it, and that it represents this process in an "incomplete and untrustworthy" fashion (Solms, 1997, p. 684).

However, Freud implicitly recognised that coming to know the unconscious part of the mind is not possible without approaching it via consciousness. "How are we to arrive at a knowledge of the unconscious? It is, of course, only as something conscious that we know it, after it has undergone transformation or translation into something conscious" (Freud, 1915e, p. 166). Yet, the idea that consciousness was the epistemological bedrock for explorations of the unconscious was probably not fully accepted by Freud. Husserl (1936) understood that what is unconscious can be discovered only on the basis of making consciousness the prior subject matter, and suggested

that the science of the unconscious would be a failure because it did
not take the understanding of consciousness as its point of departure.
I would like to touch briefly on Solms' (1997) radical interpretation
of Freud's view that both external sensory self-awareness and internal
states of mind were "perceived". Solms (1997) wrote,

> When you perceive the same apparatus through an internal sensory
> modality, you perceive it . . . as a "state of mind" . . . These two percep-
> tual realizations of yourself are on exactly the same conceptual level
> . . . although one is described as objective and the other as subjective
> . . . The only difference between them is that one represents the portion
> of reality that is "you" in an external perceptual modality, while the
> other represents "you" in an internal perceptual modality. (p. 699)

Thus, for Solms, the contents of consciousness are the data of the
senses, the data of memory and the inward appreciation of affects,
and the process is the same process that produces sensation and
perception, thought and affect. If consciousness results simply from
more complex integration of the same basic processes that produce
other mental phenomena and requires no new neural processes, then
major implications follow.

The Danish Husserlian phenomenological philosopher Dan
Zahavi (1999, 2005) has severely criticised the circularity of the "reflection theory" of self-awareness that suggests that self-consciousness
entails an act of reflective consciousness reflecting on itself by means
of a second act of reflective consciousness. Reflection described in this
way presupposes a pre-reflective act of consciousness in which self-
consciousness is anchored—it needs to be experienced if it is to be
perceived. Experience, which is supposed to be reflected upon,
already entails consciousness, so how was experience of mental states
achieved? Zahavi argues that it is improbable that our awareness of
ourselves entails exactly the same mechanism as our perception of
external objects. The circularity of "reflection theory" is due to its failure to specify a mechanism whereby mental phenomena become
available to internally directed perception.

Perhaps Freud should not have tried to circumvent phenomenology when discussing consciousness[1] because it may enable us to
distinguish between the unconscious of neuroscience (the *implicit
unconscious*, which is the concern of this volume) and our dynamic
sense of the unconscious (the "seething cauldron"), which Liz Allison

and I have called the *psychoanalytic unconscious* (Fonagy & Allison, 2016). The implicit unconscious lacks the properties of consciousness, but, in order to make sense of this and similar statements, we need to define these properties. Phenomenologists have conceptualised these in terms of the *inner horizon* within an object, which separates what is manifest or apparent about it from a latent field of possibilities, *coherence*, which is necessary to enable us to consciously perceive an object as such, and *intentionality*, which is the central structure of an experience—its quality of being directed toward, or being about, something.[2] The unique feature of consciousness from a phenomenological perspective is this striving for wholeness or, as Heidegger's ontological approach would have it, "Being", a certain quality of three-dimensionality, the experience that can be "walked around". Many psychoanalytic views of consciousness, of course, also stress the notion of bringing coherence and integration, particularly Kleinian–Bionian psychoanalysis with its emphasis on the cycling of the Ps↔D positions.[3] An act of consciousness can be viewed as an intentional synthesis of sensory givens into a coherent whole. Perception is a much more complex process than we tend to assume and when it comes to the perception of internal events, the challenge is even greater.

With colleagues, I have tried to describe the interpersonal developmental processes leading to the creation of psychic reality (Allen & Fonagy, 2006; Allen et al., 2008; Bateman & Fonagy, 2006; Fonagy et al., 2007; Fonagy et al., 2002) and we have stressed that internal representations of their constitutional states do not arise from within the infant; rather, the infant internalises the carer's visible or otherwise sensorially available representation to form a representation of the self. The infant needs closeness to another human being who, via contingent marked mirroring actions, can create an external image congruent with the infant's internal state; once internalised, this image serves as a representation of it. This initially dyadic consciousness of affect facilitates the emergence of a symbolic representational system for affective states, assists in developing affect regulation and selective attention,[4] but is linked not to consciousness but to a quality of representations captured by phenomenological descriptions as coherent or possessing an intentional quality. For the normal development of phenomenal experience (Sandler's distinction between the mental representation and the psychic structure that generates it is relevant here), the child needs to be exposed to a mind that has his mind in mind, reflecting and enabling him to reflect on his embryonic conscious intentions without overwhelming him.

The converse of this developmental assumption is that internal states that are not confirmed by contingent congruent responses from the object world will not achieve experiential status either consciously or unconsciously. It is the infant's and child's unmirrored, unreflected internal states that make up the seething cauldron of Freud's conceptualisation of the id. Sexual and aggressive impulses come to be major organisers of unconscious states of mind because they are unmirrored. In our view, the key role played by sexuality in accounts of the unconscious is not due to an inherent conflict between sexuality and adaptation to a civilised world necessitating repression, but a consequence of the bizarre human condition that infantile sexuality is an internal state that is not to be reflected on and mirrored by the attentive carer (Fonagy, 2008). The mother inevitably fails to mirror the infant's sexual excitement. Infantile aggression is another state of mind that is unlikely to be adequately mirrored by carers and can consequently become part of a residue of what, following Bion's (1963) thinking, we might refer to as "unmetabolised" internal states. But the vast bulk of what is not mirrored is what cannot be mirrored. This may be because it is not sufficiently coherent to be mirrored by another mind. It is too disconnected, insufficiently linked to what has gone before or what is evident in the present. Or it may be something that generates too much "unpleasure", triggering a biologically formed reluctance in the object to respond contingently (as could be the case with sexual excitement and aggression). It is the chaotic, the fragmentary, the destructive that are not re-presented to the child, and these are the emergent characteristics[5] of the repressed unconscious. Our unmirrored experiences will always remain unnameable and unconscious because categorisation and meaning arise out of the mirroring of experience by an attentive adult. The unconscious mind of our psychoanalytic metapsychology is a repository for internal states that remain unmanageable because they were never mirrored and, therefore, never acquired a symbolic or second-order representation. These ideas are felt to be inherently alien because they are internal experiences—that is, they are felt to be sitting within the self, but can be the object of meaningful experience (Being, in Heidegger's sense) only when they are externalised and felt as if they belonged to the other.

The assumption of the relational (or co-constructed nature of) consciousness might help to clarify an aspect of the subject matter of this volume. The unrepressed unconscious is that part of the non-phenomenologically accessible mind that has the potential for relational representation, of being mirrored or contingently responded to even in the absence of such shared experience. The pre-conscious can be conceptualised as designating mental contents that could become conscious with the help of the searchlight of attention. In our formulation, that searchlight is not guided from within. Rather, it is guided by another mind focusing on the mental world of the subject. It is the process of interaction and the simultaneous experience of thought or feeling that creates the potential for phenomenal experience. The unrepressed unconscious awaits such external validation. The repressed unconscious waits in vain as, under normal circumstances, the agent cannot contingently respond to give meaning to the experience.

Notes

1. The philosophical approach placing phenomenology at its centre (Heidegger, 1959; Husserl, 1936; Sartre, 1957) has always had considerable appeal for psychoanalysts (e.g., Laing, 1982; Loewald, 1965) but it has undoubtedly become more popular with the rise of the relational school of psychoanalysis (Bromberg, 1998; Stern, 1997). The key questions that phenomenologists concern themselves with around the nature of knowledge, truth, and understanding are also the central questions that the psychoanalysts try to answer, both in relation to the essential subject matter of their discipline (the science of the unconscious) and the phenomenological experience with which an individual patient presents them.

2. As Sartre (1957) phrased it: "intentionality is what makes up the very subjectivity of subjects" (p. 49).

3. We should note, however, that the notion of consciousness as intentional means that we cannot conceive of a "container" that houses consciousness, and it is, therefore, probably not compatible with the Bionian conceptualisation of the process of thinking (Bion, 1959).

4. The distinction we have made between primary and second-order representation may be similar to Edelman's (2004) elaboration of primary and higher not-order consciousness. Edelman considers the latter to be restricted to self-reflective ("reflective cognizing"; Kim,

2005) humans capable of turning consciousness back on itself, and bringing with it the capacity to delay judgement and refrain from responding immediately to environmental cues. There is superficial similarity between these ideas and Sartre's distinctions between "pre-reflective" and "reflective" consciousness, and consciousness and "knowledge"—only the latter being accompanied by "experience". The suggestion has also much in common with Damasio's (1999) sophisticated and beautifully argued statements about consciousness, such as: "The secret of making consciousness may well be this: the plotting of a relationship between any object and the organism becomes the feeling of a feeling" (p. 313). In pointing to a "feeling of a feeling", Damasio ascribes consciousness to a second-order state of the brain being in possession of information regarding a first-order feeling state (knowing about being the feeling of the thereby known). Damasio's conceptualisation of consciousness is as the interaction of the "self-system" and "non-self system" with very rapid shifts back and forth between "self-system" representations and the representations of sensory images (see also Edelman, 1989).

5. Emergent characteristics are ones that may be causally explained by the behaviour of elements of a system but are not the property of any of the individual elements of the system, or the summation of the properties of the elements (e.g., the liquid quality of water is explained by the combination of hydrogen and oxygen atoms into the water molecule, but neither hydrogen nor oxygen is a liquid at room temperature).

References

Allen, J. G., & Fonagy, P. (2006). *Handbook of Mentalization-based Treatment*. New York: Wiley.

Allen, J. G., Fonagy, P., & Bateman, A. W. (2008). *Mentalizing in Clinical Practice*. Washington, DC: American Psychiatric Press.

Bateman, A. W., & Fonagy, P. (2006). *Mentalization-based Treatment for Borderline Personality Disorder: A Practical Guide*. Oxford: Oxford University Press.

Bion, W. R. (1959). Attacks on linking. *International Journal of Psycho-analysis, 40*: 308–315.

Bion, W. R. (1963). *Elements of Psycho-Analysis*. London: Heinemann.

Bromberg, P. M. (1998). *Standing in the Spaces*. Hillsdale, NJ: Analytic Press.

Damasio, A. (1999). *The Feeling of What Happens: Body and Emotion in the Making of Consciousness*. New York: Harcourt Brace.

Edelman, G. M. (1989). *The Remembered Present: A Biological Theory of Consciousness*. New York: Basic Books.

Edelman, G. M. (2004). *Wider than the Sky: The Phenomenal Gift of Consciousness*. New Haven: Yale University Press.

Fonagy, P. (2008). A genuinely developmental theory of sexual enjoyment and its implications for psychoanalytic technique. *Journal of the American Psychoanalytic Association, 56*: 11–36.

Fonagy, P., & Allison, E. (2016). Psychic reality and the nature of consciousness. *International Journal of Psychoanalysis, 97*: 5–24.

Fonagy, P., Gergely, G., & Target, M. (2007). The parent–infant dyad and the construction of the subjective self. *Journal of Child Psychology and Psychiatry, 48*: 288–328.

Fonagy, P., Gergely, G., Jurist, E., & Target, M. (2002). *Affect Regulation, Mentalization, and the Development of the Self*. New York: Other Press.

Freud, S. (1900a). *The Interpretation of Dreams. S. E., 4–5*. London: Hogarth.

Freud, S. (1915e). The unconscious. *S. E., 14*: 161–215. London: Hogarth.

Freud, S. (1917a). A difficulty in the path of psycho-analysis. *S. E., 17*: 135–143. London: Hogarth.

Freud, S. (1923b). *The Ego and the Id. S. E., 19*: 3–66. London: Hogarth.

Freud, S. (1924f). A short account of psycho-analysis. *S. E., 19*: 191–212. London: Hogarth.

Freud, S. (1925e). The resistances to psycho-analysis. *S. E., 19*: 213–222. London: Hogarth.

Freud, S. (1933a). *New Introductory Lectures on Psycho-analysis. S. E., 22*. London: Hogarth.

Freud, S. (1939a). *Moses and Monotheism. S. E., 23*: 3–137. London: Hogarth.

Freud, S. (1940a). *An Outline of Psycho-Analysis. S. E., 23*: 141–207. London: Hogarth.

Freud, S. (1940b). Some elementary lessons in psycho-analysis. *S. E., 23*: 279–286. London: Hogarth.

Heidegger, M. (1959). *An Introduction to Metaphysics*. New Haven, CT: Yale University Press.

Husserl, E. (1936). Fink's appendix on the problem of the "unconscious". In: *The Crisis of European Sciences and the Transcendental Phenomenology*. Evanston, IL: Northwestern University Press, 1970.

Kim, J. (2005). *Physicalism, or Something Near Enough*. Princeton, NJ: Princeton University Press.

Laing, R. D. (1982). *The Voice of Experience*. New York: Pantheon Books.

Loewald, H. W. (Ed.) (1965). *Papers on Psychoanalysis*. New Haven, CT: Yale University Press, 1980.

Sartre, J.-P. (1957). *The Transcendence of the Ego*, F. Williams & R. Kirkpatrick (Trans.). New York: Hill and Wang.

Solms, M. (1997). What is consciousness? *Journal of the American Psychoanalytic Association*, 45: 681–703.

Stern, D. B. (1997). *Unformulated Experience: From Dissociation to Imagination in Psychoanalysis*. Hillsdale, NJ: Analytic Press.

Zahavi, D. (1999). *Self-awareness and Alterity: A Phenomenological Investigation*. Evanston, IL: Northwestern University Press.

Zahavi, D. (2005). *Subjectivity and Selfhood: Investigating the First-Person Perspective*. Cambridge, MA: Bradford Books.

Introduction

Giuseppe Craparo and Clara Mucci

What do we mean by "unrepressed unconscious"? Are there differences between the so-called "unrepressed unconscious" identified by some authors, and the "repressed unconscious", which has generally been the object of the psychoanalytical investigations of theoreticians and clinicians, starting with Freud himself? How do we understand the relationship of this "unrepressed unconscious" with the modes of implicit memory? What is the role of the unrepressed unconscious in the most recent clinical work? These are some of the questions the contributors to this volume have tried to debate and exemplify.

As is well known, Sigmund Freud was the first author to use the construct of unrepressed unconscious in relation to the emotional world, in both *The Interpretation of Dreams* (1900a) and "The unconscious" (1915e). On the relationship between the repressed and the unconscious, he maintained that "the *Ucs.* does not coincide with the repressed; it is still true that all that is repressed is *Ucs.*, but not all that is *Ucs.* is repressed" (Freud, 1923b, p. 17). According to Freud, the contents of the unrepressed unconscious are related to the emotional traces of childhood experiences, that he called "thing-representations" (*Sachvorstellung*). This concept proposed by Freud "consists in the cathexis, if not of the direct memory-images of the thing, at least of remoter memory-traces derived from these" (1915e, p. 201).

Wilfred Bion proposed a construct similar to that of unrepressed unconscious, when he wrote about "wild thoughts", or thoughts without a thinker. On the other hand, "wild thoughts" are thoughts in which "there is no possibility of being able to trace immediately any kind of ownership or even any sort of way of being aware of the genealogy of that particular thought" (1997, p. 27).

In this regard, it is also interesting to consider the interpretation given by Franco De Masi (2015), who used the term "emotional–receptive unconscious" in order to describe a specific psychic functioning "present in every human being, except when distorted or weakened in those cases of psychic illness" (De Masi, 2015, p. 99). According to this author the notion of emotional unconscious exists alongside that of repressed unconscious, representing "the necessary condition for existence and functioning of the dynamic unconscious" (2015, p. 101). If, in neurotic patients, the emotional unconscious works as a receptive organ of preverbal and presymbolic emotional experiences which are secondarily symbolised, in non-neurotic patients, we can observe, in contrast, an impairment of the emotional–unconscious, characterised by "states or phenomena that are 'not yet' or are 'proto'-psychic" (Reed et al., 2013, p. 6).

Other contemporary authors, included in this collection, such as Mark Solms, Mauro Mancia, Giovanni Liotti, Allan Schore, and ourselves highlight the relevance of implicit memory in normal functioning as well as in psychopathology, starting with the emotional regulation and dysregulation carried on between infant and carer, which connects the right brain of the one to the right brain of the other.

In his chapter, Mark Solms underlines the necessity of a revision of Freud's model of the unconscious on the basis of recent neuroscientific findings, which are: (1) it is necessary to consider Ucs. and id as two different mental systems; (2) the id is the fount of the affective, non-declarative consciousness; (3) implicit memory is related to this affective consciousness (called also primary consciousness), to be distinguished from system Cs. (or secondary conscience); (4) an important consequence of this interpretation is that implicit memory is related to the id. According to Solms, "the deep structures that generate consciousness are not only responsible for the level (quantity) but also for the core *content* (quality) of consciousness" (p. 6, this volume). Differently from reflexive or secondary consciousness, primary consciousness is characterised by states rather than images related to perception of external objects. The upper brainstem structures that generate consciousness do not map our external senses; they map the internal state of the (visceral, autonomic) body. This mapping of the internal milieu generates not perceptual objects but, rather, the subject of perception. It generates the background state of being conscious. This is of paramount importance. We may picture this core quality of consciousness as the page upon which external perceptual objects are inscribed. The objects are always perceived by an already sentient subject. Affects are valenced states of the subject. These states are thought to represent the biological meaning of changing internal conditions (e.g., hunger, sexual arousal). When internal conditions favour survival and reproductive success, they feel "good"; when not, they feel "bad". This registers biological value, which is evidently what consciousness is for. It tells the subject how well it is doing. At this level of the brain, consciousness is closely tied to homeostasis" (p. 7 in this volume)

For Solms, the id is bonded with affective consciousness, and the contents of this mental system are not characterised by repressed representations, but by emotional states related to unrepressed unconscious.

Prior to his death, Mauro Mancia, in his well known writings of 2006, posits that the right hemisphere "is the seat of implicit memory" and he further observes that

the discovery of the implicit memory has extended the concept of the unconscious and supports the hypothesis that this is where the emotional and the affective, sometimes traumatic presymbolic and preverbal experiences of the primary infant–mother relations, are stored. (p. 83)

Considering the implicit memories of the earliest relational exchanges, Giovanni Liotti underlines how, under the rubric of unrepressed unconscious, go modalities of preverbal and pre-affective consciousness and specific early experiences implicitly remembered. He also stresses how, in the earliest phases of extra-uterine life, relational experiences are memorised at the implicit level as sub-symbolic representations (Wilma Bucci's term) of what we have come to refer to, after Bowlby, as internal working models (IWM) (Bowlby, 1969). "Implicit relational knowing may be conceived as a continuous articulation of various motivational systems that works outside of the reflective consciousness" (Liotti, p. 58 of this volume), "from the cradle to the grave" (Bowlby's expression, 1969). Liotti underlines how the explicit memories, both semantic and episodic, of attachment have been extensively and systematically studied in adults using a structured interview, the adult attachment interview. Forms of dissociations between implicit and explicit memories and forms of incoherent attributions of meaning are evident in adults whose mental states with regard to attachment are "dismissing" and "preoccupied/entangled", respectively. Liotti interestingly attributes these two forms of discrepancy between implicit and explicit memories of attachment to the influence of points of view verbally expressed by the carers and their own feelings towards the child. In disorganised attachment, "the implicit memories connected to the innate disposition of attachment and survival defence normally assume an integrated form because they are conceptualised in two different spheres of experience"—that is, danger on the one hand, and desire for comfort and protection, on the other (Liotti, p. 55 in this volume). But in disorganised attachment the two sets of experience are, indeed, both directed at the same person, therefore the sub-symbolic representation of the self–other connected to the innate disposition of attachment is dissociated from that of self with the same other connected to the disposition of defence for survival. As Kernberg and colleagues confirm (Kernberg et al., 2008), forms of dissociation and splitting can be used to indicate the lack of integration between implicit representations of the self and of the carer in disorganised attachment. But, as Liotti very cogently underlines, "the cause and the psychic mechanism at the origin of this type of disintegration, however, differ significantly if we adopt the classical drive theory or the evolutionistic multi-motivational theory" (see p. 65 in this volume). Instead of seeing this disintegration as the result of the effect of two different emotions, desire and destructive aggression (as a Kleinian view would lead us to point at), in this evolutionary multi-motivational perspective, Liotti (with Main & Hesse, 1990) considers fear without solution as the pivot around which multiple affects turn: desire for help and comfort, on the one hand, rage, sadness, and helplessness, on the other.

For Allan Schore, the implicit self is located in the right brain and is the basis of the functioning of the human unconscious. He argues that "the early developing right brain generates the implicit self, an early unrepressed unconscious nucleus of the self" (p. 74 in this volume) and that "the current, expanding body of knowledge of the right hemisphere suggests a major alteration in the conceptualisation of the Freudian unconscious, the internal structural system that processes information at nonconscious levels" (2003a, p. 269). Affective phenomena cannot be understood without an understanding and consideration of affect regulation between mother and child and, for Schore, "the emotion-processing right mind is the neurobiological substrate of Freud's dynamic unconscious . . ." (Schore, 1999, p. 53). The mother as the regulator of arousal, through the right brain inter-mediation, contributes to the further self-regulation for the child; the process of this intersubjective neurobiological exchange is inscribed in implicit–procedural memory in the early developing right brain (Schore, 2003a, p. 222). Schore finally suggests that this transfer of non-conscious affect is mediated by a right amygdala–right amygdala communication. This somatic embedding of the unconscious is perfectly in line with both Freud's statement that "the unconscious is the proper mediator between the somatic and the mental" (Freud 1960, "Letter to Groddeck", 5 June, 1917) and the idea that the drive is, as we have said above, at the confine between the mental and the somatic. Moving towards psychotherapy, Schore underlines the role of implicit affect in so far as "unconscious processing of emotional stimuli is specifically associated with activation of the right and not the left hemisphere" (p. 77 in this volume).

Integrating both Allan Schore's and Giovanni Liotti's conclusions, Clara Mucci underlines how the orbitofrontal cortex, that is, the central mechanism of affect regulation in the dual hemisphere brain, accesses memory functions by implicit processing. So, that which Freud terms "preconscious" (Schore, 2003a, p. 272) is directly influenced by this regulatory activity that from external regulation becomes internal and self-regulated. The orbitofrontal cortex also exerts an essential role in co-ordinating internal states of the organism and the various representational processes, similar to the IWM (internal working models) as explained by Bowlby (1969). In the case of early relational trauma, that is, a severe dystony between the systems, and the right brains of mother and child, they might lose the possibility of integration so that dysregulated somatic states are created, which, in turn, is coherent with current day understanding of how personality disorders develop as a result of dysregulation of affect and related pathologies (Schore, 1994, 2003a, 2003b). In other words, early trauma and insecure forms of attachment, including disorganised attachment, are encoded in implicit memory.

In his chapter, Giuseppe Craparo defines two different mental processes (transference–countertransference and enactment), as related to repressed and unrepressed unconscious, respectively, present in the analytic field. In accordance with Freud's interpretation, the author suggests that transference involves the patient's past and its re–evocation under the form of a psychic acting out in the relation with the analyst. Craparo clarifies the nature of *mise en scène* of the transference–countertransference, in contrast with enactment, which assumes the characteristics of a dyadic dissociative process the patient makes use of, through his/her relationship with the analyst, to control aspects of the self that are inaccessible to reflective functioning. According to this author, in contrast with transference–countertransference that is supported by acting out, enactment is supported by projective identification which is the psychic mechanism through which the traumatic emotions present in the patient's unrepressed unconscious (disorganised) are conveyed to the analyst's unrepressed unconscious (well organised).

References

Bion, W. R. (1997). *Taming Wild Thoughts*. London: Karnac.
Bowlby, J. (1969). *Attachment and Loss*. London: Hogarth Press.
De Masi, F. (2015). *Working with Difficult Patients*. London: Karnac.
Freud, S. (1900a). *The Interpretation of Dreams*. S. E., 4–5. London: Hogarth.
Freud, S. (1915e). The unconscious. *S. E., 14*: 166–204. London: Hogarth.
Freud, S. (1923b). *The Ego and the Id*. S. E., 19: 3–66. London: Hogarth.
Freud, S. (1960). *Letters, 1873–1939*. New York: Basic Books.
Kernberg, O. F., Diamond, D., Yeomans, F. E., Clarkin, J. F., & Levy, K. N. (2008). Mentalization and attachment in borderline patients in transference focused psychotherapy. In: E. Jurist, A. Slade, & S. Bergner (Eds.), *Mind to Mind: Infant Research, Neuroscience, and Psychoanalysis* (pp. 167–198). New York: Other Press.
Main, M., & Hesse, E. (1990). Parents' unresolved traumatic experiences are related to infant disorganized attachment status: is frightened and/or frightening parental behavior the linking mechanism? In: M. T. Greenberg, D. Cicchetti, & E. M. Cunnings (Eds.), *Attachment in the*

Preschool Years: Theory, Research, Intervention. Chicago, IL: University of Chicago Press.

Mancia, M. (2006a). Implicit memory and the unrepressed unconscious: how they surface in the transference and in the dream. In: M. Mancia (Ed.), *Psychoanalysis and Neuroscience* (pp. 97–124). Milan: Springer.

Mancia, M. (2006b). Implicit memory and early unrepressed unconscious: their role in the therapeutic process (how the neurosciences can contribute to psychoanalysis. *International Journal of Psychoanalysis, 87*: 83–103.

Reed, G. S., Levine, H. B., & Scarfone, D. (2013). Introduction. In: H. B. Levine, G. S. Reed, & D. Scarfone (Eds.), *Unrepresented States and the Construction of Meaning: Clinical and Theoretical Contributions* (pp. 3–17). London: Karnac.

Schore, A. N. (1994). *Affect Regulation and the Origin of the Self. The Neurobiology of Emotional Development*. Hillsdale, NJ: Lawrence Erlbaum.

Schore, A. N. (1999). Commentary on emotions: neuropsychoanalytic views. *Neuropsychoanalysis, 1*: 49–55.

Schore, A. N. (2003a). *Affect Regulation and the Repair of the Self*. New York: W. W. Norton.

Schore, A. N. (2003b). *Affect Regulation and the Disorders of the Self*. New York: W. W. Norton.

CHAPTER ONE

"The unconscious" in psychoanalysis and neuroscience: an integrated approach to the cognitive unconscious*

Mark Solms

U sing Freud's (1915e) essay on "The unconscious" as my point of departure, I endeavour in this chapter to update Freud's classical metapsychology in the light of recent developments in cognitive and affective neuroscience. In doing so, my effort is to integrate Freud's concept of repression with contemporary notions of the cognitive—unrepressed—unconscious. My arguments are set out in eight sections.

Most mental processes are unconscious

Freud wrote, "Our right to assume the existence of something mental that is unconscious and to employ that assumption for the purposes of our scientific work is disputed in many quarters" (p. 166). (Unless otherwise indicated, all Freud citations in this chapter are from "The unconscious", 1915e.)

* This is a heavily revised version of a chapter first published as Solms, M. (2013), "'The unconscious' in psychoanalysis and neuropsychology", in S. Akhtar & M. O'Neil (Eds.), *On Freud's "The Unconscious"*. London: Karnac, pp. 101–118. I would like to thank Dr Lois Oppenheim for her many helpful editorial suggestions.

This statement no longer holds true. In cognitive science today, Freud's insistence that mental processes are not necessarily conscious is widely accepted.

However, the consensus was not won by the arguments that Freud set out in his writings; it derived from a different research tradition. Where Freud cited clinical psychopathological evidence (and the psychopathology of everyday life), modern scientists independently postulated unconscious mental processes on the basis of neuropathological and experimental evidence. Foremost were observations of "split-brain" cases in which complex psychological responses (e.g., giggling) were elicited in patients by stimuli (e.g., pornographic images) that were exposed only to the isolated right hemisphere, of which the speaking left hemisphere was unaware (Galin, 1974). Also influential were reports of 'implicit memory'; that is, significant learning effects in amnesic cases, who, following bilateral mesial temporal lobectomy, had lost the ability to encode new *conscious* memories (Milner et al., 1968). Most striking were reports of "blindsight": cases of cortical blindness where the patients could localise visual stimuli of which they had no visual consciousness (Weiskrantz, 1990). These examples provided evidence of unconscious brain processes that could only be described as *mental*: unconscious embarrassment, unconscious remembering, and unconscious seeing. Such examples could easily be multiplied.

Experimental neurophysiological studies, the most celebrated of which was Libet's (1985) demonstration that voluntary motor acts are initiated at the level of supplementary motor area before a subject becomes aware of the decision to move (i.e., unconscious volition), have only strengthened the conviction. The general view today is just as Freud put it:

> that at any given moment consciousness includes only a small content, so that the greater part of what we call conscious knowledge must in any case be for very considerable periods of time in a state of latency, that is to say, of being psychically unconscious. (p. 167)

Bargh and Chartrand (1999), for example, estimate that consciousness plays a causal role in less than 5% of cognition. It is likewise now generally agreed that some mental processes are not merely "in a state of latency"; they are not "*capable* of becoming conscious" (Freud, p. 173). In other words, on the face of it, we all seem to agree that mental activity can be divided into three grades: what Freud called *Cs.*, *Pcs.*, and *Ucs.* (the conscious, not currently conscious, never conscious). At this point, however, modern notions of the unconscious begin to diverge from Freud's.

Unconscious processes are automatised cognition

It is true that Freud himself gradually came to recognise the inadequacy of his taxonomy, especially when he realised that many secondary processes, which obey the reality principle, are *never* conscious (Freud, 1923b). But the existence of unconscious ego processes is not disputed. What is controversial is the very idea of *dynamically* unconscious processes, that is, of all the things that Freud theorised under the headings of "repression" (and "resistance" and "censorship"). For Freud, tendentious mechanisms for the avoidance of unpleasure were pivotal to his conception of the unconscious, giving rise as they do to the active exclusion of certain mental contents from awareness. With relatively rare exceptions (e.g., Anderson et al., 2004; Ramachandran, 1994), the unconscious of contemporary cognitive scientists is theorised without any reference to psychodynamic processes; that is, the unconscious outside of psychoanalysis has no special relationship to affect. It is a purely cognitive entity. In contemporary science, the unconscious is a repository of automatic and automatised information processing and behavioural capacities (see Kihlstrom, 1996 for review). In cognitive neuroscience today there is, in short, no conception of the "id".

Consequently, it makes no sense for modern cognitive scientists to speak of the "special characteristics of the system Unconscious" as Freud did (1915e, p. 186). Although some neuropsychoanalysts draw attention to clinical neurological evidence and experimental psychological findings that confirm Freud's conception (e.g., Kaplan-Solms & Solms, 2000; Shevrin et al., 1996), cognitive scientists generally characterise unconscious mental systems in very different terms (e.g., Schacter & Tulving, 1994).

Typically, they do not even speak of "conscious" *vs.* "unconscious" systems; they refer instead to "explicit" *vs.* "implicit" and "declarative" *vs.* "non-declarative" systems. This difference, as we shall see, is not entirely accidental.

Consciousness is endogenous

It is important to draw attention to the fact, perhaps not widely recognised among psychoanalysts, that the behavioural neurosciences are just as riven by competing "schools" as psychoanalysis is. Most pertinent for our purposes is the division between *cognitive* and *affective* neuroscientists. Affective neuroscientists (e.g., Panksepp, 1998) bemoan the anthropocentrism of their cognitive colleagues, and their excessive focus on cortical processes. They argue that the cognitive approach overlooks the fundamental part played in mental life by phylogenetically ancient subcortical structures, and by the instinctual and affective processes associated with them. The affective neuroscience tradition, which relies more on animal than human research, can be traced back to Darwin's *The Expression of Emotions in Man and Animals* (1872) via Paul Maclean (1990) to the work of Jaak Panksepp (1998)—who actually coined the term "affective neuroscience".

What I said about cognitive neuroscientists still having no conception of the id does not apply to affective neuroscientists. What Freud called the "id" is the principle object of study in affective neuroscience (Solms & Panksepp, 2012). Panksepp identifies his research focus as the "primary processes" of the mammalian brain, the raw instinctual affects. He argues that these are evolutionarily conserved in humans, where they play a fundamental but largely unrecognised role in behaviour. His findings in this respect are, therefore, of the utmost relevance to psychoanalysts (see Panksepp & Biven, 2012).

Unlike his cognitive colleagues, Panksepp would have little difficulty agreeing with this statement of Freud's:

> The content of the *Ucs.* may be compared with an aboriginal population in the mind. If inherited mental formations exist in the human being – something analogous to instinct in animals – these constitute the nucleus of the *Ucs.* Later there is added to them what is discarded during childhood development as unserviceable; and this need not differ in nature from what is inherited. (p. 195)

But there is one crucial respect in which Panksepp and colleagues *would* disagree with this statement, and this pulls the carpet right out from under we psychoanalysts. He would not agree that the core content of what Freud first called the system *Ucs.* and subsequently called the id—that is, the deepest stratum of the mind—*is unconscious.* Panksepp, with Damasio (2010) and an increasing number of other scientists (e.g., Merker, 2009), would argue that the primitive brain structures that process what Freud called instincts[1]—"the stimuli originating from within the organism and reaching the mind, as a measure of the demand made upon the mind for work in consequence of its connection with the body" (1915c, p. 122)—are the *very fount of consciousness* (see Solms, 2013; Solms & Panksepp, 2012). According to these scientists, consciousness derives from the activating core of the upper brainstem, a very ancient arousal mechanism.

We have known this for many years. A mere decade after Freud's death, Moruzzi and Magoun (1949) first demonstrated that the state of being conscious, in the sense measured by EEG activation, is generated in a part of the brainstem thereafter called the "reticular activating system". Total destruction of exogenous sensory inputs had no impact on the endogenous consciousness-generating properties of the brainstem (e.g., sleep/waking). Moruzzi and Magoun's conclusions were confirmed by Penfield and Jasper (1954), whose studies led them to the view that absence seizures (paroxysmal obliterations of consciousness) could only be reliably triggered at an upper brainstem site. They were also impressed by the fact that removal of large parts of the human cortex under local anaesthetic, even total hemispherectomy, had limited effects on consciousness. Cortical removal did not interrupt the presence of the sentient self, *being* conscious, it merely deprived the patient of "certain forms of information" (Merker, 2009, p. 65). Lesions in the upper brainstem, by contrast, rapidly destroyed all consciousness, just as the induced seizures did. These observations demonstrated a point of fundamental importance: consciousness always depends upon the integrity of upper brainstem structures. This contradicted an assumption of nineteenth-century behavioural neurology, which was that consciousness was derived from perception and attached to higher cortical functions. According to the affective neuroscientists cited above, there appears to be no such thing as intrinsic cortical consciousness; the upper brainstem supplies it all.

Freud never questioned what is now called the "corticocentric fallacy". Despite occasional disclaimers to the effect that "our psychical topography has *for the present* nothing to do with anatomy" (p. 175), Freud repeatedly asserted that his system *Pcpt.-Cs.* was anatomically localisable and that it was a cortical system. For example:

What consciousness yields consists essentially of perceptions of excitations coming from the external world and of feelings of pleasure and unpleasure which can only arise from within the mental apparatus; it is therefore possible to assign to the system *Pcpt.-Cs.* a position in space. It must lie on the borderline between inside and outside; it must be turned towards the external world and must envelop the other psychical systems. It will be seen that there is nothing daringly new in these assumptions; *we have merely adopted the views on localization held by cerebral anatomy, which locates the "seat" of consciousness in the cerebral cortex* – the outermost, enveloping layer of the central organ. Cerebral anatomy has no need to consider why, speaking anatomically, consciousness should be lodged on the surface of the brain instead of being safely housed somewhere in its inmost interior. (Freud, 1923b, p. 24, my emphasis)

Ironically, as it turns out, consciousness *is* housed in the inmost interior of the brain. The observations of Moruzzi and Magoun (1949) and Penfield and Jasper (1954) have stood the test of time, but greater anatomical precision has been added (see Merker, 2009, for review). Significantly, the peri-aquaductal grey, *an intensely affective structure*, appears to be a nodal point in the brain's "activating" system. This is the smallest region of brain tissue in which damage leads to complete obliteration of consciousness. This fact underscores a major change in recent conceptions of the brain's ascending activating system: the deep structures that generate consciousness are not only responsible for the *level* (quantity) but also for the core *content* (quality) of consciousness. The conscious states generated in the upper brainstem are inherently *affective*. This realisation is now revolutionising consciousness studies.

The classical conception is turned on its head. Consciousness is not generated in the cortex; it is generated in the brainstem. Moreover, consciousness is not inherently perceptual; it is inherently affective.

Basic (brainstem) consciousness consists in *states* rather than *images* (cf., Mesulam, 2000). The upper brainstem structures that generate consciousness do not map our external senses; they map the internal state of the (visceral, autonomic) body. This mapping of the internal milieu generates not perceptual objects but rather the *subject* of perception. It generates the background state of *being* conscious. This is of paramount importance. We might picture this core quality of consciousness as the page upon which external perceptual objects are inscribed. The objects are always perceived by an already sentient subject.

Affects are valenced states of the subject. These states are thought to represent the biological meaning of changing internal conditions (e.g., hunger, sexual arousal). When internal conditions favour survival and reproductive success, they feel "good"; when not, they feel "bad". This registers biological *value*, which is evidently what consciousness is *for*. It tells the subject how well it is doing. At this level of the brain, consciousness is closely tied to homeostasis. All of this is entirely consistent with Freud's conception of affect:

> The id, cut off from the external world, has a world of perception of its own. It detects with extraordinary acuteness certain changes in its interior, especially oscillations in the tension of its instinctual needs, and these changes become conscious as feelings in the pleasure–unpleasure series. It is hard to say, to be sure, by what means and with the help of what sensory terminal organs these perceptions come about. But it is an established fact that self-perceptions – coenaesthetic feelings and feelings of pleasure–unpleasure – govern the passage of events in the id with despotic force. The id obeys the inexorable pleasure principle. (Freud, 1940a, p. 198)

Affect may accordingly be described as an interoceptive sensory modality, but that is not all it is. Affect is an intrinsic property of the brain. This property is also *expressed* in emotions; emotions are, above all, peremptory forms of motor discharge. This reflects the fact that the changing internal conditions mentioned above are closely tied to changing external conditions. This is because, first, vital needs (represented as deviations from homeostatic set-points) can only be satisfied through interactions with the external world. Second, certain changes in external conditions have predictable implications for survival and reproductive success. Therefore affects, although inherently subjective, are typically directed towards objects (implicating, thereby, the philosophical notion of intentionality, the idea that subjective awareness, conscious or unconscious, is always perceptually directed toward the object of its perception): "I feel this about that." Damasio (1999) defines the object relation "I feel like this about that" as the basic unit of consciousness.

In this view, consciousness derives from the deepest strata of the mind, it is inherently affective, and it is only secondarily "extended" (to use Damasio's term) upwards to the higher perceptual and cognitive mechanisms that Freud described as the systems *Pcpt.-Cs.* and

Pcs. In other words, it is the *higher* systems that are unconscious in themselves. They borrow consciousness via associative links from the lower system, not the other way round.

Despite this apparently fundamental contradiction of Freud's model, a moment's reflection reveals that it could not be otherwise. If the reality principle inhibits the pleasure principle, as it obviously must do, then where do the inexorable feelings of pleasure (and unpleasure) come from? Surely not from above. "The id obeys the inexorable pleasure principle" (Freud, 1940a). The pleasure principle is not a top-down control mechanism; quite the opposite. And how can one speak of *feelings* of pleasure and unpleasure without speaking of consciousness? Consciousness (or, at least, affective consciousness) must, therefore, come from below.

But this is not how Freud saw it:

> The process of something becoming conscious is above all linked with the perceptions which our sense organs receive from the external world. From the topographical point of view, therefore, it is a phenomenon which takes place in the outermost cortex of the ego. It is true that we also receive information from the inside of the body – the feelings, which actually exercise a more peremptory influence on our mental life than external perceptions; moreover, in certain circumstances the sense organs themselves transmit feelings, sensations of pain, in addition to the perceptions specific to them. Since, however, these sensations (as we call them in contrast to conscious perceptions) also emanate from the terminal organs *and since we regard all these as prolongations or offshoots of the cortical layer*, we are still able to maintain the assertion made above. The only distinction would be that, as regards the terminal organs of sensation and feeling, the body itself would take the place of the external world. (Freud, 1940a, pp. 161–162, my emphasis)[2]

There is a clear contradiction here. The pleasure principle cannot simultaneously be a bottom-up force *and* a top-down sensory "offshoot of the cortical layer".

Affect is always conscious

Nevertheless, Freud had no difficulty in recognising that affectivity is "more primordial, more elementary, than perceptions arising externally" (p. 22), in other words, that it is a more ancient form of consciousness than perception (see Freud, 1911b, p. 220). He also readily admitted that affects are consciously felt from the start; that *there is no such thing as unconscious affect*, nothing analogous to unconscious ideas:

> It is surely of the essence of an emotion that we should be aware of it, i.e. that it should become known to consciousness. Thus the possibility of the attribute of unconsciousness would be completely excluded as far as emotions, feelings and affects are concerned. (p. 177)

Freud explained,

> The whole difference arises from the fact that ideas are cathexes – basically of memory-traces – whilst affects and emotions correspond to processes of discharge, the final manifestation of which are perceived as feelings. In the present state of our knowledge of affects and emotions we cannot express this difference more clearly. (1911b, p. 220)

In other words, affects are not stable *structures* that persist in the mind whether activated or not; they discharge the activation itself. Freud put this more clearly in his earliest metapsychological writings (1894a), when he still theorised activation as "quotas of affect . . . spread over the memory-traces of ideas somewhat as an electric charge is spread over the surface of a body" (p. 60). Later, however, he conceived of the activating process as unconscious drive energy, only the terminal discharge of which was perceived as affect.

Strachey added a footnote to the last sentence of the quotation above (where Freud says that "in the present state of our knowledge of affects and emotions we cannot express this difference more clearly") referring the reader to a passage in *The Ego and the Id* that is of such fundamental importance that I quote it in full, despite its length:

> Whereas the relation of *external* perceptions to the ego is quite perspicuous, that of *internal* perceptions to the ego requires special investigation. It gives rise once more to a doubt whether we are really right in referring the whole of consciousness to the single superficial system *Pcpt.–Cs.* Internal perceptions yield sensations of processes arising in the most diverse and certainly also the deepest strata of the mental apparatus. Very little is known about these sensations and feelings;

those belonging to the pleasure–unpleasure series may still be regarded as the best examples of them. They are more primordial, more elementary, than perceptions arising externally and they can come about even when consciousness is clouded. I have elsewhere expressed my views about their greater economic significance and the metapsychological reasons for this. These sensations are multilocular, like external perceptions; they may come from different places simultaneously and may thus have different and even opposite qualities. Sensations of a pleasurable nature have not anything inherently impelling about them, whereas unpleasurable ones have in the highest degree. The latter impel towards change, towards discharge, and that is why we interpret unpleasure as implying a heightening and pleasure a lowering of energic cathexis. Let us call what becomes pleasure and unpleasure a quantitative and qualitative "something" in the course of mental events; the question then is whether this "something" can become conscious in the place where it is, or whether it must first be transmitted to the system *Pcpt*. Clinical experience decides for the latter. It shows us that this "something" behaves like a repressed impulse. It can exert driving force without the ego noticing the compulsion. Not until there is resistance to the compulsion, a hold-up in the discharge reaction, does the "something" at once become conscious as unpleasure. . . . It remains true, therefore, that sensations and feelings, too, only become conscious through reaching the system *Pcpt.*; if the way forward is barred, they do not come into being as sensations, although the "something" that corresponds to them in the course of the excitation is the same as if they did. We then come to speak, in a condensed and not entirely correct manner, of "unconscious feelings", keeping up an analogy with unconscious ideas which is not altogether justifiable. Actually the difference is that, whereas with *Ucs. ideas* connecting links must be created before they can be brought into *Cs.*, with *feelings*, which are themselves transmitted directly, this does not occur. In other words: the distinction between *Cs.* and *Pcs.* has no meaning where feelings are concerned; the *Pcs.* here drops out – and feelings are either conscious or unconscious. Even when they are attached to word-presentations, their becoming conscious is not due to that circumstance, but they become so directly. (1923b, pp. 21–23)

Two points must be noted here. The first is that research in affective neuroscience strongly suggests that Freud's "something" *can and does* become conscious "in the place where it is" (in the upper brainstem and associated subcortical structures). There are multiple lines of evidence for this (see Merker, 2009 and Damasio, 2010 for reviews), but perhaps the most striking is the fact that children who are born without cortex (without any system *Pcpt.–Cs.*) display abundant evidence of affective consciousness.

These children are blind and deaf, etc.,[3] but they are not unconscious. They display normal sleep–waking cycles, and they suffer absence seizures in which their parents have no trouble recognising the lapses of consciousness and when the child is "back" again. Detailed clinical reports (Shewmon et al., 1999) give further proof that the children not only qualify as "conscious" by the behavioural criteria of the Glasgow Coma Scale, they also show vivid emotional reactions:

> They express pleasure by smiling and laughter, and aversion by "fussing," arching of the back and crying (in many gradations), their faces being animated by these emotional states. A familiar adult can employ this responsiveness to build up play sequences predictably progressing from smiling, through giggling, to laughter and great excitement on the part of the child. (Merker, 2009, p. 79)

They also show associative emotional learning. They

> take behavioral initiatives within the severe limitations of their motor disabilities, in the form of instrumental behaviors such as making noise by kicking trinkets hanging in a special frame constructed for the purpose ("little room"), or activating favorite toys by switches, presumably based upon associative learning of the connection between actions and their effects. Such behaviors are accompanied by situationally appropriate signs of pleasure and excitement on the part of the child. (Merker, 2009, p. 79)

Although there is in these children significant degradation of the types of consciousness that are normally associated with adult cognition, there can be no doubt that they are conscious, both quantitatively and qualitatively. They are not only awake and alert, but also experience and express a full range of instinctual emotions. In short, subjective "being" is fully present. The fact that cortex is absent in these cases proves that core consciousness is both generated *and felt* subcortically—that instinctual energy can become conscious "in the place where it is", without being transmitted to the system *Pcpt.–Cs.* This contradicts the theoretical assumptions of Freud, quoted above, to the effect that "feelings, too, only become conscious through reaching the system *Pcpt.*". It appears that affects truly are *conscious in themselves*.

The only possible reason to doubt this is the fact that children without cortex cannot *tell* us what they feel (they cannot "declare" their feelings). The same applies to animals. They also cannot declare their feelings to themselves; that is, they can feel their feelings but they cannot *think about* them. This leads to a second point that needs to be made with regard to the lengthy quotation from *The Ego and the Id*.

Not all consciousness is declarative

In the closing sentences of the long extract above, Freud says,

> Actually the difference is that, whereas with *Ucs. ideas* connecting links must be created before they can be brought into Cs., with *feelings*, which are themselves transmitted directly, this does not occur. In other words: the distinction between Cs. and Pcs. has no meaning where feelings are concerned; the Pcs. here drops out – and feelings are either conscious or unconscious. Even when they are attached to word-presentations, their becoming conscious is not due to that circumstance, but they become so directly. (Freud, 1923b, p. 23)

In "The unconscious", Freud adds,

> The system *Ucs.* is at every moment overlaid by the *Pcs.* which has taken over access to motility. Discharge from the system *Ucs.* passes into somatic innervations that leads to the development of affect; but even this path of discharge is, as we have seen, contested by the *Pcs.* By itself, the system *Ucs.* would not in normal conditions be able to bring about any expedient muscular acts, with the exception of those already organized as reflexes. (pp. 187–188)

What is introduced here is a *developmental* point of view. Initially, the *Ucs.* has direct access to affectivity and motility, which are normally controlled by the *Cs.* (see p. 179), but this control is gradually "contested" and eventually "taken over" (p. 187) by the *Pcs.*

Freud concludes,

> We are describing the state of affairs as it appears in the adult human being, in whom the system *Ucs.* operates, strictly speaking, only as a preliminary stage of the higher [*Pcs.*] organization. The question of what the content and connections of that system are during the development of the individual, and of what significance it possesses in animals – these are points on which no conclusion can be deduced from our descriptions: they must be investigated independently. (p. 189)

This greatly clarifies the point at hand. The primordial plan of the mental apparatus (which pertains to many animals and young children) probably did not include the *Pcs.* organisation to which Freud attributes control of motility and consciousness (including, to a limited extent, affect).

The *Pcs.* organisation is bound up, more than anything else, with "word-presentations". Thus, we learn that, for Freud, consciousness in adult human beings is largely dependent upon *language*.

Let us make Freud's position absolutely clear:

> We now seem to know all at once what the difference is between a conscious and an unconscious presentation. . . . The conscious presentation comprises the presentation of the thing plus the presentation of the word belonging to it, while the unconscious is the presentation of the thing alone. The system *Ucs.* contains the thing-cathexes of the objects, the first and true object-cathexes; the system *Pcs.* comes about by this thing-presentation being hypercathected through being linked with the word-presentations corresponding to it. It is these hypercathexes, we may suppose, that bring about a higher psychical organization and make it possible for the primary process to be succeeded by the secondary process which is dominant in the *Pcs.* . . . A presentation which is not put into words, or a psychical act which is not hypercathected, remains thereafter in the *Ucs.* in a state of repression. . . . Moreover, by being linked with words, cathexes can be provided with quality even when they represent only the *relations* between presentations of objects and are thus unable to derive any quality from perceptions. (pp. 210–212)

What this conception precludes is the distinction between what is nowadays called "primary" *vs.* "secondary" consciousness (Edelman, 1993). *Freud's usage of the word "consciousness" typically refers to* secondary *consciousness*; that is, to *awareness of* consciousness as opposed to consciousness *itself*. Secondary consciousness is given various names by different theorists, such as "declarative" consciousness, "reflective" consciousness, "access" consciousness, "autonoetic" consciousness, "extended" consciousness, "higher-order" thought, etc. Primary consciousness, by contrast, refers to the direct, concrete, phenomenal *stuff* of sentience. As we have seen, Freud was dimly aware of this distinction, but he did not think through the implications.

In the light of contemporary knowledge, we can clarify: alongside the secondary (declarative, reflective) form of consciousness that Freud typically emphasised, two other (primary) forms of consciousness exist: *affective* consciousness and pre-reflexive perceptual consciousness. These latter forms are not dependent on language. *Primary affective consciousness is the "something" that Freud referred to in the long extract above.* It is *not* unconscious. It can be felt but it cannot be thought about.[4]

As we have seen already, despite his topographic uncertainties, Freud recognised the primary nature of affective consciousness. He seems also to have indirectly recognised that even pre-reflexive perceptual consciousness is activated endogenously. Consider the following passage (which has several equivalents elsewhere in his writings):

> Cathectic innervations are sent out and withdrawn in rapid periodic impulses from within into the completely pervious system *Pcpt.–Cs.* So long as that system is cathected in this manner it receives perceptions (which are accompanied by consciousness) and passes the excitation onwards to the unconscious mnemic systems; but as soon as the [endogenous] cathexis is withdrawn, consciousness is extinguished and the functioning of the system comes to a standstill. It is as though the unconscious stretches out feelers, through the medium of the system *Pcpt.–Cs.*, towards the external world and hastily withdraws them as soon as they have sampled the excitations coming from it. (Freud, 1925a, p. 231)

Please note that—for Freud—it is "the unconscious"[5] that stretches out the feelers of perception "from within". However, the cathexes in question remain unconscious until the feelers reach the cortical system *Pcpt.–Cs.* This reveals that even simple perceptual consciousness, in Freud's model, is ultimately endogenous. If we now add that he was *mistaken* in thinking that the cathectic "feelers" cannot generate consciousness until they reach the cortex (as we must do; see above) then we arrive at a different formulation—one that is more consistent with the findings of modern neuroscience: consciousness is *affective* until it reaches the cortex, at which point it becomes conscious *perception* (". . . *about that*"). This gives rise to primary consciousness of objects, which may or may not then be *re-represented* in words (in "declarative" secondary consciousness: "this feeling belongs to me and I am feeling it about that").

The systems Pcpt.–Cs. and Pcs. are unconscious in themselves

This formulation has substantial implications for Freudian metapsychology, some of which are addressed elsewhere (see Solms, 2013, as well as endnote 5). In this section, I address only the most basic implication of the insight that the cognitive systems *Pcpt.–Cs.* and *Pcs.* are unconscious in themselves. In the next section, I will consider the implications for the system *Ucs.*

I begin by returning to an observation I have cited twice already, which is that vision can occur unconsciously ("blindsight"). This implies that perception itself is an unconscious process, and poses the question: what does consciousness *add* to perception? The significance of this question cannot be overstated.

The answer is that consciousness adds *feeling* (Damasio, 1999, 2010), ultimately derived from the pleasure–unpleasure series. That is, consciousness adds *valence* to perception; it enables us to know: "how do I feel about this; is this good or bad for me?" In terms of the scale of biological values that gave rise to consciousness in the first place, it enables us to decide: "does this situation enhance or reduce my chances of survival and reproductive success?" This is what consciousness adds to perception. It tells us what a particular situation *means*, and, thereby, tells us what to *do* about it—in the simplest terms: whether to approach or withdraw. Some such decisions are "unconditioned"; that is, they are made automatically. This is what instinctual responses are; they provide generic predictive models that spare us the dangers inherent in learning for ourselves.[6]

Such automatic responses are accounted for by the primitive mode of mental functioning that Freud called the "pleasure principle".

However, a vast number of situations occur in life that cannot be predicted by stereotyped instincts. This is the purpose of *learning* from experience, and, therefore, of the whole mode of functioning that Freud called the "reality principle". The reality principle utilises secondary process inhibition (the mode of cognition that dominates in the *Pcs.*) to constrain the pleasure principle, and replaces instinct with the flexible solutions that only *thinking* can provide. The purpose of the reality principle, therefore, is to construct an *individualised* predictive model of the world.

Freud refers to thinking as "experimental action" (i.e., virtual or imaginary action). In contemporary neuropsychology, this is called "working memory". Working memory, whose relationship to thinking is further clarifed in a section below, is conscious by definition. (Not all cognition is conscious, but here we are concerned only with conscious cognition.) The function of working memory is to "feel your way through" a problem until you find a solution. The feeling tells you how you are doing within the biological scale of values described above, which determines when you have hit upon a good solution (cf. Freud's concept of "signal anxiety").

Thinking is only necessary when problems arise. This (the problem) generates the conscious "presence" of affect, and, thereby, *attention* to the objects of perception and cognition. However, the whole purpose of the reality principle (of learning from experience) is to improve one's predictive model; that is, to minimise the chances of surprise—to solve problems—and, thereby, to *minimise the need for consciousness*. The classical model, therefore, is again turned on its head.

Freud's secondary process rests on the binding of "free" drive energies. Such binding (i.e., inhibition) creates a reserve of tonic activation that can be utilised for the function of thinking, just described, which Freud attributed to the *Pcs.* ego. In fact, Freud's earliest conception of the ego defined it as a network of "constantly cathected" neurons which exert collateral inhibitory effects on each other (Freud, 1950[1895]). This prompted Carhart-Harris and Friston (2010) to equate Freud's ego "reservoir" with the "default mode network" of contemporary neuroscience. Be that as it may, Karl Friston's work is grounded in the same Helmholtzian energy concepts as Freud's (see Friston, 2010). His model (in terms of which prediction-error or "surprise"—equated with free energy—is minimised through the encoding of more accurate models of the world, resulting in better predictions) is entirely consistent with Freud's. His model reconceptualises Freud's reality principle in computational terms, with all of the advantages this entails for quantification and experimental modelling. In this view, *free energy is untransformed affect*—energy released from the bound state, or blocked from the bound state, due to prediction errors (see Solms & Friston, 2014).

It is of the utmost interest to note that, in Friston's model, prediction error (mediated by surprise), which increases "incentive salience" (and, therefore, conscious attention) in perception and cognition, *is a bad thing* biologically speaking. The more veridical the brain's predictive model of the world, the less surprise, the less salience, the less attention, the more automaticity, the better. One is reminded of Freud's "Nirvana principle".

The very purpose of the reality principle, which first gave rise to secondary process cognition, is to find solutions via learning from experience. Once a solution is found, it is automatised in the form of an unconscious predictive model: "When this happens, I just do that; I don't even think about it." Thinking is no longer necessary once a problem is solved. The goal of thinking, therefore, is non-thinking, *automaticity*, which obviates the need for the subject to "feel its way through" unpredictable situations. In other words, *the ideal purpose of cognition is to forego conscious processing, and replace it with automatised processing*—to shift from representational "episodic" to associative "procedural" modes of functioning (and, thereby, from cortical to subcortical circuits). It appears that consciousness in cognition is intended only to be a temporary measure: a compromise. (Cf., Freud's "constancy principle".)

With reality being what it is—always uncertain and unpredictable, always full of surprises—there is little risk that we shall in our lifetimes actually reach the zombie-like state of Nirvana that we now learn is what cognition aspires to. Affect is not so easily overcome.

Repression is premature automatisation

I shall now reformulate the metapsychology of repression, and link it with the role that consciousness plays in thinking. I have described this role already, but wish now to point out that the aim of thinking (of problem solving) is the updating of memory traces: a process currently called "reconsolidation" (see Nader & Einarsson, 2010).

Reconsolidation is the neural process by which previously consolidated memories are made labile again through *reactivation* of the consolidated memory traces.

My principle claim is that repressed memories are *prematurely consolidated solutions*—that is, non-solutions—predictions that constantly give rise to errors. Hence, the ever-present threat of a "return of the repressed", which causes neurotic symptom formation.

Why do we automatise inadequate solutions? The answer is that *cognitive consciousness is an extremely limited resource*. As we know from clinical neuropsychology, the typical human brain is capable of holding only seven (plus or minus one) bits of information in working memory at any one moment. Comparing this paltry figure with the amount of information that is permanently stored gives some indication of the extent of our need to automatise. I would, therefore, propose the following: when confronted with an insoluble problem, *it is better to automatise an inadequate solution than to devote the precious resources of working memory to a lost cause*.

Needless to say, insoluble problems are more ubiquitous in childhood than in adulthood. How does the child ever solve problems such as: "I want to be big like him, I want a job like him, I want a wife like him, I want *his* wife, I want to make babies with her", etc.? It is also clear why mental *conflicts* are particularly apt to become repressed. "Conflict", in this context, is just another word for "insoluble problem". ("I want this *and* I want that although I can't have both.")[7]

The tragedy of repression (of premature automatisation) is that it renders childish solutions immune to updating. Hence, *the central task in psychoanalytic therapy is to de-automatise*, to render conscious once more, to permit reconsolidation to take place, and then to automatise better solutions.

The purpose of learning is not to maintain veridical records of the past so much as to guide future behaviour on the basis of past experience. The purpose of learning is, in short, to shape predictions, predictive models of reality, predictive models of how we can meet our needs in the world.

That is why memory functions implicitly for the most part; it serves no useful purpose to be consciously aware of the past basis of your present actions, so long as the actions in question bring about the predicted (desired) outcomes. In fact, *conscious reflection upon an automatised motor programme undermines the intended behaviour because it destabilises the underlying programme.* It only becomes necessary to bring past experience to consciousness when predicted outcomes fail to materialise, when prediction error ("surprise") occurs. Prediction error renders the basis of present actions salient again—and deserving of attention (of consciousness) once more—precisely because the prediction that was generated by the past learning episode is now in need of revision. Reconsolidation, then, simply improves prediction.

Biologically successful memories are reliable predictive algorithms—what Helmholtz (1866) called "unconscious inferences". There is no need for them to be conscious. In fact, as soon as they become conscious they no longer deserve to be called memories, because at that point they become labile again. *This seems to be what Freud had in mind when he famously declared that* "consciousness arises instead of a memory-trace" (1920g, p. 25). The two states—consciousness and automatised algorithm—are mutually incompatible. They cannot arise from the same neural assemblage at the same time.

In short: the "cognitive" unconscious does not consist only in viable predictive algorithms. While it is true that the ultimate aim of learning is the generation of perfect predictive models—a state of affairs in which there is no need for consciousness (Nirvana)—the complexity of life is such that this ideal is unattainable. Real life teems with uncertainty and surprise, and, therefore, with consciousness. That is to say, it teems with unsolved problems. As a result, we frequently have to automatise less-than-perfect predictive algorithms so that we can get on with the job of living, considering the limited capacity of cognitive consciousness. Many behavioural programmes, therefore, have to be automatized—rendered unconscious—before they adequately predict how to meet a need in the world. This applies especially to predictions generated in childhood, when it is impossible for us to achieve the things we want—when there is so much about reality that we cannot master.

The consequently rampant necessity for premature automatisation is, I believe, the basis of repression. I hope this makes clear why repressed memories are always threatening to return to consciousness. They do not square with reality. (For example, in the transference.) I hope this also clarifies why the repressed part of the unconscious is the part of the mind that most urgently demands reconsolidation, and, therefore, most richly rewards psychotherapeutic attention.

Most important, I also hope it is clear that the above formulation *does away with the distinction between the cognitive and the dynamic unconscious.* The dynamic unconscious is formed in just the same way as the cognitive unconscious; the only difference is the legitimacy of the basis upon which the automatised predictions are formed.

Conclusions

This review of Freud's metapsychology of "The unconscious" in relation to some findings of contemporary cognitive and affective neuroscience suggests that his model is in need of major revision:

1. The core processes of the system *Ucs.* (the processes that Freud later called "id") are not unconscious. *The id is the fount of consciousness,* and consciousness is primarily affective. I, therefore, propose that *the Ucs. and the id are different mental systems, and that they should be located separately.*
2. The primary consciousness generated in the id is of a kind different from that generated in Freud's system *Cs.* Freud's systems *Pcpt.–Cs.* and *Pcs.* are concerned primarily with what is now called secondary, or "declarative", consciousness.
3. The systems *Pcpt.–Cs.* and *Pcs.* (the systems that Freud later called "ego") are *unconscious in themselves,* and by inhibiting the id, *they aspire to remain so.* They inhibit the id in order to supplement stereotyped instincts with learning from experience. Unsuccessful instinctual predictions generate affective consciousness (prediction error; free energy), which can only be tamed through thinking (problem solving).
4. The ego systems borrow consciousness as a compromise measure, they *tolerate* consciousness, in order to solve problems and resolve uncertainties (to bind affect). Once a realistic solution is found for an id demand, however, the *raison d'être* of consciousness disappears. *Then a memory-trace arises instead of consciousness.* This is "Nirvana".
5. The system *Ucs.* includes all such automatised predictions. This system is not the id; the *Ucs.* is hived off from the ego. The "dynamic" part of the *Ucs.* is simply the part of it that malfunctions,

that causes prediction errors (causes affect; reawakens the id). The dynamic ("repressed") part of the Ucs., therefore, *tends to reattract consciousness*. This is the threat of the "return of the repressed".

6. The task of psychoanalytic therapy is to connect the affect (the "free energy" of the id) generated by prediction errors (by "surprises", in reality) with the illegitimately automatised predictions that gave rise to it (the "repressed" in the Ucs.). This enables the individual (the conscious ego) to *think* its way through an unsolved problem once more, and then to *reconsolidate* (to reautomatise in the unconscious ego) the memory traces in question. Conscious thinking is, thus, a temporary state, located half way between affect on the one hand (problems) and automatised behaviour on the other (solutions).

Notes

1. Actually, Freud's term was "drives", *Triebe* in German.
2. Freud's localisation of the system Cs. changed over the years. Initially, he made no distinction between perceptual and affective consciousness (Freud, 1894a). Rather, he distinguished between *memory traces of perception* ("ideas") and the *energy that activates them*. This distinction coincided with the conventional assumptions of British empiricist philosophy, but Freud interestingly described the activating energy as "quotas of affect" which are "spread over the memory-traces of ideas somewhat as an electric charge is spread over the surface of a body" (Freud, 1894a, p. 60). Strachey (1962, p. 63) rightly described this as the "most fundamental of all [Freud's] hypotheses" but there is every reason to believe that Freud envisaged such activated memory traces of "ideas" as *cortical* processes. In his more elaborated (1895[1950]) "Project" model, he explicitly attributed consciousness to a special system of cortical neurons (ω), which he located at the *motor* end of the forebrain. This location enabled consciousness to register discharge (or lack thereof) of the energy that accumulates inside the system of memory traces (then called the ψ system) from both endogenous and sensory sources. Please note: from 1895 onward, Freud described mental energy as being *unconscious* in itself; it was no longer described as a "quota of affect". Consciousness, which Freud now divided into two forms, arose from

the manner in which the energy excited the ω neurons. It gave rise to *affective* consciousness when differences in the quantitative level of energy in the ψ system (caused by degrees of motor discharge) was registered in ω as pleasure–unpleasure; and it gave rise to *perceptual* consciousness when differences in qualitative aspects of exogenous energies (e.g., wavelength or frequency) derived from the different sense organs were transmitted, via perceptual (ϕ) neurons, through the memory traces of ideas (ψ), on to ω. In an 1896 revision of this "Project" model, Freud moved the ω neurons to a position between ϕ and ω, and simultaneously acknowledged that all energy in the mental apparatus was endogenously generated; energy did not literally enter the apparatus through the perceptual system. (Freud seemed to forget this later; for example, 1920g.) In *The Interpretation of Dreams* (1900a), however, Freud reverted to the "Project" arrangement, and again located the perceptual and consciousness systems at opposite (sensory and motor) ends of the mental apparatus. His indecision in this respect seems mainly to have derived from the fact that his perceptual (sensory) and consciousness (motor) systems formed an integrated functional unit, since motor discharge necessarily produced kinaesthetic (sensory) information. Freud accordingly settled (in 1917d) on a hybrid localisation of the perceptual and consciousness systems. In this final arrangement, ϕ (renamed '*Pcpt*' in 1900) and ω (renamed '*Cs*') were combined into a single functional unit, the system '*Pcpt–Cs*'. At this point Freud clarified that the *Pcpt–Cs* system is really a single system which is *excitable from two directions*: exogenous stimuli generate perceptual consciousness, endogenous stimuli generate affective consciousness. However, he again emphasised that this combined system is *cortical* (Freud, 1923b, p. 24). Freud also retreated at this point from the notion that affective consciousness registers the quantitative "level" of excitation within the ψ system, and suggested instead that it—like perceptual consciousness—registers something qualitative, like wavelength (i.e., fluctuations in the level of energy within the *Pcs* system over a unit of time; see Freud 1920g). The main thing to notice in this brief history of Freud's localisation of consciousness is that it was, from first to last, conceptualised as a cortical process. (Although Freud did seem to have fleeting doubts about this at times; for example, 1923b, p. 21.) See Solms (1997) for a first intimation that something was wrong with Freud's superficial localisation of the internal (affective) surface of the system *Pcpt–Cs*. See also Solms (2013).

3. They lack perceptual *consciousness*. This does not mean they cannot process perceptual *information* via subcortical pathways. Consciousness is not prerequisite for perception (cf. "blindsight").
4. This has massive clinical implications. For one thing, it implies that both patient and analyst register the relevant affects directly; they just do not know what they *mean*. This, then, becomes the principle analytic task: to attach (or re-attach) missing ideas to troublesome affects. I also think these affects are the principle source of the countertransference, that they are the medium by which patient and analyst communicate "unconsciously". I am inclined to paraphrase Freud's famous assertion about hysterics suffering mainly from reminiscences and say: our patients suffer mainly from *feelings*.
5. This despite the fact that he was writing in 1925. He should have said "the id". And as we have seen above, the id is conscious. (See my concluding section below.)
6. Please note: I am using the word "instinctual" in the modern sense here, not in the misleading way that Strachey used it to translate Freud's term *Trieb* ("drive"). See note 1, above.
7. Hence the "tolerance of mutual contradiction" in the system *Ucs*. In the following sentence we discover the basis for its "timelessness" (cf. Freud, 1915e).

References

Anderson, M., Ochsner, K., Kuhl, B., Cooper, J., Robertson, E., Gabrieli, S., Glover, G., & Gabrieli, J. (2004). Neural systems underlying the suppression of unwanted memories. *Science, 303*: 232–235.

Bargh, J., & Chartrand, T. (1999). The unbearable automaticity of being. *American Psychologist, 54*: 462–479.

Carhart-Harris, R., & Friston, K. (2010). The default mode, ego functions and free energy: a neurobiological account of Freudian ideas. *Brain, 133*: 1265–1283.

Damasio, A. (1999). *The Feeling of What Happens*. New York: Harvest.

Damasio, A. (2010). *Self Comes to Mind*. New York: Pantheon.

Darwin, C. (1872). *The Expression of Emotions in Man and Animals*. London: John Murray.

Edelman, G. (1993). *Bright Air, Brilliant Fire*. New York: Basic Books.

Freud, S. (1894a). The neuro-psychoses of defence. *S. E., 3*: 45–61. London: Hogarth.

Freud, S. (1896). Letter from Freud to Fliess, January 1, 1896. In: *The Complete Letters of Sigmund Freud to Wihelm Fliess, 1887–1904* (pp. 158–162). London: Hogarth.

Freud, S. (1900a). *The Interpretation of Dreams. S. E., 4 & 5.* London: Hogarth.

Freud, S. (1911b). Formulations on the two principles of mental functioning. *S. E., 12*: 215–226. London: Hogarth.

Freud, S. (1915c). Instincts and their vicissitudes. *S. E., 14*: 117–140. London: Hogarth.

Freud, S. (1915e). The unconscious. *S. E., 14*: 166–204. London: Hogarth.

Freud, S. (1917d). Metapsychological supplement to the theory of dreams. *S. E., 14*: 222–235. London: Hogarth.

Freud, S. (1920g). *Beyond the Pleasure Principle. S. E., 18*: 7–64. London: Hogarth.

Freud, S. (1923b). *The Ego and the Id. S. E., 19*: 12–59. London: Hogarth.

Freud, S. (1925a). A note upon "the mystic writing-pad". *S. E., 16*: 227–232. London: Hogarth.

Freud, S. (1940a). *An Outline of Psychoanalysis. S. E., 23*: 144–207. London: Hogarth.

Freud, S. (1950)[1895]. Project for a scientific psychology. *S. E., 1*: 281–397. London: Hogarth.

Friston, K. (2010). The free-energy principle: a unified brain theory? *Nature Reviews Neuroscience, 11*: 127–138.

Galin, D. (1974). Implications for psychiatry of left and right cerebral specialization. *American Journal of Psychiatry, 31*: 572–583.

Helmholtz, H. (1866). Concerning the perceptions in general, J. Southall (Trans.). In: *Treatise on Physiological Optics* (3rd edn). New York: Dover.

Kaplan-Solms, K., & Solms, M. (2000). *Clinical Studies in Neuropsychoanalysis.* London: Karnac.

Kihlstrom, J. (1996). Perception without awareness of what is perceived, learning without awareness of what is learned. In: M. Velmans (Ed.), *The Science of Consciousness: Psychological, Neuropsychological and Clinical Reviews* (pp. 23–46). London: Routledge.

Libet, B. (1985). Unconscious cerebral initiative and the role of conscious will in voluntary action. *Behavioral & Brain Sciences, 8*: 529–539.

Maclean, P. (1990). *The Triune Brain in Evolution.* New York: Plenum.

Merker, B. (2009). Consciousness without a cerebral cortex: a challenge for neuroscience and medicine. *Behavioral Brain Science, 30*: 63–134.

Mesulam, M. M. (2000). Behavioral neuroanatomy: large-scale networks, association cortex, frontal syndromes, the limbic system and hemispheric lateralization. In: *Principles of Behavioral and Cognitive Neurology* (2nd edn) (pp. 1–120). New York: Oxford University Press.

Milner, B., Corkin, S., & Teuber, H.-L. (1968). Further analysis of the hippocampal amnesic syndrome: 14 year follow-up study of HM. *Neuropsychologia, 6*: 215–234.

Moruzzi, G., & Magoun, H. (1949). Brain stem reticular formation and activation of the EEG. *Electroencephalography and Clinical Neurophysiology, 1*: 455–473.

Nader, K., & Einarsson, E. (2010). Memory reconsolidation: an update. *Annals of the New York Academy of Sciences, 1191*: 27–41.

Panksepp, J. (1998). *Affective Neuroscience*. New York: Oxford University Press.

Panksepp, J., & Biven, L. (2012). *Archaeology of Mind*. New York: Norton.

Penfield, W., & Jasper, H. (1954). *Epilepsy and the Functional Anatomy of the Human Brain*. Oxford: Little, Brown.

Ramachandran, V. (1994). Phantom limbs, neglect syndromes, repressed memories, and Freudian psychology. *International Review of Neurobiology, 37*: 291–333.

Schacter, D., & Tulving, E. (1994). *Memory Systems*. Cambridge, MA: MIT.

Shevrin, H., Bond, J., Brakel, L., Hertel, R., & Williams, W. (1996). *Conscious and Unconscious Processes: Psychodynamic, Cognitive and Neurophysiological Convergences*. New York: Guilford Press.

Shewmon, D., Holmse, D., & Byrne, P. (1999). Consciousness in congenitally decorticate children: developmental vegetative state as a self-fulfilling prophecy. *Development Medicine and Child Neurology, 41*: 364–374.

Solms, M. (1997). What is consciousness? *Journal of the American Psychoanalytic Association, 45*: 681–778.

Solms, M. (2013). The conscious id. *Neuropsychoanalysis, 15*: 5–19.

Solms, M., & Friston, K. (2014). Consciousness by surprise. Oral presentation (Solms) and discussion (Friston) at the International Psychoanalytical Association Research Conference, Sigmund Freud Institute, Frankfurt (www.youtube.com/watch?v=xP8Y2f1I0jE).

Solms, M., & Panksepp, J. (2012). The id knows more than the ego admits. *Brain Sciences, 2*: 147–175.

Strachey, J. (1962). The emergence of Freud's fundamental hypotheses. *S. E., 3*: 62–68.

Weiskrantz, L. (1990). *Blindsight*. New York: Oxford University Press.

CHAPTER TWO

Implicit memory and early, unrepressed unconscious: their role in the therapeutic process

How the neurosciences can contribute to psychoanalysis*

Mauro Mancia

This chapter concerns the various systems of long-term memory studied by neuroscience, and their relationship to the unconscious. It suggests that analytic work on these memory systems is essential for the success of the therapeutic process.

Memory and neurosciences

Memory, its relationship to neurosciences, and its role in the therapeutic process have, in recent years, been studied intensively by many authors (e.g., Modell, 1993, 2004; Semenza, 2001; Shevrin, 2002). In particular, Pally (1997) has applied neurological findings on memory to her clinical work, so as to recover, in the course of the treatment, those primary emotions deriving from the mother–infant relationship. Such emotions belong to infantile amnesia and cannot be remembered.

---

* Originally published in 2006 in *International Journal of Psychoanalysis; 87*: 83–103.

Fonagy (1999) has in turn underlined the therapeutic role of ex-periences stored in the implicit memory, which can be recovered by analysis even without recollection.

More recently, Pugh (2002) has emphasised the role of the amyg-dala and the basal nuclei, structures which develop earlier than the hippocampus, in the organisation of the implicit memory and in the unconscious elaboration of cognitive functions.

In summary, it is known through neuroscience that there exist in our brain two memory systems, each with different functions. One system concerns explicit (or declarative) memory and another implicit (or non-declarative) memory (Schacter, 1995; Squire, 1994). The first can be retrieved consciously and verbalised. It concerns specific events of one's life and allows one to give meaning to the recollections of experiences. Thus, explicit memory allows, through remembering, a reconstruction of one's personal history.

Neuropsychology has used imaging techniques such as PET (positron emission tomography) and MRI (magnetic resonance imag-ing) to study brain-injured patients, and has shown that explicit memory relies on the integrity of the medial temporal lobe (rhinal, perirhinal, and parahippocampal cortex), the frontal–basal areas and the bilateral functionality of the hippocampus. The amygdala is mainly responsible for the emotional component in the process of information storage (see Gazzaniga, 1999; Mancia, 2000b, 2004b, 2006), and can modulate both the encoding and the storage of hippocampal-dependent memories (Phelps, 2004).

Implicit memory, by contrast, is not conscious and concerns data that can be neither remembered nor verbalised. It presides over the learning of various skills:

1. *Priming*, which is the ability of an individual to choose an object to which he has previously been exposed subliminally.
2. *Procedural memory*, which concerns cognitive and sensorimotor experiences such as motor skills learning, everyday activities, playing instruments, or playing certain sports.
3. *Emotive and affective memory*,[1] which concerns emotional experi-ences, as well as the phantasies and defences linked to the first relations of the child with the environment and, in particular, with the mother. It is likely that this memory also concerns the experiences of the foetus during the last period of gestation,

when it is in close relation with the mother, her rhythms, and, in particular, her voice. These stimuli constitute a pattern of continuity, rhythm, and musicality around which the first representations of the infant from birth (or protore-presentations) are organised (Mancia, 1981). It is well known that the sensorimotor experiences of the foetus can be memorised (De Casper & Fifer, 1980). The voice of the mother can also be memorised (see Kolata, 1984), and when re-experienced in the first months of life, in particular during breastfeeding, it can influence the cardiac frequency and even the suction rate of the infant. (Mehler et al., 1978)

The child, developing its symbolic system and language during its first two years of life, goes through very important affective and emotional experiences. It is very likely that these experiences are memorised. As for language, the infant is particularly sensitive, at a very early stage of its development, to the prosody (intonation and rhythm) of the maternal language. After learning the prosodic structure of the mother tongue, the child is able, at about the sixth month of life, to represent its sequential intonations of vowels and consonants (Mehler & Christophe, 1995).

Some of the child's primary experiences will be positive and essential for the physical and mental growth of the child. Others may be traumatic: neglect, parental inadequacy, or possible mental illness, physical or psychological violence, child abuse, even of a sexual nature, as well as the constant frustrations and disillusionments that lead the child to organise his defences and boost his phantasies. All these experiences cannot be repressed because the hippocampus, necessary for the explicit memory, which is in turn indispensable for repression, is not mature in early infancy (R. Joseph, 1996; Siegel, 1999). In contrast, the amygdala, which promotes the organisation of the implicit memory, undergoes an earlier maturation (R. Joseph, 1996). Therefore, these early experiences, including those that concern the organisation of language, can only be deposited in this latter form of memory and they contribute to the formation of an early, unrepressed, unconscious nucleus of the self (Mancia, 2003a, 2006).

The structures and circuits of implicit memory have not yet been accurately defined by neuropsychological research. It does not rely upon the integrity of the temporal medial lobe or the hippocampus.

The amygdala does seem to have an essential role in the processing of emotions (Bennett & Hacker, 2005; Damasio, 1999; LeDoux, 2000) and is, thus, involved in the organisation of implicit memory. The basal ganglia are also involved in this kind of memory and the cerebellum seems to play a role in the experience of fear (Sacchetti et al., 2004). Indirect evidence suggests that implicit memory might have its site in the posterior temporal–occipital and parietal areas (angular gyrus and supramarginal gyrus areas, or Broadman areas 39 and 40) of the right hemisphere. The latter is considered the emotive hemisphere *par excellence* (Gainotti, 2001). It is the seat of implicit memory in relation to words (Gabrieli et al., 1995).

The discovery of implicit memory was made by Warrington and Weiskrantz (1974) who studied with priming experiments patients affected by Korsakov's amnesia, in which the structures of explicit memory are damaged. Subsequently, the *procedural dimension* of implicit memory has been confirmed. As well as this, the *emotional and affective dimension* of implicit memory is of particular interest for psychoanalysis. It is linked to the earliest, most significant experiences of the infant with the mother and the surrounding environment.

A more recent contribution to the study of implicit memory comes from the experiments with a spatial organisation computer game on amnesic patients (Stickgold et al., 2000). Damage to the bilateral temporal lobe and hippocampus had caused the loss of explicit memory. However, despite being unable to recall the game, these patients were able to dream of it at sleep onset. This observation is interesting, as it shows that learning can be memorised without the contribution of explicit memory, which requires the activation of the hippocampus and of the temporal and basal cortex. In the cases observed by Stickgold and colleagues, the explicit memory was definitely impaired, but a non-explicit and non-conscious kind of memory was left and could emerge in dreams. This observation shows that an experience can be stored in the implicit memory and can be represented symbolically in dreams.

The contribution of molecular biology

After the pioneering experiments obtained with post-tetanic potentiation (Bliss & Lomo, 1973) and with long-term potentiation of the hippocampus, the molecular biologist Rose (1992) demonstrated a genetic memory located in chromosomal DNA. This kind of memory supports behaviour linked to the survival of the species.

Furthermore, this author has demonstrated that learning is accompanied by protein synthesis facilitating the formation of new synapses and, therefore, of new circuits, allowing long-term assimilation of the information received. More recent are the experiments by Kandel and colleagues (1996) on *Aplysia californica*, and their subsequent extension to mammals (Kandel, 2001). This author stimulated in *Aplysia* a simple reflex in the gill and syphon, inducing two opposite forms of learning that the animal could memorise: habituation and sensitisation. He demonstrated that storage of information happens at synaptic level through stimulation of gene expression and protein synthesis. This process permanently modifies synaptic transmission, acting at the level of the ionic channels of the presynaptic membrane, decreasing the passage of divalent calcium ($Ca2+$) ions, progressively reducing the synaptic transmission, and, thus, inducing habituation. Alternatively, it can increase the passage of $Ca2+$ions, thus facilitating in a stable way the synaptic transmission and so inducing sensitisation. An important transmitter such as dopamine facilitates in mammals the fixation of the protein expressed by genes on the specific synapses which preside over the memory of some given experiences (Kandel, 2003). It is worth noting that dopamine is also an active transmitter at the level of the accumbens nucleus (Ikemoto & Panksepp, 1999), thus having a role in the system which presides over pleasure and sexuality (Gessa & Tagliamonte, 1974). This system can, therefore, create a condition of "synaptic plasticity" as the organisational basis of long-term memory (implicit and explicit).

These observations enabled Kandel (1999) to make links between the molecular biology of memory and psychology and to put forward some extremely interesting hypotheses. I list them briefly:

- all mental processes, normal or pathological, derive from operations of the brain;
- genes and protein expression determine the pattern of interconnection of neuronal synapses; therefore, a component of mental function (both normal and pathological) is linked to genes;
- relational and social factors can exert an action on the brain, modifying permanently the function of the genes, which is to say

their protein expression as concerns the synapses, and, therefore, the neuronal circuits—it follows that "culture" can express itself as "nature";

- psychical anomalies induced by traumatic relational and social situations can occur through modification of gene expression and protein synthesis;

- psychotherapy (and, *a fortiori*, psychoanalysis) can bring about long-term changes of behaviour and of various functions of the mind, exerting an action on the gene expression of proteins that modify the structure and potency on neuronal synapses (and, thus, of the specific circuits controlling specific areas of the brain).

The transformations induced by psychoanalytic therapy would be due to the effect of the cure on the plasticity of the central nervous system.

Memory and unconscious

Memory and the unconscious are inseparable; therefore, the unconscious function of the mind can be identified with the memory functions. Freud considered the unconscious to be the expression of an active process of repression, beginning in early infancy (primal repression) and carrying on through life (as repression proper) (Freud, 1915d, 1915e). It is obvious that this concept of repression is intimately linked to the instinctual model of the mind and to the storage of experience in the explicit memory. The result of this operation is, according to Freud, the formation of a dynamic unconscious which influences conscious life and manifests itself in various ways: through free associations, slips of the tongue, dreams, and everyday life psychopathology.

However, it was precisely in those years when he was working on his theory of dreams that Freud became interested in the way the experiences of early years are forgotten. He was almost intuiting the concept of implicit memory, but, in effect, he introduced a different one: the concept of "screen memory", understood as the result of the repression of some events or of their displacement into contiguous ones. According to Freud (1899a), screen memories are purposeful falsifications of the memory, acting to repress and replace disturbing experiences, a role not dissimilar to the manifest content of a dream in relation to the latent. As the focus of his theory was the Oedipus complex, Freud overlooked the importance of the earliest pre-oedipal, preverbal and presymbolic experiences. The latter are stored in the implicit memory and are not, therefore, susceptible to being repressed. This is why, in "Remembering, repeating and working-through" (1914g), Freud refers to the explicit memory which can be recovered through the free associations of the analysand, even though he writes, "There is one special class of experiences of the utmost importance for which no memory can as a rule be recovered . . . One gains a knowledge of them through dreams . . ." (1914g, p. 149). This was a wonderful intuition which Freud could not develop as he could not know of the existence of the implicit memory. Indeed, he (wrongly) considered this kind of memory as another expression of primal repression.

Freud returns to the issue of memory in "A note on the 'mystic writing-pad'" (1925a), in which he emphasises the analogies between the mystic pad and our memory. This is because our psychical apparatus is able to offer us both functions of the pad, dividing itself between the two different systems that he mentions in "Project for a scientific psychology" (1950a[1895]): the systems ϕ and ψ. Later, in *Civilization and its Discontents* (1930a), Freud returns to the subject of memory with a historic–archaeological metaphor, stating that what has been experienced cannot be erased. Analytical work orientates towards a past that emerges in the present through transference. The latter allows the re-experience in the present of emotional situations belonging to the past. To be precise, Freud refers to the past as "surviving" in the present. This means that a given experience is present but not necessarily remembered. It can survive in the *recollection* and in the *non-recollection*. This is an important point for the hypothesis of the unrepressed unconscious that I am proposing here, in so far as it cannot be accessed through recollection.

The archaeological metaphor, with which Freud (1937d) compared the analyst's work to that of the archaeologist who brings to light *all* that time has buried, seems now incomplete and in need of modification. The analyst is a historian at the same time. He is a historian *sui generis* who has to trust hidden documents that he will never be able to consult directly, but can retrieve indirectly through attention to particular details. In order to achieve this, the analyst/historian, as well as relying on the patient's verbal material (Ferro, 2002), must concentrate his attention on the modalities of his communication such as intonation, rhythms, and tempi of speech, in particular on the musicality of the voice, and on the most obviously "reconstructive" dimension of dreams. All this will allow the emergence, besides recollection, of emotions that concern the most archaic and meaningful relational experiences, and that belong to unrepressed unconscious material.

Ricoeur's philosophical reflection on time and memory (1998) is helpful in suggesting the analyst be considered as a historian whose work enables the patient to acquire a *historical consciousness of his unconscious*. Following on from the work of Koselleck (1985), Ricoeur suggests that historical consciousness can be the result of the dialectic between two poles: the "space of experience" formed by the *entire* heritage of the past, and the "horizon of expectations", constituted by the projects and the anticipations projected into the future. Historical consciousness concerning the unconscious can, therefore, be regarded, in analysis, as the expression of a dialectic taking place in the present, in the here and now of the relationship, between the most archaic past, starting from the earliest preverbal and presymbolic experiences which are unconscious and unrepressed, and the project of the future intended as the result of a *transformation* taking place during analysis.

I describe here the unrepressed unconscious as having its foundations in the sensory experiences the infant has with his mother (including hearing her voice, which recalls for the infant prosodic experiences in the womb). It is through these sensory experiences that the mother sends to the infant messages of affectivity, emotionality, reliability, happiness, and dedication. But she can also send messages that the infant can experience as traumatic, terrifying, threatening, non-reassuring, or strongly frustrating. The latter will disrupt the attachment patterns of the child (Bowlby, 1969) and his reflective capacity (Fonagy & Target, 1997), threatening seriously the organisation of its self (Stern, 1985). These traumas will cause what Money-Kyrle (1978) calls "unconscious misconceptions". They cannot be repressed because the structures that concern the explicit memory, indispensable for repression, are lacking (R. Joseph, 1996; Siegel, 1999). They will organise, instead, an early unrepressed unconscious nucleus of the self (Mancia, 2003a,b, 2004a).

The concept of unrepressed unconscious that I propose differs greatly from the one described by Freud (1923b), in which a part of the ego is unconscious, as it derives from the id through the action on it of the *Pcpt–Cs* (perception–consciousness) system. It also differs from the "past unconscious" proposed by Sandler and Sandler (1987), which is considered as the result of repression. In my elaboration, it is the result of the storage in the implicit memory of experiences, phantasies, and defences that belong to the presymbolic and preverbal stage of development and cannot, therefore, be remembered. Nevertheless, they can condition the affective, emotional, cognitive, and sexual life even of the adult. This unrepressed unconscious can reveal itself in the transference and in dreams, as I shall show later.

Modern discoveries in neuropsychology concerning the organisation of memory now allow us to hypothesise that some synaptical cortical and subcortical circuits form the seat of unconscious mental functions. The possibility of identifying, in the explicit and implicit memory respectively, the repressed and unrepressed unconscious opens new and stimulating perspectives for an integration of neuroscience with psychoanalysis, and for a possible anatomic localisation of the functions of these two different forms of unconscious. This depends on a presupposition: that the experiences, emotions, phantasies, and defences which each contribute to the organisation of an individual's unconscious psychic reality, from birth throughout life, are stored in the nervous structures concerning memory, both implicit and explicit. This is, after all, in line with Freud's conviction: "latent conceptions, if we have any reason to suppose that they exist in the mind – as we had in the case of memory – let them be denoted by the term 'unconscious'" (1912g, p. 260).

On these grounds, it is possible to suggest that the repressed unconscious finds its own location in the structures of explicit, or autobiographic, memory. Supporting this hypothesis is the recent observation by Anderson and colleagues (2004), who demonstrated that the deliberate forgetting of mental experiences, which they compare to Freudian repression[2] is accompanied by an increase of activity in the dorsolateral prefrontal areas and a parallel reduction of the hippocampus activity. This phenomenon is opposed to the "derepressive" character of dreams (in rapid eye movement (REM) sleep), during which an increase of hippocampal activity and a deactivation of the dorsolateral prefrontal cortex (Braun et al., 1998) have been observed. By contrast, the unrepressed unconscious may find in the implicit memory its own organisation, promoted by the activation of the amygdala which presides over the emotions (Damasio, 1999; LeDoux, 2000; Bennett & Hacker, 2005). It seems to be located in the posterior associative cortical areas (temporal–occipital–parietal) of the right hemisphere, as well as in the basal ganglia and in the cerebellum. In favour of this hypothesis are the following experimental and clinical tests: implicit experiences have an emotional component which engage the amygdala and, for some emotions (such as fear), the cerebellum also (Sacchetti et al., 2004); the right hemisphere, through its temporal–occipital–parietal areas, is considered the hemisphere of emotions (Gainotti, 2001). It is also the seat of implicit memory, in particular of the information related to speech (Gabrieli et al., 1995); the above areas of this hemisphere are more active during REM sleep (and, therefore, in the dream), when compared to the corresponding areas of the left hemisphere (Antrobus, 1983; Bertini & Violani, 1984). They correspond to the angular and supramarginal gyri (Brodman areas 39 and 40) in which the maximum of sensory integration (somatic, auditory, and visual) is observed. These areas are engaged in the most sophisticated processes concerning symbolic, gnostic, and praxic functions (Bisiach et al., 1977; Critchley, 1953; Geschwind, 1965a,b; Hyvärinen, 1982). Furthermore, in patients with a section of the corpus callosum, they regulate the geometrical–spatial functions and those related to art and music (Sperry, 1974). Even a partial injury of these areas can abolish dream activity (Solms, 1995; Bischof & Bassetti, 2004).

Therapeutic functions and work on memory

I come now to the core of my reflections on what makes our memory work with patients therapeutic.

According to Freud, the therapeutic effect of psychoanalysis is essentially linked to a reconstructive process that happens through working on the autobiographical memory. The very concept of "working through" (Freud, 1914g) has been considered as the expression of the process of working on and recovering repressed experiences stored in the explicit memory (a process that we may call derepression), and overcoming the opposing resistances (Gill, 1983). This aspect of the therapeutic function of psychoanalysis, already criticised by some epistemologists (Grünbaum, 1993), has been the object of a profound revision by current psychoanalysis. Strachey (1934), already, had talked of the analyst as a "new object", whom patients need to introject into their superego to modify its severity and harshness. Later, various authors tried to capture the therapeutic effect of psychoanalysis as something different from mere recovery of repressed infantile memories (Fonagy, 1999; Winnicott, 1956). For instance, Loewald (1960) argued that the analyst should make himself available for the development of a new "object relation" with the patient. Klein (1932) emphasised the idea that the therapeutic action is, above all, linked to the recovery of parts of the self projectively identified in the object, and to the retrospective discovery, in the transference, of the infantile experiences which made possible the projective identification (Steiner, 1989). Bion (1991) considered that one of the aims of psychoanalysis is that of offering to the patient the opportunity to develop his own α-function of the mind, so as to confer a new order to the β-elements reaching it.

More recently, Gabbard and Westen (2003) drew attention to three main themes concerning the therapeutic action of psychoanalysis: (a) the reduced importance of interpretation compared to the relationship as such and the acknowledgement of a multiplicity of modes for a therapeutic action of psychoanalysis; (b) a shift of the emphasis from *reconstruction* to *construction* in the here and now of the session;[3] and (c) the importance of *negotiation* of the therapeutic atmosphere created between analyst and patient. For these authors, the insight reached through interpretation and the transformations that can be obtained through the relational experience work in synergy.

In fact, the emphasis on reconstruction has in recent years considerably decreased, in favour of the interaction in the here and now of the session, allowing the patient to gain an insight into the influences of the past on his present conflicts and object relations (Arlow, 1987; Gabbard, 1997). My point of view, now, is that of re-evaluating reconstruction, but from a new epistemological stance. This concerns a standpoint of observation and interpretation that focuses on the phantasies, representations, and defences stored in the implicit memory of the patient and is, therefore, reconstructive. However, the material observed comes from the work in the here and now of the session. The latter is essentially constructive, as it focuses on the relationship, on the transference and countertransference, as well as on the analysis of dreams. Particularly important, in this kind of work, are the experiences inherent to the analytic relationship that emerge in the session; they reactivate those emotions which are not remembered but belong to the unrepressed unconscious of the past. The kind of reconstruction to which I am referring has many analogies with the concept elaborated by Blum (1994), who considered reconstructive activities to be complementary to transference interpretations, and a necessary process for the understanding and resolution of the transference.

The transference is to be grasped in its total dimension (B. Joseph, 1985), and, therefore, in its narrative elements, but also, and above all, through the extra- and infra-verbal elements. By extra-verbal I mean the patients' behaviour in the analytic setting, the expression of their faces, their posture, their movements, which are related to the unrepressed unconscious and to the procedural dimension of the implicit memory (Clyman, 1991), and even their clothes and general way of relating to the analyst. The infra-verbal elements belong to the signifier concept of the signified–signifier semantic dyad (de Saussure, 1960). It concerns those modes of communication of the patient in which the voice has fundamental importance. In the analytic encounter, in which speech acquires a very important role, the voice is the vehicle by which words create sounds and convey affects. From this perspective, the voice is an "experience" of one's self actualised in the act of speech (Ogden, 2001), but is, at the same time, an experience of the self in relation to the other. The voice constitutes a "transference current" which recalls a sensory dimension associated with the maternal voice (Godfrind, 1993). These elements of communication include the rhythm, tone, timbre, and musicality of a sentence, as well as the syntax and tempi of speech. All this constitutes, in the analytic encounter, the "musical dimension" of the transference (Mancia, 2003a,b,c). This dimension has also been described by Knoblauch (2000) as the "musical edge of therapeutic dialogue", in the sense of a "shared musical performance" of the analytic couple. According to this author, this dimension has analogies with what happens with jazz.

The musical dimension of the analytical encounter refers to a conception of music as a language *sui generis*, whose symbolic structure is isomorphic with that of our emotional and affective world (Di Benedetto, 2000; Langer, 1942; Ognibene, 1999). This dimension facilitates the transferential metaphor, beyond the content of narrative (Ferro, 2002), of affective, emotional, and cognitive (traumatic) experiences which have shaped the implicit model of the patient's mind. Such a process is rooted in language, in particular in the emotional tone of the maternal voice, which the child acquires before the semantic meaning that it conveys. It gives to the mother's speech a privileged access to feelings (Amati Mehler et al., 1993). The maternal voice can be considered as a metaphorical area of exchange in which very primitive processes of projection and introjection take place. Therefore, in the analytic relationship, the analysand and the analyst use their voices to communicate their affects and to facilitate or prevent their own reciprocal affective investment (Rizzuto et al., quoted in Etchegoyen, 2004). The semantic element in the analysand's (and in the therapist's) speech is profoundly influenced by its emotional significance, which belongs to the patient's early unconscious history and is based on the prosody of the speech learnt before the development of language. Such a prosodic and musical dimension can only belong to the unrepressed unconscious, in as much as it is linked to the most primitive emotional experiences. It can be easily split and projectively identified in the analyst and is capable, therefore, of piercing his countertransferential skin more than any other semantic content of the narrative. It is the task of the analyst, the sensitive listener, to capture, in the here and now of the session, the unrepressed, unconscious meaning of this specific transferential modality (and, in particular, the most archaic quality of those affects which are split and projectively identified). The analyst must then put it into words, thus giving it a symbolic meaning and linking it to the past.

It is to this aspect of the countertransference that Pally (1997) refers when she states that analysts' reverie, their empathic resonance and sensitiveness to patients' non-verbal communications, are precious instruments for reaching the experiences encoded in the implicit memory of the patient. Similarly, Fonagy (1999), quoting B. Joseph (1989), underlines how the primitive emotions of the patient are revealed through the feelings that they are able to evoke in the analyst. More recently, Cimino and Correale (2005) have referred to implicit emotions of the patient's mind being projectively identified in the analyst. However, in the above works, the link between the experiences stored in the implicit memory and the unrepressed unconscious of the patient is not always obvious.

In this context, I stress the importance of recent neuropsychological observations, showing that the areas presiding over pain (anterior part of the cingulate and of the insula) are activated also in an affectively concerned person witnessing a suffering subject, following an extra-verbal (Singer et al., 2004) or even verbal (Osaka et al., 2004) communication from the latter. Even smell stimuli that induce disgust in a subject activate in an observer the same structures (inferior part of the insula and, to a lesser extent, of the cingulate, Wicker et al., 2003). At the neuronal level, investigations of the so-called "mirror neurons" (Gallese, 2001, 2003) also provided evidence of an exchange of feelings and sensations among individuals, forming the physiological basis of a process which could be defined as having a projective identification nature.

These possible neurological modifications of functions in individuals communicating with each other constitute an area of integration of neuroscience with psychoanalysis. The therapist's countertransference is based on these same principles.

The repetitive and implicit processes of communication that I have described might have some analogies with those modifications in affective and interactive connections which Lyons-Ruth and colleagues (1998) call implicit relational knowing. They concern the structure of the patient's mind and can emerge in those particular "encounter moments", described by the Process of Change Study Group (PCSG) (1998) as playing a key role in the reorganisation of affective implicit experiences. However, it is my impression that the implicit models described by these authors do not feature the same unrepressed unconscious characteristics of those experiences, defences, and phantasies that I describe in this chapter. It is possible that "implicit relational knowing" is part of the unrepressed unconscious related to the implicit memory that I discuss here. However, on a more purely clinical level, the PCSG group considers as therapeutic in itself any moment of encounter which highlights the implicit knowing, whereas I think that the unrepressed unconscious of infancy needs an interpretation or a possibility of representation (particularly as it concerns work on dreams) if it is to be reconstructive and therapeutically useful.

Grasping in the transference these complex modalities is one of the best ways of reaching the most archaic aspects of a patient's unconscious, so obtaining a "reconstruction" of their past. It will be, however, a reconstruction *sui generis*, as the experiences stored in this kind of memory cannot, in fact, be "remembered". They can only be re-experienced emotionally and enacted in the intersubjective relationship. They may also be represented in the dream, the theatre *par excellence* of the implicit (as well as explicit) memory, whose curtains open on the transference (Mancia, 2000a, 2003a).

The dream can be the privileged representation giving insight into the phantasies, affects, and defences that emerge in the transference, as well as into the reconstructive elements, related to the preverbal and presymbolic experiences that characterise the implicit structures of the patient. The function of the dream is indeed that of creating images able to fill the void of non-representation, representing symbolically experiences that were originally presymbolic. Their interpretation will facilitate the reconstructive process that is necessary for the psyche to improve its abilities to mentalize experiences that could, originally, neither be represented nor thought about. Although still not remembered, these experiences will be rendered thinkable.

Following from these reflections, the defining element of the therapeutic action of current psychoanalysis appears to be that of transforming symbolically and putting into words the early implicit structures of the patient's mind. This is where highly emotional experiences, rooted in the affective sphere of the primary relationships, are stored. They are condensed in language and in the prosodic tone of the preverbal stage, rather than in the autobiographic memories of later stages. If the implicit structures of patients' minds and the unconscious modes with which they function are made thinkable, patients will be able to represent the non-representable material of their unrepressed unconscious and to recover those parts of the self which have either been denied or split and projected in the early development of their minds. This is not to say that work on explicit memory has no role in the reconstructive and therapeutic process of analysis. An excessive use of autobiographic memories in the here and now of the session can, of course, be a defence against the more painful experiences of the patient and, therefore, a resistance to analysis. However, it is necessary to recognise that the narrations of the patient and the recollection of facts stored in the explicit memory have a role in the constructive and reconstructive process. Therefore, they play their part in the transformations observed in analysis (Ferro, 2004). Nevertheless, this must not distract us from paying constant attention to what the patient neither tells nor remembers, but which is "enacted" or communicated in the session in infra-verbal forms.

These communications are extremely significant from the point of view of the transference and countertransference. Lacan (1966) points this out when he writes that the essential property of analytic speech is to communicate what it does not say.

In summary, both implicit and explicit memory experiences can be present in the transference, influencing each other just as they do in the normal development of the infantile mind (Siegel, 1999). If the work on implicit memory can facilitate the emergence of phantasies and memories stored in the explicit memory, so the work of reconstruction, which relies on the autobiographic memory, can facilitate the emergence in the transference and in the dreams of the most archaic experiences, with their relevant phantasies and defences, stored in the implicit memory of the patient. This corresponds to Davis's (2001) description of declarative and non-declarative processes in the psychoanalytic perspective.

Last, but not least, I come to the negotiation of the therapeutic climate between analyst and patient, which forms the basis of the therapeutic alliance (Greenson, 1967; Zetzel, 1970). This relational element can play a key role in establishing a situation emotionally conducive to the encounter and to the emergence of repressed and unrepressed material in the course of the analytic process. Moments of tension, rage, and resentment on the part of the patient (and sometimes also of the analyst) can jeopardise the way in which the couple's affective climate is negotiated. The analyst must be able to understand the feelings that, at any given time, obstruct a good negotiation. Practitioners will need to find out which parts of the patients are active and dominating in that particular transferential moment, as well as the nature of their countertransference. They must be able to decide, often with rapidity, which part of the patient needs gratification and which needs frustration. Analysts will then have to verbalise to patients the reasons for their dissent and why they have been drawn to emphasise one part of patients' personality as opposed to another one active at the same time. Dreams can be of great help, both for choosing the appropriate interpretative intervention and for letting patients understand what is being represented in the theatre of their minds, so justifying patients' emotions and analysts' choices. All this is in the belief that at moments when the negative transference risks compromising the possibility of letting the libidinal part of the patient prevail, or even putting at risk the analytic relationship itself, the correct understanding and interpretation can often be of valuable help. They can contain and transform the negative transference itself and promote progress in the therapeutic process.

A clinical case

To illustrate clinically what I have discussed, I present a segment of an analysis with one of my patients. This forty-year-old lady, whom I will call Luisa, the fourth of five children, requested analysis because of profound death anxieties, brought on by the diagnosis of breast cancer. After surgical intervention, this patient started a four-times-per-week analysis. During analysis, she undertook several treatments of chemotherapy. A fundamental characteristic which emerged immediately in Luisa's transference was the prosody of her language and her way of communicating in the sessions: her speech was slow, fragmented, interrupted by long intervals, and delivered with a very low voice, producing an atmosphere of expectation as to the content of her narrative. The slowness, the monotony, and the sense of distance that her speech evoked induced in me uneasiness, anxiety, and feelings of boredom. Her voice and her way of talking conveyed a continuous and desperate lament whose elaboration seemed impossible. Session after session, the (justified) worry about her physical health would conceal rage and resentment towards a destiny selecting her to represent suffering and the fear of separating from the world. However, the destiny was, in her unconscious, her mother and, in the transference, myself. She would project into me the rage and resentment for having had an inadequate, unjust, and insensitive mother, unable to understand the miserable, ill, and angry child that she had been. These feelings, conveyed in the transference by her voice and her words, and projectively identified into myself, would make me feel distant and incapable of either understanding or helping her. This was a repetition of a frustrating relationship with her mother, who preferred her other children and neglected Luisa's needs and desires.

Outside the transference, the patient's rage and resentment were enacted in the relation with her husband, who was accused of not doing enough for her, of not having any interests, of being boring, and of expecting from her a sexual proficiency that she was unable to offer. Husband and analyst were, of course, the objects in which she would put, through projective identification, the rage, the dissatisfaction, and the resentment of her infantile part related to a mother perceived as absent, boring, and incapable of taking care of her. The interpretative work on this aspect of the transference revealed by the prosody of her language, had allowed the patient to grasp some of the most emotional aspects of her (unrepressed) unconscious, those which concerned her early relationship with a depressed, distant, frustrating, and inadequate mother.

The patient's father never entered in the analytic relationship, except as the expression of an indifferent and absent internal object unable to help his daughter to undo her identification with the mother and to promote a positive identification with him. This explained the patient's total lack of interest in sexuality and, consequently, the difficulty in accepting a satisfactory sexual relation with her husband.

Correlating the work on transference, significant dreams emerged which helped to draw some reconstructive hypotheses concerning the patient's earliest stages. The work on these dreams allowed the patient to re-experience emotionally in the sessions traumatic experiences that she had never thought about or remembered, and to rewrite the story of her early affective relation with her mother. In one of these dreams,

the patient is talking while lying in bed and I am behind some curtains. When the curtains are drawn back, I am not there.

Having listened to this dream, I wondered whether my absence was temporary or whether I had always been absent with this patient, just as her mother had been distant and uninterested in her.

On a countertransference level, I experienced Luisa as a complaining, boring patient, who often conveyed, through her voice and words, rage, resentment, and hatred. Sometimes, during the session, I had a fleeting fantasy of leaving the consulting room in order to alleviate the heaviness of the encounter. I was almost overwhelmed by those feelings of uneasiness that Luisa would force into me through an intense projective identification. On the basis of these feelings, I was able to offer her a "constructive" interpretation. It was linked to the here and now of the session and aimed at making her aware of the affects that she conveyed with her voice, her speech, and her way of being in the session.

At the same time, however, I would feel as if I was the symbolic representative of an always absent mother, without reverie, unaffective, depressed, and distant. This led me to suggest to the patient a "reconstructive" hypothesis, offering the image of a little girl left alone with her rage, resentment, and hatred arising from not being looked after and nourished adequately by a mother always too busy with the other numerous siblings. I also mentioned that, as a baby, she had not felt physically contained and reassured through the sensory contact of skin against skin.

Luisa remained silent and the following day she brought this dream:

> I am with my husband at the computer and on the keyboard there is a thick layer of carpet that prevents me from feeling the keys. I am trying to reduce the thickness of the carpet, but it is still impossible for me to feel the keys.

In a lamenting tone, Luisa spoke again of the difficulties with her husband, but also of the great worry that I might get tired of her grievances and abandon her. I linked this dream to a "sensory" phantasy: that of not experiencing the analyst–mother as emotionally close. The lack of perception of a physical skin contact made her feel uncontained, and fearful of being left alone with her despair. Luisa told me of a painful separation that she had to accept from a close friend who abandoned her. Then, after a silence, she said, "I had a catastrophic phantasy. I wondered how far you are prepared to stay close to me, should things go wrong." (She was obviously referring to her tumour.)

The fear of being abandoned and of dying activated in Luisa very regressive defences. She told me, during that period, a dream in which "I feel transformed into a vegetal, pre-human being, with tree branches on my head instead of hair". Chemotherapy had, in reality, made all her hair fall out and the presence of the tumour had accentuated her death anxieties and the phantasies of disappearing as a human being. Although acknowledging this reality, I interpreted the dreams as symbolising very archaic experiences, still anchored in her memory without an actual recollection, and representing a transformation of herself into a cold and insensitive vegetal being, with tree branches on her head, similar to emotions without thoughts. I added that this transformation could be a defence against an unthinkable pain, produced by a mother without reverie, cold and of a vegetal, pre-human nature. This dream and the work on it created between us a very moving encounter that increased the insight of the patient and reduced significantly her anxiety.

Shortly before an analytic separation, Luisa described another dream: "there is a tree representing the face of a lamenting person". The words are not intelligible, but the tone of the voice and the atmosphere created by that face evoke suffering. Luisa complained of living with a depressed and boring husband. She added that before analysis she had never realised how many feelings his way of talking could convey. She complained again about her fate, the illness that might kill her, the void she felt inside her, the uselessness of our work, since she feared her life might be extinguished. I commented that not only the illness, but also the approach of our separation, made her feel like a miserable child, alone, without a mother–analyst within her able to contain her despair and neutralise her fear of dying. She interrupted by saying, "It is true. You have just described my mother. I cannot remember it, but your words have just formed for me the image of an inadequate, unsatisfied, depressed, and complaining mother, who has had, just like her own mother, a hard life."

During that period, her ninety-year-old mother died. In the session following the day of the death, she said, in a clear voice and with an aggressive tone, "I am ashamed to say that I do not feel any pain for the death of my mother. There is in me hate which I cannot control, a bad part of me which invades and neutralises my good part." I ventured the possibility that the little girl who now hates her mother was the victim, a long time ago, of painful and traumatic experiences which fuelled in her a resentful, bad part; this was her response to a mother who did not contain her and did not understand her needs. She interrupted me by saying, "As far as I remember, my mother's body repelled me. It was repugnant. It used to emit disgusting sounds and I was ashamed for her. I was disgusted just by the touch of her skin. I remember that my little sister developed a very serious erythema in the genitalia. In fact, my mother would often say that newborns repelled her." I was able, at this point, to link for her these phantasies to the image of her as a baby who does not feel contained by her mother, whose skin induces disgust in her. This baby had to cohabit with a maternal body full of vulgar noises that created in her a resentful, bad part that hates the mother and is happy at her death.

This session produced for the patient a profound insight and allowed her, through the work on the dreams and on the transference, to think about and verbalise frequent and extremely traumatic experiences, which were, in origin, unthinkable. This happened without the actual recollection of these experiences, by virtue only of their emotional recovery in the session.

In conclusion, and in order to link this clinical experience to the theory which I propose in this chapter, I wish to emphasise how the interpretations offered to the patient, concerning her voice and the prosody of her language, together with the images of the dreams, reproduced in the adult part of her the emotional essence of her infantile experience. The emphasis on these elements allowed the patient to re-experience emotionally the earliest traumatic experiences in the relationship with her mother, which she could not remember. She was, by then, able to integrate the different moments of her affective development with the unconscious significance of the experiences verbalised in the present of the transference. The therapeutic aspect of this process was its bridging function, which allowed the patient to put into narrative the unconscious traumatic experiences of the past. She was then able to think of, verbalise, and transform such experiences, conferring on them a new meaning.

Notes

1.   Pally (1997) calls this dimension "emotional memory". It presents analogies with that described by Klein (1957) as "memory in feeling".
2.   One objection can be made to Anderson and colleagues (2004), which is that Freudian repression would be unconscious, while suppression is conscious. However, the authors themselves suggest that, according to Freud, repression could be both conscious and unconscious. The limitation of repression to the unconscious was essentially due to Anna Freud (Erdelyi, 2001).
3.   For a discussion on constructions and reconstructions in the analytic process, see Mancia (1993) and Blum (1994).

References

Amati Mehler, J., Argentieri, S., & Canestri, J. (1993). *The Babel of the Unconscious: Mother Tongue and Foreign Languages in the Psychoanalytic Dimension*. Madison, CT: International Universities Press.

Anderson, M. C., Ochsner, K. N., Kuhl, B., Cooper, J., Robertson, E., Gabrieli, S. W., Glover, G. H., & Gabrieli, J. D. (2004). Neural systems underlying the suppression of unwanted memories. *Science, 303*: 232–235.

Antrobus, J. (1983). REM and NREM sleep reports: comparison of word frequencies by cognitive classes. *Psychophysiology, 5*: 562–568.

Arlow, J. A. (1987). The dynamics of interpretation. *Psychoanalytic Quarterly, 56*: 68–87.

Bennett, M. R., & Hacker, P. M. S. (2005). Emotion and cortical–subcortical function: conceptual developments. *Progress in Neurobiology, 75*: 29–52.

Bertini, M., & Violani, C. (1984). Cerebral hemisphere, REM sleep and dreaming. In: M. Bosinelli & P. Cicogna (Eds.), *Psychology of Dreaming* (pp. 131–135). Bologna: Clueb.

Bion, W. R. (1991). *Cogitations.* London: Karnac.

Bischof, M., & Bassetti, C. L. (2004). Total dream loss: a distinct neuropsychological dysfunction after bilateral PCA stroke. *Annals of Neurology, 56*: 583–586.

Bisiach, E., Denes, F., De Renzi, E., Faglioni, P., Gainotti, G., Pizzamiglio, L., Spinnler, H. R., & Vignolo, V. A. (1977). *Neuropsicologia clinica* [Clinical Neuropsychology]. Milan: Franco Angeli.

Bliss, T. V. P., & Lomo, T. (1973). Long-lasting potentiation of synaptic transmission in the dentate area of the anaesthetized rabbit following stimulation of the perforant path. *Journal of Physiology, 232*: 331–356.

Blum, H. P. (1994). *Reconstructions in Psychoanalysis. Childhood Revisited and Recreated.* New York: International Universities Press.

Bowlby, J. (1969). *Attachment and Loss, Volume 1: Attachment.* London: Hogarth.

Braun, A. R., Balkin, T. J., Wesensten, N. J., Carson, R. E., Varga, M., Baldwin, P., Belenky, G., & Herscovitch, P. (1998). Dissociated pattern of activity in visual cortices and their projections during human rapid eye movement sleep. *Science, 279*: 91–95.

Cimino, C., & Correale, F. (2005). Projective identification and consciousness alteration: a bridge between psychoanalysis and neuroscience? *International Journal of Psychoanalysis, 86*: 51–60.

Clyman, R. B. (1991). The procedural organization of emotions: a contribution from cognitive science to the psychoanalytic theory of therapeutic action. *Journal of the American Psychoanalytic Association, 39*(Suppl): 349–382.

Critchley, M. (1953). *The Parietal Lobes.* London: Arnold.

Damasio, A. R. (1999). *The Feeling of What Happens: Body and Emotion in the Making of Consciousness*. San Diego, CA: Harcourt Brace.

Davis, J. T. (2001). Revising psychoanalytic interpretations of the past: an examination of declarative and non-declarative memory processes. *International Journal of Psychoanalysis, 82*: 449–462.

De Casper, A. J., & Fifer, W. P. (1980). Of human bonding: newborns prefer their mothers' voices. *Science, 208*: 1174–1176.

De Saussure, F. (1960). *Course in General Linguistics*, G. Wolf (Ed.). London: Owen.

Di Benedetto, A. (2000). *Prima della parola: L'ascolto psicoanalitico del non detto attraverso le forme dell'arte* [Before speech: Psychoanalytical Listening of the non-said through Art Forms]. Milan: Angeli.

Erdelyi, M. H. (2001). Defense processes can be conscious or unconscious. *American Psychologist, 56*: 761–762.

Etchegoyen, L. (2004). Language and affects in the analytic practice. *International Journal of Psychoanalysis, 85*: 1479–1483.

Ferro, A. (2002). *In the Analyst's Consulting Room*, P. Slotkin (Trans.). Hove: Routledge.

Ferro, A. (2004). *Seeds of Illness, Seeds of Recovery: The Genesis of Suffering and the Role of Psychoanalysis*, D. Birksted-Breen (Ed.), P. Slotkin (Trans.). Hove: Routledge.

Fonagy, P. (1999). Memory and therapeutic action. *International Journal of Psychoanalysis, 80*: 215–223.

Fonagy, P., & Target, M. (1997). Attachment and reflective function: their role in self-organization. *Development and Psychopathology, 9*: 679–700.

Freud, S. (1899a). Screen memories. *S. E., 2*: 303–322. London: Hogarth.

Freud, S. (1912g). A note on the unconscious in psycho-analysis. *S. E., 12*: 260–266. London: Hogarth.

Freud, S. (1914g). Remembering, repeating and working-through (Further recommendations on the technique of psycho-analysis, II). *S. E., 12*: 147–156. London: Hogarth.

Freud, S. (1915d). Repression. *S. E., 14*: 146–158. London: Hogarth.

Freud, S. (1915e). The unconscious. SE 14, p. 166–204. London: Hogarth.

Freud, S. (1923b). *The Ego and the Id. S. E., 19*: 12–66. London: Hogarth.

Freud, S. (1925a). A note upon the 'mystic writing-pad'. *S. E., 14*: 227–232. London: Hogarth.

Freud, S. (1930a). *Civilization and its Discontents. S. E., 21*: 64–145. London: Hogarth.

Freud, S. (1937d). Constructions in analysis. *S. E., 23*: 257–269. London: Hogarth.

Freud, S. (1950a). Project for a scientific psychology. *S. E., 1*: 295–391. London: Hogarth.

Gabbard, G. O. (1997). Challenges in the analysis of adult patients with histories of childhood sexual abuse. *Canadian Journal of Psychoanalysis*, 5:1–25.

Gabbard, G. O., & Westen, D. (2003). Rethinking therapeutic action. *International Journal of Psychoanalysis, 84*: 823–841.

Gabrieli, J. D. E., Fleishman, D. A., Keane, M. M., Reminger, S. L., & Morrell, F. (1995). Double dissociation between memory systems underlying explicit and implicit memory in the human brain. *Psychological Science, 6*: 76–82.

Gainotti, G. (2001). Components and levels of emotion disrupted in patients with unilateral brain damage. In: F. Boller & J. Grafman (Eds.), *Handbook of Neuropsychology, Vol. 5: Emotional Behavior and its Disorders* (2nd edn) (pp. 161–180). Amsterdam: Elsevier.

Gallese, V. (2001). The 'shared manifold' hypothesis. From mirror neurons to empathy. *Journal of Consciousness Studies, 8*: 33–50.

Gallese, V. (2003). The manifold nature of interpersonal relations: the quest for a common mechanism. *Philosophical Transactions of the Royal Society of London, Series B, Biological Sciences, 358*: 517–528.

Gazzaniga, M. S. (Ed.) (1999). *The New Cognitive Neurosciences* (2nd edn). Cambridge, MA: MIT Press.

Geschwind, N. (1965a). Disconnection syndromes in animals and man—I. *Brain, 88*: 237–274.

Geschwind, N. (1965b). Disconnection syndromes in animals and man—II. *Brain, 88*: 585–644.

Gessa, G. L., & Tagliamonte, A. (1974). Possible role of brain serotonin and dopamine in controlling male sexual behavior. *Advances in Biochemical Psychopharmacology, 11*: 217–228.

Gill, M. M. (1983). *Analysis of Transference, Volume 1: Theory and Technique*. New York: International Universities Press.

Godfrind, J. (1993). *Les deux courants du transfert* [The Two Currents of Transference]. Paris: PUF.

Greenson, R. R. (1967). The technique and practice of psycho-analysis. London: Hogarth.

Grünbaum, A. (1993). *Validation in the Clinical Theory of Psychoanalysis: A Study in the Philosophy of Psychoanalysis*. Madison, CT: International Universities Press.

Hyvärinen, J. (1982). *The Parietal Cortex of Monkey and Man*. Berlin: Springer.

Ikemoto, S., & Panksepp, J. (1999). The role of nucleus accumbens dopamine in motivated behavior: a unifying interpretation with special reference to reward-seeking. *Brain Research Reviews, 31*: 6–41.

Joseph, B. (1985). Transference: the total situation. *International Journal of Psychoanalysis, 66*: 447–454.

Joseph, B. (1989). Defence mechanism and phantasy in the psychoanalytic process. In: M. Fedelman & E. Bott Spillius (Eds.), *Psychic Equilibrium and Psychic Change: Selected Papers of Betty Joseph* (pp. 116–126). Hove: Routledge.

Joseph, R. (1996). *Neuropsychiatry, Neuropsychology and Clinical Neuroscience: Emotion, Evolution, Cognition, Language, Memory, Brain Damage, and Abnormal Behavior* (2nd edn). Baltimore, MD: Lippincott Williams & Wilkins.

Kandel, E. R. (1999). Biology and the future of psychoanalysis: a new intellectual framework for psychiatry revisited. *American Journal of Psychiatry, 156*: 505–524.

Kandel, E. R. (2001). The molecular biology of memory storage: a dialogue between genes and synapses. *Science, 294*: 1030–1038.

Kandel, E. R. (2003). From the sea snail to the human brain: science without frontiers. Magistral Lecture, University of Milan-Bicocca, 21 November.

Kandel, E. R., Schwartz, J. H., & Jessel, T. M. (Eds.) (1996). *Principles of Neural Science* (3rd edn). East Norwalk, CT: Appleton & Lange.

Klein, M. (1932). *The Psycho-analysis of Children*. London: Hogarth.

Klein, M. (1957). *Envy and Gratitude: A Study of Unconscious Sources*. London: Hogarth.

Knoblauch, S. H. (2000). *The Musical Edge of Therapeutic Dialogue*. Hillsdale, NJ: Analytic Press.

Kolata, G. (1984). Studying learning in the womb. *Science, 225*: 302–303.

Koselleck, R. (1985). *Futures Past: On the Semantics of Historical Time*, K. Tribe (Trans.). Cambridge, MA: MIT Press.

Lacan, J. (1966). *Écrits: Le champ freudien*. Paris: Seuil.

Langer, S. K. (1942). *Philosophy in a New Key: A Study in the Symbolism of Reason, Rite, and Art*. Cambridge, MA: Harvard University Press.

LeDoux, J. E. (2000). Emotion circuits in the brain. *Annual Review of Neuroscience, 23*: 155–184.

Loewald, H. W. (1960). On the therapeutic action of psychoanalysis. *International Journal of Psychoanalysis, 41*: 16–33.

Lyons-Ruth, K., Bruschweiler-Stern, N., Harrison, A. M., Morgan, A. C., Nahum, J. P., Sander, L., Stern, D. N., & Tronick, E. Z. (1998). Implicit relational knowing: its role in development and psychoanalytic treatment. *Infant Mental Health Journal, 19*: 282–289.

Mancia, M. (1981). On the beginning of mental life in the foetus. *International Journal of Psychoanalysis*, 62: 351–357.

Mancia, M. (1993). *In the Gaze of Narcissus: Memory, Affects, and Creativity*. London: Karnac.

Mancia, M. (2000a). Il sogno: una fi nestra aperta sul transfert [Dreaming: an open window to transference]. *Rivista Psicoanalisi*, 46: 225–268.

Mancia, M. (2000b). Sulle molte dimensioni della memoria: neuroscienze e psicoanalisi a confronto [On the various dimensions of memory: a debate between neuroscience and psychoanalysis]. *Psiche*, 2: 181–192.

Mancia, M. (2003a). Dream actors in the theatre of memory: their role in the psychoanalytic process. *International Journal of Psychoanalysis*, 84: 945–952.

Mancia, M. (2003b). Implicit memory and unrepressed unconscious: their role in creativity and transference. *Israel Psychoanalytic Journal*, 3: 331–349.

Mancia, M. (2003c). Il sonno della memoria genera mostri [The sleep of memory generates monsters]. *Rivista Psicoanalisi*, 4: 691–708.

Mancia, M. (2004a). Coscienza e inconscio, sogno e memoria: possibili contaminazioni tra neuroscienze e psicoanalisi [Consciousness and unconscious, dream and memory: possible influences between neuroscience and psychoanalysis]. *Psiche*, 1: 75–89.

Mancia, M. (2004b). *Feeling the Words. Resonant Archives of the Implicit Memory and Musicality of the Transference*. Hove: Routledge.

Mancia, M. (2006). The dream in the dialogue between neurosciences and psychoanalysis. In: M. Mancia (Ed)., *Psychoanalysis and Neuroscience* (pp. 97–123). Milan and New York: Springer.

Mehler, J., & Christophe, A. (1995). Maturation and learning of language in the first year of life. In: M. F. Gazzaniga (Ed.), *The Cognitive Neurosciences* (pp. 943–954). Cambridge, MA: MIT Press.

Mehler, J., Bertoncini, J., Barrière, M., & Jassik-Gerschenfeld, D. (1978). Infant recognition of mother's voice. *Perception*, 7: 491–497.

Modell, A. H. (1993). *The Private Self*. Cambridge, MA: Harvard University Press.

Modell, A. H. (2004). The construction of meaning and the unconscious. Paper presented at: Dialogue of Psychoanalysis and Neurobiology: Theoretical and Therapeutic Aspects, Athens, 6 November.

Money-Kyrle, R. (1978). *The Collected Papers of Roger Money-Kyrle*, D. Meltzer (Ed.). Strathtay: Clunie Press.

Ogden, T. H. (2001). *Conversations at the Frontiers of Dreaming*. Northvale, NJ: Jason Aronson.

Ognibene, A. (1999). La spinta di Eros: Dalle rappresentazioni al linguaggio [The drive of Eros: From representation to language]. In: A. Bimbi (Ed.), *Eros e psiche* (pp. 27–37). Tirrenia (Pisa): Cerro.

Osaka, N., Osaka, M., Morishita, M., Kondo, H., & Fukuyama, H. (2004). A word expressing affective pain activates the anterior cingulate cortex in the human brain: an fMRI study. *Behavioral Brain Research, 153*: 123–127.

Pally, R. (1997). Memory: brain systems that link past, present and future. *International Journal of Psychoanalysis, 78*: 1223–1234.

Phelps, E. A. (2004). Human emotion and memory: interactions of the amygdala and hippocampal complex. *Current Opinion in Neurobiology, 14*: 198–202.

Process of Change Study Group (PCSG) (1998). Non-interpretative mechanisms in psychoanalytic therapy: the 'something more' than interpretation. *International Journal of Psychoanalysis, 79*: 903–921.

Pugh, G. (2002). Freud's 'problem': cognitive neuroscience and psychoanalysis working together on memory. *International Journal of Psychoanalysis, 83*: 1375–1394.

Ricoeur, P. (1998). *Das Rätsel der Vergangenheit: Erinnen—Vergessen—Verzeihen* [The Puzzle of the Past: Memory—Forgetting—Forgiveness]. Göttingen: Wallstein.

Rose, S. (1992). *The Making of Memory: From Molecules to Mind.* London: Bantam.

Sacchetti, B., Scelfo, B., Tempia, F., & Strata, P. (2004). Long-term synaptic changes induced in the cerebellar cortex by fear conditioning. *Neuron, 42*: 973–982.

Sandler, J., & Sandler, A.-M. (1987). The past unconscious, the present unconscious and the vicissitudes of guilt. *International Journal of Psychoanalysis, 68*: 331–341.

Schacter, D. L. (1995). Implicit memory: a new frontier for cognitive neuroscience. In: M. S. Gazzaniga (Ed.), *The Cognitive Neurosciences* (pp. 815–824). Cambridge, MA: MIT Press.

Semenza, C. (2001). Psychoanalysis and cognitive neuropsychology: theoretical and methodological affinities. *Neuro-Psychoanalysis, 3*: 3–10.

Shevrin, H. (2002). A psychoanalytic view of memory in the light of recent cognitive and neuroscience research. *Neuro-Psychoanalysis, 4*: 131–138.

Siegel, D. J. (1999). *The Developing Mind: Toward a Neurobiology of Interpersonal Experience.* New York: Guilford Press.

Singer, T., Seymour, B., O'Doherty, J., Kaube, H., Dolan, R. J., & Frith, C. D. (2004). Empathy for pain involves the affective but not sensory components of pain. *Science, 303*: 1157–1162.

Solms, M. (1995). New findings on the neurological organization of dreaming: implications for psychoanalysis. *Psychoanalytic Quarterly*, 44: 43–67.

Sperry, R. W. (1974). Lateral specialization in the surgical separated hemispheres. In: F. D. Smith & F. G. Worden (Eds.), *The Neurosciences. Third Study Program* (pp. 5–19). Cambridge, MA: MIT Press.

Squire, L. R. (1994). Declarative and nondeclarative memory: multiple brain system supporting learning and memory. In: D. L. Schacter & E. Tulvin (Eds.), *Memory Systems* (pp. 203–231). Cambridge, MA: MIT Press.

Steiner, J. (1989). The aim of psychoanalysis. *Psychoanalytic Psychotherapy*, 4: 109–120.

Stern, D. N. (1985). *The Interpersonal World of the Infant: A View from Psychoanalysis and Developmental Psychology*. New York: Basic Books.

Stickgold, R., Malia, A., Maguire, D., Roddenberry, D., & O'Connor, M. (2000). Replaying the game: hypnagogic images in normals and amnesics. *Science, 290*: 350–353.

Strachey, J. (1934). The nature of the therapeutic action of psychoanalysis. *International Journal of Psychoanalysis, 15*: 127–159.

Warrington, E. K., & Weiskrantz, L. (1974). The effect of prior learning on subsequent retention in amnesic patients. *Neuropsychologia, 12*: 419–428.

Wicker, B., Keysers, C., Plailly, J., Royet, J. P., Gallese, V., & Rizzolatti, G. (2003). Both of us disgusted in my insula: the common neural basis of seeing and feeling disgust. *Neuron, 40*: 655–664.

Winnicott, D. W. (1956). On transference. *International Journal of Psychoanalysis, 37*: 386–388.

Zetzel, E. R. (1970). *The Capacity for Emotional Growth*. London: Chatto & Windus.

CHAPTER THREE

Attachment, implicit memory, and the unrepressed unconscious

Giovanni Liotti

After extensive research into the different modes in which recollections of events can be conserved in the memory, experimental psychology now distinguishes between an explicit, declarative mode that is fully conscious and an implicit mode in which the contents of memory are expressed through enactment unaccompanied by conscious memory of how those contents were acquired (Schacter, 1987). Of particular interest to the clinician are the implicit memories of the earliest relational exchanges. Since it is not possible to invoke repression for the absence of a conscious memory of the mode of acquisition of the earliest implicit memories, it has been proposed that they be considered in the conceptual category of the unrepressed unconscious (Mancia, 2006). Reflections on this theme have led, on the one hand, to an extended conception of the unrepressed unconscious as a general modality of preverbal and prereflective consciousness that operates throughout the arc of a lifetime (implicit relational knowing: Lyons-Ruth et al., 1998; Stern, 2004) and, on the other hand, to a more restricted view of the unrepressed unconscious that focuses on *specific experiences* implicitly remembered in the earliest phases of life (Mancia, 2006).

Attachment theory (Bowlby, 1969) and the empirical research it inspired can provide us with a useful perspective from which to compare the two views, extended and restricted, of what is meant by unrepressed unconscious. In this chapter, I begin by recalling some of the basic tenets of attachment theory that, although necessary for an understanding of the specifics of the theory, are often neglected even by those authors who admire Bowlby's work and use it in their own studies.

The evolutionary and motivational foundations of attachment theory

Bowlby studied attachment in a framework of Darwinian thought, considering it to be one among many behavioural dispositions that are the result of evolution. Attachment, in this conceptual framework, can be traced back to one of the many classical Darwinian adaptations, or modules, selected because of the evolutionary advantage they offered. Since the beginning of life, these modules direct behaviour, operating outside of consciousness, towards goals that have an adaptive value. Some of the behavioral modules selected by evolution involve specific forms of social exchange. Attachment behaviour is just one among these relational modules (Cortina & Liotti, 2014). The relational goal of attachment behaviour is protection from environmental danger obtained through closeness to a member of the social group (primarily the mother, but potentially every known member of the social group). Different modules have different relational goals: the offer of care and protection (caring), the definition of the social order of dominance and subordination (social ranking), sexual mating, and co-operation in view of shared goals (Tomasello and his collaborators have recently called attention to this disposition towards egalitarian co-operation: Tomasello, 1999, 2009; Warneken et al., 2006). The operations of the relational modules involve the limbic system, which is evolutionarily more recent than the archaic areas of the brain involved in carrying out the innate dispositions that regard interaction with the non-social environment (exploration of the surrounding environment, territoriality, procuring food through predatory aggression, and defence from environmental threats through flight or fight). A careful reading of the first volume in Bowlby's trilogy (1969) reveals that the British psychoanalyst had clearly understood the need to study, throughout the entire period of development, the dynamic interaction between the attachment disposition and the other evolved dispositions (Liotti, 2015).

As early as in the earliest phases of extra-uterine life, relational experiences involving conduct regulated by the various evolved dispositions are memorised at the implicit level as sub-symbolic representations that, in attachment theory, are conceptualised as dynamic processes of memory and expectation functioning as operative rules (cf. the concept of internal working model, IWM, in Bowlby, 1969, and Bretherton, 2005). The IWM, then, is an organised set of implicit memories that combine with innate dispositions to constitute a corresponding system of behavioural control (motivational system). The IWM expresses, in an individualised manner, depending on the particular interactive experience of each child, the innate tendencies to pursue specific relational goals. The motivational systems of attachment (Bowlby, 1969) and of co-operative interaction (Tomasello, 1999) take shape within the first year of life. The first signs of the formation of the caring system (conduct that expresses a tendency towards gestures of rescue–comfort and protective affection) and the competitive system (opposition to adult orders, behaviour aimed at achieving dominance or displaying submissiveness) have been noticed by experts in infant observation during the second year of life. Controlled observations suggest that when the attachment system has developed in a safe environment, the behaviour typical of the caring system manifests itself more clearly, while a marked tendency to aggressiveness and competiveness are observed in two-year-olds whose attachment system was developed in an unsafe environment (Sroufe et al., 2005a,b).

The evolutionary multi-motivational theory that began to develop with the work of Bowlby (Cortina & Liotti, 2014) suggests that from the very earliest phases and throughout the life span there are continuous interactions or dynamic tensions between the various motivational systems. These tensions vary greatly from person to person because they are formed by individual memories (IWM) working at the level of implicit knowledge (Cortina & Liotti, 2007). This is the conceptual base on which rests the extended view of the unrepressed unconscious as "implicit relational knowing" (Lyons-Ruth et al., 1998; Stern, 2004). Implicit relational knowing might be conceived as a continuous articulation of various motivational systems that works outside of the reflective consciousness "from the cradle to the grave" (Bowlby, 1979a, p. 129). Mancia (2006) criticises this extended view of the unrepressed unconscious for the distance it takes from the classical concept of unconscious mental activity and for its approach instead to the conscious (although non-verbalised) dimension of relations. Consequently, Mancia (2006) proposes limiting the concept of unrepressed unconscious: rather than applying it to the complex procedure of implicit relational knowing as a whole, it could be applied to precise early experiences that, since the beginning of life, have been memorised only on an implicit level and dissociated from explicit memory. Throughout life, these early implicit memories influence oneiric activity and transference, manifesting themselves in oneiric symbols or with emotions that do not correspond to any recollection that can be considered as originally explicit and then successively repressed. Mancia's proposal suggests that, apart from the intrinsic difficulty in relating early implicit knowledge to successive explicit knowledge structures, other obstacles, potentially very interesting from a clinical point of view, might exist to the reformulation at the explicit level (fully conscious) of the memories built from the beginning of life at the implicit level. These obstacles could lead to a radical dissociation of some aspects of the implicit memory from those aspects of the explicit memory that should correspond but, instead, end up being collocated in meaning domains that are notably different and separate. Although part of a different conceptual framework, the reflections of Stern (2003) on unformulated experience appear to proceed in this direction.

Research on attachment supplies us with knowledge on the various forms of early intersubjective experience that lead to the establishment of the unrepressed unconscious in Mancia's restricted sense of that term, as well as knowledge of the processes that could lead to dissociation of the implicit from the explicit memories.

Research on attachment from infancy to adulthood

Attachment patterns in children at the end of their first and the beginning of their second year of life have been studied using a standardised procedure (strange situations procedure, SSP) in which the behaviour of children is observed during a sequence of brief separations followed by reunions (Ainsworth et al., 1978). As a result, three patterns of attachment behaviour have been identified: secure, insecure–avoidant and insecure–resistant (or ambivalent). In addition to these three patterns of attachment, subsequent research has demonstrated that it is possible for attachment behaviour to be disorganised at the end of the first year of life. Each pattern of attachment has, according to Bowlby's theory, a corresponding type of IWM (i.e., a different structure of the implicit memory of attachment).

The explicit memories, semantic and episodic, of attachment have been extensively and systematically studied in adults using a structured interview called the adult attachment interview (AAI). This research has demonstrated the existence of three organised mental states related to attachment: secure (free of defences), dismissing, and preoccupied (or entangled). Besides these three coherent or organised states of mind, a disorganised or incoherent mental state has been identified. It has been called "unresolved" because it is characterised by unresolved memories of traumas or bereavements undergone in relation to attachment.

A series of controlled researches lasting over decades and based on the comparison between the SSP of children and the AAI of their principal carer (usually the mother) have demonstrated notable correlations between the attachment pattern of the children and the mental state towards attachment of the adults who cared for them (for a recent survey of studies in this regard, see Shah et al., 2010), leading to the concept of intergenerational transmission of attachment (Bretherton, 1990).The adult mental state known as "secure" (or "free of defences", because it is characterised by the capacity to remember both positive and negative episodes from one's personal history of childhood attachment) predicts in statistically significant measure the security of the pattern of attachment of the child cared for by that adult. The intergenerational transmission of security in attachment is only slightly influenced by genetic factors (Fearon et al., 2006). The adult mental states called "dismissing" (denying the value of attachment needs) and "entangled" (hyper-involved in attachment issues) are characterised by a reduced capacity of mentalization and they predict two different types of insecure attachment in children: avoidant and resistant (or ambivalent). The adult mental states that are not integrated in thought and discourse because of unresolved memories of trauma or bereavement predict an analogous disorganisation in the attachment behaviour of the child (Sroufe et al., 2005a,b). The conclusion that can be drawn from this research is that, from the beginning of life, interactive experiences related to attachment, different for each child in regard to the function of the mental state of his adult carer, are memorised at the implicit level (IWM) and are manifested in corresponding styles of behaviour that express in an individualised way the universal need for attachment. The extended version of the concept of unrepressed unconscious (implicit relational knowing) could find support in the observation that the construction of individualised memories of attachment interactions is a universal process. However, it can also be argued that attachment theory and research support the restricted version of the concept in so far as only a few of the results of the universal process of constructing individualised IWMs lead to a lasting dissociation between early implicit memories of attachment and the explicit memories reported in the AAI (see the findings of the five longitudinal research studies on the vicissitudes of attachment from childhood to adulthood in Grossmann et al., 2005).

Forms of dissociation between implicit and explicit memories of attachment

The longitudinal studies cited above suggest the existence in adults of both explicit memories coherent with the implicit memories of early attachment and at least three forms of dissociation between these memories.

Adults whose mental states are classified as "secure" by the AAI do not show any evident discrepancies between: (a) their memories of positive and negative experiences as reported in response to the interview questions, and (b) their probable early experiences of attachment. The coherence between the implicit and explicit levels of memory is evidenced, not only by the contents and the forms of their answers to AAI questions, but also by two research findings: (1) children who have received care from these adults tend to show security in attachment in statistically significant percentages; (2) data from the longitudinal studies provide evidence of the continuity between security in the attachment assessed in the child through the SSP and the young adult through the AAI (Main et al., 2005; Sroufe et al.,

2005b). Therefore, when early attachment is secure, there is no evidence of a tendency to dissociation between implicit and explicit memories of attachment.

Adults whose AAI mental states are categorised as "dismissing" (the importance of attachment) give instead the impression of a dissociation between: (a) the formally coherent but unrealistically positive (idealised) descriptions they give when speaking of the attachment figure, and (b) clear indications that their early experiences of attachment were unhappy (as can be inferred from the responses they give when asked to exemplify their generic idealised descriptions with episodic memories). The longitudinal studies support this impression, evidencing correlations between the patterns of early attachment classified as "insecure" that were observed in children through the SSP and the mental state concerning attachment classified "dismissing" in the AAI.

A different form of dissociation between implicit and explicit memories of attachment is suggested by the mental state classified in the AAI as "preoccupied" or "entangled" (hyper-involved in the inconclusive attempt to attribute a unitary meaning to their own experience of attachment). Rather than an idealisation of the attachment figure that is far removed from the probable implicit memory of the real interaction, here there is instead a sequence of incoherent attributions of meaning to the memory of the attachment experience, as if the explicit memory were continually engaged in a futile search for meanings (even though multiple) for the underlying implicit memory. A recent longitudinal study shows that an inconclusive search for stable meaning while responding to the AAI may be found not only in adults whose early attachment in the SSP had ben ambivalent (resistant), but also in some adults whose infant attachment had been avoidant (Shah et al., 2010).

These two forms of dissociation between early implicit memories and successive explicit memories of attachment can be traced back, hypothetically, to the influence of points of view verbally expressed by the carers about relational events and about their own feelings towards the child. In the course of the development of personality and of cognitive capacity, the child might be repeatedly exposed to pressures from the carer that belie the potential meaning of his direct or implicit experience or that discourage him from focusing attention and his growing reflective capacity on familial events and on evident aspects of his parents' behaviour and personalities. These pressures, whether they are explicit and direct or subtle and indirect, exploit children's intense desire to be loved, approved of, and protected, inducing them to make the carer's point of view their own at the level of explicit memory even though that point of view is incompatible with implicit memories (Bowlby, 1979b). Consequently, during the AAI, some adults might affirm that they always trusted their parents and found them to be responsive to their requests for affection, while both the video registration of their behaviour in the SSP when they were one year old and their current style of attachment testify to the existence of implicit memories that are much less positive. Considerably different from these influences that lead to the dissociation between the implicit and explicit areas of the memory are the conditions that cause disorganised attachment. Here, the dissociation is already present directly at the implicit level much before the dissociation between the early implicit memory and the successively constructed explicit memory. This third type of dissociation is expressed in the AAI in serious incoherence of thought and speech and it manifests itself in infancy as disorganised attachment behaviour during the SSP (Main, et al., 2005). Because of its clinical relevance and its importance for an understanding of the unrepressed unconscious, disorganised attachment warrants a detailed analysis.

Infant attachment disorganisation and the unrepressed unconscious

Attachment disorganisation in the first year of life is attributable to an unresolvable conflict between two innate dispositions, attachment and survival defence from environmental threats (Liotti, 2011, 2013). During mammal evolution, the first, completely individual level involving defence against environmental threats through fleeing or fighting (survival defence system) was integrated with a second level that centred on the active seeking out of protective closeness to a member of the social group (attachment system). The young in most species of mammals tend to flee from threats of danger in the environment (for example, the approach of a predator) to seek out protection in being close to an adult member of the social group (usually the mother). This functional harmony, achieved through evolution, between the survival defence system and the attachment system is transformed into an unresolvable conflict when a threat to the child's survival is repeatedly made by the attachment figure—a phenomenon that, although rarely observed in other mammals, is not uncommon in the human species. Two types of conduct on the part of the carer can give rise in the child to an unresolvable conflict between the attachment system and the survival defence system. The first is the repetition of violent aggression by the carer that abruptly interrupts the caring behaviour. The second involves neglect or a fear-stricken impotence when the child, alarmed by the perception of a threat in the environment or by physical pain, seeks closeness to the protective figure (Lyons-Ruth & Jacobvitz, 2008; Main & Hesse, 1990). In the first case, the survival defence system is activated in children towards the same persons that they perceive at the same time as the source of comfort and protection. In the second case, the terror-stricken impotence or neglect of the carer in reaction to the child's intense alarm or suffering activates the defence system by default, while the attachment system is still active. It is as if an unconscious calculation of the possibilities of getting help reveals to the child that there is no possibility at all, thereby triggering a mechanism of self-defence against the potential threats. In both cases, the attachment system and the defence system are simultaneously at work in the child, but, rather than functioning together in harmony, they enter into an unresolvable conflict with each other (see the description of "fright without solution" that characterises attachment disorganisation in Main & Hesse, 1990). Because of the similarity of the effect on the attachment of the child by the two types of the carers' behaviour— violent and fearful although not explicitly maltreating—disorganised attachment has been considered an early relational trauma. In both cases, there is the disharmonic and ineffective simultaneous activation of the survival defence and the attachment systems that characterises all post-trauma disorders (Schore, 2009).

The implicit memories connected to the innate dispositions of attachment and survival defence normally assume an integrated form because they are contextualised in two different spheres of experience (in one sphere, there is the source of danger from which the child flees, and, in the other, the carer in whose arms the child seeks protection and comfort). Since, in disorganised attachment, the two innate dispositions, attachment and survival defence, are both directed simultaneously at the same person, it becomes impossible to integrate the memory of the interaction in an implicit representation that is unified and cohesive: the sub-symbolic representation of the self-with-other co-ordinated with the innate disposition of attachment is dissociated from that of self with the same other connected to the disposition of defence for survival. Long before the dissociation between implicit and explicit typical of insecure organised (avoidant and ambivalent) attachment has a chance to establish itself, in infant disorganised attachment the dissociation appears within the implicit level.

The IWM of disorganised attachment then lacks from the outset the degree of unity and coherence that characterises the precocious implicit memories of other types of attachment: it is dis-integrated (that is, composed of multiple elements that are dissociated from each other) as has been argued through a careful analysis of attachment disorganisation observed in the SSP (Main & Morgan, 1996). A number of controlled researches, including some longitudinal studies, evidenced that disorganised attachment in early childhood predisposes a child to dissociated mental processes during the entire period of his development and into adulthood (for a synthetic review of this research, see Liotti, 2014).

The following two paragraphs present further reflections on the psychic mechanisms of dis-integration among the implicit memories of the disorganised IWM, and a synthesis of the research on the sequels of infant attachment disorganisation up to the age when the child enters school. These will be brought to bear, in the final section, on the two views, the extended and the concentrated, of the unrepressed unconscious.

The IWM of disorganised attachment

On a formal level, the psychoanalytic concept of splitting can be compared with the idea of dissociation at the implicit level between the memories of self-with-other characterising the IWM of infant disorganised attachment. Kernberg and colleagues (2008, p. 89) recently acknowledged that it is possible to use both the concepts, dissociation and splitting, to indicate the lack of integration between the implicit representations of the self and of the career in disorganised attachment. The cause and the psychic mechanism at the origin of this type of dis-integration, however, differ significantly depending on whether we adopt the classical drive theory or the evolutionistic multi-motivational theory. Splitting is a pre-oedipal defensive mechanism activated by the conflict between the libido and destructive aggression directed towards the object of a drive. The dissociation that characterises the IWM of disorganised attachment is, instead, explained by the multi-motivational theory as the result of the failure of the cognitive process that normally integrates sub-symbolic representations of the self-with-other: this failure is not caused by an intrapsychic defence mechanism, but by the intrinsic incompatibility between the implicit representations related to attachment and those related to survival defence when the two systems are both simultaneously directed towards the same person.

If we adopt classical drive theory and think of splitting in terms of an archaic intrapsychic defence, then we are led to theorise that the dis-integration that occurs among the implicit memories of the unrepressed unconscious essentially involves two opposing representations of the self and the drive object, which have two distinct emotional correlates, desire and destructive aggression. If, instead, we adopt the evolutionary multi-motivational perspective, we are led to consider fear without solution (Main & Hesse, 1990) as the pivot on which multiple affects turn: desire for help and comfort, rage, sadness, and helplessness. Thus, the dis-integration of the IWM regards more than two implicit representations of self-with-other and can be traced back, metaphorically, to the concept of the "drama triangle" proposed by Karpman (1968) in the theoretical context of transactional analysis (Liotti, 2004, 2011).

The three basic roles of the drama triangle that, according to Karpman, underpin the transactions between the main characters of both fairy tales and the tragedies of classic theatre, are the powerful rescuer, the equally powerful persecutor, and the powerless victim. Being at least potentially available and willing to help and comfort the infant, parents and other carers are perceived by the disorganised children as rescuers. When they are subtly hostile or prone to episodes of aggression, the same carers are perceived as persecutors. Simultaneously, because they express their helplessness, fear, and suffering (usually caused by the unresolved traumatic memories) while taking care of their infants, the parents of disorganised children are perceived as victims. The implicit self-representations of the infants disorganised in their attachments shifts in a quite similar manner between the roles of the powerless victim, the persecutor (self construed as the cause of the parent's expressed suffering) and the rescuer (self able and willing to soothe the carer's suffering: for a more detailed argument concerning this aspect of the drama triangle within the infant's disorganised IWM, see Liotti, 2004, p. 479). These reciprocally incompatible (and, therefore, reciprocally not integrated) representational prototypes are the base for implicitly construing the behaviour of self and others during later attachment interactions.

The evolutionary multi-motivational view also suggests that, besides the attachment and the survival defence systems, other innate motivational systems might also be activated in a disharmonic manner in the course of development, during the relational exchanges influenced by disorganised attachment (notably the caring system and the dominance–subordination system, and in contexts where experience of sexual abuse at an early age is present; also the sexual system). Each of these other systems influences the construction of the corresponding representations of self-with-other with the construction of meaning structures very different from those related to attachment and survival defence. As a consequence, the IWM of disorganised attachment might end up being linked at the implicit level to multiple memory structures that cannot be translated with corresponding coherent structures in the explicit consciousness. Research on the sequences of disorganised attachment from the third to the sixth year of life supplies data that clarify and support this hypothesis.

Sequels of infant disorganised attachment during childhood personality development

Empirical research evidenced that the majority of children who have been disorganised in their infant attachments develop, before school age, one of two types of interpersonal strategies, called controlling: either a controlling punitive or a controlling caring strategy (Lyons-Ruth & Jacobvitz, 2008). Controlling caring strategies in children (also known as inverted attachment) are identified by solicitous, caring behaviour directed toward the carer. Controlling punitive strategies are identified by attempts to punish or embarrass the carer through harsh criticism. The emergence of the controlling strategies in children who have been disorganised in their infant attachments may be explained as a case of reciprocal inhibition between different motivational systems (Liotti, 2011). The argument runs as follows.

The attachment system, as has been stated at the beginning of this chapter, is one among a number of different motivational systems that regulate social interactions in all mammals. These systems are the result of evolutionary processes and can be conceptualised as universal, inborn dispositions aimed at pursuing each a specific biosocial goal (Gilbert, 1989). They comprehend, besides the attachment system (whose goal is care-seeking), a caring system, a ranking system aimed at achieving dominance through competitive behaviour, a sexual mating system, and a co-operative system. Although the simultaneous activation of two or more of these systems is a possibility at the level of implicit mental processes during social exchanges, at the explicit (conscious) level, only one of them tends to prevail over the others in the conscious experience of the exchange (see Dennet, 1991, for a detailed argument concerning the dynamic tensions between parallel distributed processes involving the simultaneous activation of different mental systems at the level of implicit knowledge and the single version, dictated by only one prevailing system, that tends to emerge in the serial mental process that characterises consciousness).

In this conceptual framework, the activation of a motivational system in the serial, explicit process of consciousness inhibits the surfacing in consciousness of the other systems that might remain active at the implicit level of parallel processing. The development of the controlling strategies that typically appear in pre-schoolers who have been disorganised in their infant attachments might, thus, be explained by a repeated inhibition of the surfacing in consciousness of the persisting operations of the attachment system, achieved through co-opting regularly another motivational system during the daily interactions with the carer. When a disorganised IWM dominates them since infancy, there is a good reason to inhibit the activities of the attachment system as often as possible throughout development: a defensive inhibition of the attachment system protects both children and their relationship with parents from the unbearably chaotic experience of disorganisation. The activation of the caring system in the service of such a self-protecting inhibition of the attachment system yields a controlling caring strategy in the child. The activation of the dominance–submission inborn strategies (competitive or ranking system: Gilbert, 1989) lies at the base of controlling punitive strategies.

While the controlling punitive and controlling caring strategies have been well documented in longitudinal studies of the sequels of early attachment disorganisation, one could hypothesise, on clinical and theoretical grounds, that some children develop other strategies to cope with the shattered states brought on by the activation of the disorganised IWM. Other inborn, evolved, social dispositions— besides caring and dominance—might intervene instead of the attachment system to regulate the interactions between child and parent, so that behaviour and intersubjective experience can achieve at least a degree of organisation. For instance, abnormally sexualised parent–child interactions can be hypothetically linked, through evolutionary and anthropological analyses of incest avoidance (Erikson, 2000), to a preceding disorganisation of the attachment motivational system in the infant. According to this hypothesis, some disorganised children resort to the activation of the sexual system to protect themselves, through a sexualised controlling strategy, from the unbearable fragmentation in the experience of self-with-other contingent upon attachment motivations plagued by the operations of a disorganised IWM. Erikson (2000) revisited the concept of the oedipal complex on the basis of this line of evolutionary thinking.

Concluding remarks

Attachment theory and research provide abundant and clinically relevant material for a description of the structures of implicit memory that can serve in constructing a model of the unrepressed unconscious according to the restricted concept proposed by Mancia (2006). The examples described in this chapter concern the implicit memory content of the IWM that take form during the first years of life in avoidant and ambivalent attachments and, above all, in disorganised attachment, where memories are radically unintegrated among themselves. Although these structures of implicit memory usually remain dissociated throughout the entire period of development, this dissociation does not involve the classical defensive mechanisms of repression or splitting. As Mancia (2006) has emphasised, these memories of the unrepressed unconscious manifest themselves in dreams and in transference, but never in the self-reflective consciousness.

However, attachment theory—especially if it is cast in a multi-motivational evolutionary perspective—provides support also to the extended view of the unrepressed unconscious (implicit relational knowing) proposed by Daniel Stern (2004) and Karlen Lyons-Ruth (Lyons-Ruth et al., 1998). The reflections reported in this chapter on the conflict between the attachment and the survival defence systems, and on the genesis of control strategies in pre-school children as a sequel of infant attachment disorganisation, illustrate the complexity of the dynamic tensions between the various motivational systems that operate at the implicit level in the processes that lead to knowledge of the self-with-other. These dynamic tensions unfold in a mental scenario that is so radically unconscious as to elude the criticism Mancia (2006) directed at the extended version of the concept of unrepressed unconscious. It is, in fact, difficult to imagine that pre-school children implement an inhibition of the attachment system, through the co-option of another innate motivational systems, in a manner that, approximating conscious non-verbal experience, is far removed from the psychoanalytic concept of the unconscious (the main argument advanced by Mancia to refute the extended view of the unrepressed unconscious as implicit relational knowing). The process of co-opting one innate motivational system in order to inhibit another innate system seems to rest on the overall dynamic properties of the multiple inborn systems constituting the unrepressed unconscious (extended view) at least as much as it rests on the direct effect of the implicit memory (disorganised IWM) of a single set of experiences (restricted view).

From the perspective of attachment theory and of the evolutionary multi-motivational theory of which attachment theory is a part, there is, then, no reason to consider the restricted and the extended versions of the concept of unrepressed unconscious as alternatives to each other. Specific implicit memories that are intrinsically dissociated (disorganised IWM), may put in motion radically unconscious processes of co-option of other motivational systems in the place of the system to which those specific implicit memories are linked (the attachment system). If this analysis of the theory and research on attachment disorganisation is correct, then there is no basic incompatibility prohibiting the use together, in clinical practice, of both the restricted and the extended versions of the concept of unrepressed unconscious.

References

Ainsworth, M. D. S., Blehar, M. C., Waters, E., & Wall, S. (1978). *Patterns of Attachment: A Psychological Study of the Strange Situation.* Hillsdale, NJ: Lawrence Erlbaum.
Bowlby, J. (1969). *Attachment and Loss. Volume 1: Attachment.* London: Hogarth Press.
Bowlby, J. (1979a). *The Making and Breaking of Affectional Bonds.* London: Tavistock.
Bowlby, J. (1979b). On knowing what you are not supposed to know, and on feeling what you are not supposed to feel. *Canadian Journal of Psychiatry, 24:* 403–408.
Bretherton, I. (1990). Communication patterns, internal working models, and the intergenerational transmission of attachment relationships. *Infant Mental Health Journal, 11:* 237–252.
Bretherton, I. (2005). In pursuit of the internal working model construct and its relevance to attachment relationship. In: K. E. Grossmann, K. Grossmann, & Waters, E. (Eds.), *Attachment from Infancy to Adulthood: The Major Longitudinal Studies* (pp.13–47). New York: Guilford Press.
Cortina, M., & Liotti, G. (2007). New approaches to understanding unconscious processes: implicit and explicit memory systems. *International Forum of Psychoanalysis, 16:* 204–212.
Cortina, M., & Liotti, G. (2014). An evolutionary outlook on motivation: implications for the clinical dialogue. *Psychoanalytic Inquiry, 34:* 864–899.
Dennet, D. C. (1991). *Consciousness Explained.* New York: Little, Brown.
Erikson, M. T. (2000). The evolution of incest avoidance: Oedipus and the psychopathology of kinship. In: P. Gilbert & K. Bailey (Eds.), *Genes on the Couch: Explorations in Evolutionary Psychotherapy* (pp. 211–231). Hove: Brunner-Routledge.
Fearon, R. M., Van IJzendoorn, M. H., Fonagy, P., Bakermans-Kranenburg, M. J., Schuengel, C., & Bokhorst, C. L. (2006). In search of shared and nonshared environmental factors in security of attachment: a behavior-genetic study of the association between sensitivity and attachment security. *Developmental Psychology, 42:* 1026–1040.
Gilbert, P. (1989). *Human Nature and Suffering.* London: LEA.
Grossmann, K. E., Grossmann, K., & Waters, E. (Eds.) (2005). *Attachment from Infancy to Adulthood: The Major Longitudinal Studies.* New York: Guilford Press.
Karpman, S. (1968). Fairy tales and script drama analysis. *Transactional Analysis Bulletin, 7:* 39–43. www.karpmandramatriangle.com/pdf/DramaTriangle.pdf.

Kernberg, O. F., Yeomans, F., Clarkin, J. F., & Levy, K. N. (2008). Transference focused psychotherapy: overview and update. *International Journal of Psychoanalysis, 89*: 601–620.

Liotti, G. (2004). Trauma, dissociation and disorganized attachment: three strands of a single braid. *Psychotherapy: Theory, Research, Practice, Training, 41*: 472–486.

Liotti, G. (2011). Attachment disorganization and the controlling strategies: an illustration of the contributions of attachment theory to developmental psychopathology and to psychotherapy integration. *Journal of Psychotherapy Integration, 21*: 232–252.

Liotti, G. (2013). Phobias of attachment-related inner states in the psychotherapy of adult survivors of childhood complex trauma. *Journal of Clinical Psychology, 69*: 1136–1147.

Liotti, G. (2014). Disorganized attachment in the pathogenesis and the psychotherapy of borderline personality disorder. In: A. N. Danquah & K. Berry (Eds.), *Attachment Theory in Adult Mental Health* (pp 113–128). London: Routledge.

Liotti, G. (2015). Psicoterapia ispirata dalla teoria dell'attaccamento: Una prospettiva basata sulla teoria evoluzionista dei sistemi motivazionali [Attachment informed psychotherapy: an approach based on the evolutionary theory of motivational systems]. *Attaccamento e Sistemi Complessi* (Attachment and Complex Systems), 2: 11–26.

Lyons-Ruth, K., & Jacobvitz, D. (2008). Attachment disorganization: genetic factors, parenting contexts and developmental transformation from infancy to adulthood. In: J. Cassidy & P. Shaver (Eds.), *Handbook of Attachment* (2nd edn) (pp. 666–697). New York: Guilford Press.

Lyons-Ruth, K., Bruschweiler-Stern, N., Harrison, A. M., Morgan, A. C., Nahum, J. P., Sander, L., Stern, D. N., & Tronick, E. Z. (1998). Implicit relational knowing: its role in development and psychoanalytic treatment. *Infant Mental Health Journal, 19*: 282–289.

Main, M., & Hesse, E. (1990). Parents' unresolved traumatic experiences are related to infant disorganized attachment status: is frightened and/or frightening parental behavior the linking mechanism? In: M. T. Greenberg, D. Cicchetti, & E. M. Cummings (Eds.), *Attachment in the Preschool Years* (pp. 161–182). Chicago, IL: Chicago University Press.

Main, M., & Morgan, H. (1996). Disorganization and disorientation in infant Strange Situation behavior: phenotypic resemblance to dissociative states? In: L. Michelson & W. Ray (Eds.), *Handbook of Dissociation* (pp. 107–137). New York: Plenum Press.

Main, M., Hesse, E., & Kaplan, N. (2005). Predictability of attachment behavior and representational processes at 1, 6 and 19 years of age.

In: K. E. Grossmann, K. Grossmann, & E. Waters (Eds.), *Attachment from Infancy to Adulthood: The Major Longitudinal Studies* (pp. 245–304). New York: Guilford Press.

Mancia, M. (2006). Implicit memory and unrepressed unconscious: how they surface in the transference and in the dream. In: M. Mancia (Ed.), *Psychoanalysis and Neuroscience* (pp. 97–123). New York: Springer.

Schacter, D. L. (1987). Implicit memory: history and current status. *Journal of Experimental Psychology: Learning, Memory, and Cognition*, 13: 501–518.

Schore, A. N. (2009). Attachment trauma and the developing right brain: origins of pathological dissociation. In: P. F. Dell & J. A. O'Neill (Eds.), *Dissociation and the Dissociative Disorders* (pp. 107–141). New York: Routledge.

Shah, P. E., Fonagy, P., & Strathearn, L. (2010). Is attachment transmitted across generations? The plot thickens. *Clinical Child Psychology and Psychiatry*, 15: 329–345.

Sroufe, L. A., Egeland, B., Carlson, E., & Collins, W. A. (2005a). Placing early attachment experiences in developmental context. In: K. E. Grossmann, K. Grossmann, & E. Waters (Eds.), *Attachment from Infancy to Adulthood: The Major Longitudinal Studies* (pp. 48–70). New York: Guilford Press.

Sroufe, L. A., Egeland, B., Carlson, E., & Collins, W. A. (2005b). *The Development of the Person: The Minnesota Study of Risk and Adaptation from Infancy to Adulthood*. New York: Guilford Press.

Stern, D. B. (2003). *Unformulated Experience: From Dissociation to Imagination in Psychoanalysis*. Hillsdale, NJ: Analytic Press.

Stern, D. N. (2004). *The Present Moment in Psychotherapy and Everyday Life*. New York: Norton.

Tomasello, M. (1999). *The Cultural Origins of Human Cognition*. Cambridge, MA: Harvard University Press.

Tomasello, M. (2009). *Why We Cooperate*. Cambridge, MA: Boston Review Books.

Warneken, F., Chen, F., & Tomasello, M. (2006). Cooperative activities in young children and chimpanzees. *Child Development*, 77: 640–663.

CHAPTER FOUR

The right brain implicit self: a central mechanism of the psychotherapy change process

Allan N. Schore

After a century of disconnection, psychoanalysis is returning to its psychological *and* biological sources, and this reintegration is generating a palpable surge of energy and revitalisation of the field. At the centre of both theoretical and clinical psychoanalysis is the concept of the unconscious. The field's unique contribution to science has been its explorations of the psychic structures and processes that operate beneath conscious awareness in order to generate essential survival functions. In the past ten years, implicit unconscious phenomena have finally become a legitimate area of not only psychoanalytic, but also scientific, enquiry. Writing to the broader field of psychology, Bargh and Morsella (2008, p. 73) now conclude, "Freud's model of the unconscious as the primary guiding influence over every day life, even today, is more specific and detailed than any to be found in contemporary cognitive or social psychology".

An important catalyst of this rapprochement is the contact point between modern neuropsychoanalysis and contemporary neuroscience. Current neurobiological researchers now conclude, "The right hemisphere has been linked to implicit information processing, as opposed to the more explicit and more conscious processing tied to the left hemisphere" (Happaney et al., 2004, p. 7). Indeed, over the past two decades, I have provided a substantial amount of interdisciplinary evidence which supports the proposition that the early developing right brain generates the implicit self (Schore, 1994, 1997, 2003a, 2005, 2007, 2009b, 2012), an early unrepressed unconscious nucleus of the self (Mancia, 2006). My ongoing studies in regulation theory focus on the essential right brain structure–function relationships that underlie the psychobiological substrate of the human unconscious, and they attempt to elucidate the origin, psychopathogenesis, and psychothera-peutic treatment of the early forming subjective implicit self.

In this chapter, I demonstrate that current clinical and experimen-tal studies of the unconscious, implicit domain can do more than sup-port a clinical psychoanalytic model of treatment, but, rather, this interdisciplinary information can elucidate the mechanisms that lie at the core of psychoanalysis. The body of my work strongly suggests the following organising principles. The concept of a single unitary "self" is as misleading as the idea of a single unitary "brain". The left and right hemispheres process information in their own unique fash-ions, and this is reflected in a conscious left lateralised self system ("left mind") and an unconscious right lateralised self system ("right mind"). Despite the designation of the verbal left hemisphere as "dominant" due to its capacities for explicitly processing language functions, it is the right hemisphere and its implicit homeostatic survival and affect regulation functions that are truly dominant in human existence (Schore, 2003a, 2009b). Over the life span, the early-forming unconscious implicit self continues to develop to more complexity, and it operates in qualitatively different ways from the later-forming conscious explicit self. Recall Freud's (1916–1917) asser-tion that the unconscious is "a special realm, with its own desires and modes of expression and peculiar mental mechanisms not elsewhere operative". In essence, my work is an exploration of this "special realm".

With the emergence of modern neuropsychoanalysis and its direct connections with contemporary neuroscience, the right brain's domi-nance for an "emotional" and "corporeal" sense of self (Devinsky, 2000; Schore, 1994) is now common ground to both disciplines. This integration clearly demonstrates that evolutionarily adaptive implicit bodily based socio-emotional functions represent the output of the unique developmental, anatomical, and psychobiological properties of the right brain. Indeed, the implicit functions and structures of the right brain represent the inner world described by psychoanalysis since its inception. From its origin in "The project for a scientific psychology", Freud's explorations of the deeper levels of the human mind have exposed the illusion of a single state of surface conscious-ness, and revealed the essential contributions of a biological substra-tum of unconscious states that indelibly impact all levels of human existence. The temporal difference of right implicit and left explicit processing is described by Buklina (2005, p. 479):

> [T]he more "diffuse" organization of the right hemisphere has the effect that it responds to any stimulus, even speech stimuli, more quickly and, thus, earlier. The left hemisphere is activated after this and performs the slower semantic analysis . . . the arrival of an indi-vidual signal initially in the right hemisphere and then in the left is more "physiological". (See Figure 4.1.)

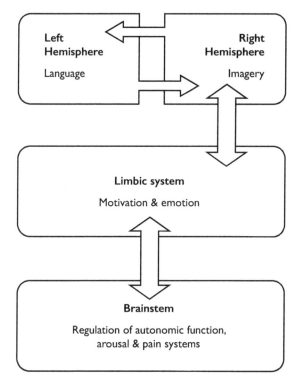

Figure 4.1.   Implicit processing of right brain and subsequent connections into left brain explicit system.

Another reason for the strong attraction of psychoanalysis to the right brain is found in its unique survival functions, processes that are disturbed in various psychopathologies. Schutz (2005) highlights the adaptive functions uniquely subserved by this "emotional brain":

> The right hemisphere operates a distributed network for rapid responding to danger and other urgent problems. It preferentially processes environmental challenge, stress and pain and manages self-protective responses such as avoidance and escape . . . Emotionality is thus the right brain's "red phone", compelling the mind to handle urgent matters without delay. (p. 15)

A more profound and comprehensive understanding of the organising principles of this rapid acting and, therefore, non-conscious right brain "physiological" implicit core system can provide not only essential and relevant clinical and experimental data, but also a theoretical lens which can illuminate and penetrate the fundamental problems addressed by psychoanalytic science. Just as studies of the left brain, dominant for language and verbal processing, can never elucidate the unique non-verbal functions of the right, studies of the output of the explicit functions of the conscious mind in verbal transcripts or narratives can never reveal the implicit psychobiological dynamics of the unconscious mind (Schore, 1994, 2002, 2003a; Schore & Schore, 2008).

This neuropsychoanalytic perspective echoes Freud's fundamental assertion that the central questions of the human condition, which psychoanalysis directly addresses, can never be found in knowledge of how the conscious mind of the explicit self system works, but, rather, in a deeper understanding of the implicit psychobiological mechanisms of the unconscious mind. Other fields of study are currently appreciating the importance of this unconscious realm in all levels of human existence. Thus, not only psychoanalysis, but a large number of disciplines in both the sciences and the arts are experiencing a paradigm shift from explicit conscious cognition to implicit unconscious affect. In a recent editorial of the journal *Motivation and Emotion*, Richard Ryan asserts, "After three decades of the dominance of cognitive approaches, motivational and emotional processes have roared back into the limelight" (2007, p. 1). A large number of interdisciplinary studies are converging upon the centrality of these implicit right brain motivational and emotional processes that are essential to adaptive functioning.

Right brain implicit processes in contemporary psychoanalysis

In this section, I describe a surface, verbal, conscious, analytic explicit self *vs* a deeper non-verbal, non-conscious, holistic, emotional, corporeal implicit self. These two lateralised systems contain qualitatively different forms of cognition and, therefore, ways of "knowing", as well as different memory systems and states of consciousness. However, I will argue that implicit (non-conscious) functions are much more than just learning, memory, and attention, processes highlighted by cognitive psychology. A psychological theory of cognition, even unconscious cognition, cannot penetrate the fundamental questions of development, psychopathology, and the change process of psychotherapy.

In addition to implicit cognition (right brain unconscious processing of exteroceptive information from the outer world and interoceptive information from the inner world), the implicit concept also includes implicit affect, implicit communication, and implicit self-regulation. The ongoing paradigm shift from the explicit cognitive to the implicit affective realm is driven by both new experimental data on emotional processes and updated clinical models for working with affective systems.

Freud (1915e) stressed that the work of psychotherapy is always concerned with affect states. In my first book, I expanded upon this therapeutic principle, asserting that affects are "the center of empathic communication" and that "the regulation of conscious *and* unconscious feelings is placed in the center of the clinical stage" (Schore, 1994, pp. 448–449). Consonant with these ideas, the essential clinical role of implicit affect is underscored in current neuroscience research reporting that unconscious processing of emotional stimuli is specifically associated with activation of the right and not the left hemisphere (Morris et al., 1998), and documenting a "right hemispheric dominance in processing of unconscious negative emotion" (Sato & Aoki, 2006, p. 261) and a "cortical response to subjectively unconscious danger" (Carretie et al., 2005, p. 615). This work establishes the validity of the concept of unconscious (and also dissociated) affect, a common focus of the treatment of pathological defences.

In this same volume, I offered a model of implicit communications within the therapeutic relationship, whereby transference–countertransference right brain to right brain communications represent interactions of the patient's unconscious primary process system and the therapist's primary process system (Schore, 1994, 2009c). Neuroscience documents that although the left hemisphere mediates most linguistic behaviours, the right hemisphere is important for the broader aspects of communication. This research also indicates that "the right hemisphere operates in a more free-associative, primary process manner, typically observed in states such as dreaming or reverie" (Grabner et al., 2007, p. 228).

Congruent with this model, Dorpat (2001) describes the implicit process of "primary process communication" expressed in "both body movements (kinesics), posture, gesture, facial expression, voice inflection, and the sequence, rhythm, and pitch of the spoken words" (p. 451). According to his formulation, affective and object-relational information are transmitted predominantly by primary process communication, while secondary process communication has a highly complex and powerful logical syntax, but lacks adequate semantics in the field of relationships. In the light of the fact that the left hemisphere is dominant for language but the right is dominant for emotional communication, I have proposed that the psychotherapy process is best described not as "the talking cure", but "the communicating" cure (Schore, 2005, p. 841). Chused (2007) now asserts, "I suspect our field has not yet fully appreciated the importance of this implicit communication" (p. 879).

With regard to implicit cognition, I have recently suggested that primary process cognition underlies clinical intuition, a major factor in therapeutic effectiveness (Schore & Schore, 2008). Indeed, the definition of intuition, "the ability to understand or know something immediately, without conscious reasoning" (Soanes & Hawker, 2005) clearly implies right and not left brain processing. Bohart (1999) contends that, in the psychotherapy context, "what I extract perceptually and intuitively from lived experience is far more compelling than thought information" (p. 294). In an important article on this theme, Welling (2005) concludes that the psychotherapist who considers his or her methods and decisions to be exclusively the result of conscious reasoning is most likely mistaken. He asserts that no therapist can reasonably deny following hunches, experiencing sudden insights, choosing directions without really knowing why, or having uncanny feelings that turn out to be of great importance for therapy, and points out that all these phenomena are occurrences of intuitive modes of functioning.

The central theme in all of my writings is the essential function of implicit affect regulation in the organisation of the self. Citing my work, Greenberg (2007) proposes:

> . . . an issue of major clinical significance then is generating theory and research to help understand to what extent automatic emotion processes can be changed through deliberate processes and to what extent only through more implicit processes based on new emotional and/or relational experiences. Stated in another way the question becomes how much emotional change requires implicit experiential learning vs. explicit conceptual learning. (p. 414)

In agreement with current trends in modern relational psychoanalysis, Greenberg (2007, p. 414) concludes, "The field has yet to pay adequate attention to implicit and relational processes of regulation". Recall that an inability to implicitly regulate the intensity of emotions is a major outcome of early relational trauma, a common history of a large number of psychiatric disorders.

In the following, I overview my work on the centrality of unconscious processes and right brain structures from the perspective of regulation theory (Schore, 1994, 2003a,b). I begin with a description of implicit affective processes in psychotherapeutic change processes. I then focus on the dynamics of the right brain unconscious mechanisms in affect-laden enactments, expressions of the unrepressed dissociative unconscious, and in the therapist's moment-to-moment navigation through these heightened affective moments not by explicit secondary process cognition, but by implicit primary process clinical intuition. Direct access to implicit processes of the unrepressed unconscious will be shown to be central to effective treatment.

Right brain implicit processes in psychotherapy

Over the course of my work, I have provided interdisciplinary evidence to show that implicit right brain to right brain attachment transactions occur in both the carer–infant and the therapist–patient relationships (the therapeutic alliance). I suggest that not left brain verbal explicit patient–therapist discourse, but right brain implicit non-verbal affect-laden communication directly represents the attachment dynamic embedded within the alliance. During the treatment, the empathic therapist is consciously, explicitly attending to the patient's verbalisations in order to objectively diagnose and rationalise the patient's dysregulating symptomatology. But she is also listening and interacting at another level, an experience-near subjective level, one that implicitly processes moment-to-moment socio-emotional information at levels beneath awareness (Schore, 2003a). Just as the left brain communicates its states to other left brains via conscious linguistic behaviours, so the right brain non-verbally communicates its unconscious states to other right brains that are tuned to receive these communications.

On this matter Stern (2005) suggests,

> Without the nonverbal it would be hard to achieve the empathic, participatory, and resonating aspects of intersubjectivity. One would only be left with a kind of pared down, neutral "understanding" of the other's subjective experience. One reason that this distinction is drawn is that in many cases the analyst is consciously aware of the content or speech while processing the nonverbal aspects out of awareness. With an intersubjectivist perspective, a more conscious processing by the analyst of the nonverbal is necessary. (p. 80)

Studies show that sixty per cent of human communication is non-verbal (Burgoon, 1985).

Writing on therapeutic "nonverbal implicit communications" Chused (2007) asserts that

> it is not that the information they contain cannot be verbalized, only that sometimes only a non-verbal approach can deliver the information in a way it can be used, particularly when there is no conscious awareness of the underlying concerns involved. (p. 879)

These ideas are echoed by Hutterer and Liss (2006), who state that non-verbal variables such as tone, tempo, rhythm, timbre, prosody, and amplitude of speech, as well as body language signals, might need to be re-examined as essential aspects of therapeutic technique. It is well established that the right hemisphere is dominant for non-verbal (Benowitz et al., 1983) and emotional (Blonder et al., 1991) communication.

Recent neuroscientific information about the emotion-processing right brain is also directly applicable to models of the psychotherapy change process. Uddin and colleagues (2006) conclude, "The emerging picture from the current literature seems to suggest a special role of the right hemisphere in self-related cognition, own body perception, self-awareness and autobiographical memories" (p. 65). This hemisphere is centrally involved in "implicit learning" (Hugdahl, 1995, p. 235), and implicit relational knowledge stored in the nonverbal domain is currently proposed to be at the core of therapeutic change (Stern et al., 1998).

Describing the right hemisphere as "the seat of implicit memory" and the locus of the "unrepressed unconscious", Mancia (2006) observes that,

> the discovery of the implicit memory has extended the concept of the unconscious and supports the hypothesis that this is where the emotional and affective—sometimes traumatic—presymbolic and preverbal experiences of the primary mother–infant relations are stored. (p. 83)

Right brain autobiographical memory (Markowitsch et al., 2000), which stores insecure attachment histories, is activated in the therapeutic alliance, especially under relational stress. Cortina and Liotti (2007) point out that "experience encoded and stored in the implicit system is still alive and carried forward as negative expectations in regard to the availability and responsiveness of others, although this knowledge is unavailable for conscious recall" (p. 207). Such affective memories are transmitted within the therapeutic alliance. These affective communications "occur at an implicit level of rapid cueing and response that occurs too rapidly for simultaneous verbal transaction and conscious reflection" (Lyons-Ruth, 2000, pp. 91–92).

More specifically, spontaneous non-verbal transference–countertransference interactions at preconscious–unconscious levels represent implicit right brain to right brain face-to-face non-verbal communications of fast acting, automatic, regulated, and especially dysregulated bodily based stressful emotional states between patient and therapist (Schore, 1994, 2009c). Transference is, thus, an activation of right brain autobiographical memory, as autobiographical negatively valenced, high intensity emotions are retrieved from specifically the right (and not the left) medial temporal lobe (Buchanan et al., 2006). Updated neuropsychoanalytic models of transference (Pincus et al., 2007) contend that "no appreciation of transference can do without emotion"

(p. 634), and that "transference is distinctive in that it depends on early patterns of emotional attachment with caregivers" (p. 636). Current clinical models define transference as a selective bias in dealing with others that is based on previous early experiences and which shapes current expectancies, and as an expression of the patient's implicit perceptions and implicit memories (Schore, 2003a, 2009c).

Right brain implicit processes in clinical enactments

The quintessential clinical context for a right brain transferential–countertransferential implicit communication of a dysregulated emotional state is the heightened affective moment of a clinical enactment. There is now agreement that enactments, "events occurring within the dyad that both parties experience as being the consequence of behavior in the other" (McLaughlin, 1991, p. 611), are fundamentally mediated by non-verbal unconscious relational behaviours within the therapeutic alliance (Schore, 2003a). These are transacted in visual–facial, auditory–prosodic, and tactile–proprioceptive emotionally charged attachment communications, as well as in gestures and body language, rapidly expressed behaviours that play a critical role in the unconscious interpersonal communications embedded within the enactment. This dyadic psychobiological mechanism allows for the detection of unconscious affects, and underlies the premise that "an enactment, by patient or analyst, could be evidence of something which has not yet been 'felt' by them" (Zanocco et al., 2006, p. 153).

In my book, *Affect Regulation and the Repair of the Self*, I offered a chapter entitled "Clinical implications of a psychoneurobiological model of projective identification" (Schore, 2003a). This entire chapter on moment-to-moment implicit communications within an enactment focuses on phenomena that take place in "a moment", literally a split second. In it, I offer a slow-motion analysis of the rapid dyadic psychobiological events that occur in a heightened affective moment of the therapeutic alliance. This analysis discusses how a spontaneous enactment can either blindly repeat a pathological object relation through the therapist's deflection of projected negative states and intensification of interactive dysregulation, or provide a novel relational experience via the therapist's autoregulation of projected negative states and co-participation in interactive repair. Although these are the most stressful moments of the treatment, in an optimal context, the therapist potentially can act as an implicit regulator of the patient's conscious and dissociated unconscious affective states. This dyadic psychobiological corrective emotional experience can lead to the emergence of more complex psychic structure by increasing the connectivity of right brain limbic–autonomic circuits.

Consonant with this conception of implicit communication (and citing my right brain neurobiological model), Ginot (2007) concludes, "Increasingly, enactments are understood as powerful manifestations of the intersubjective process and as inevitable expressions of complex, though largely unconscious self-states and relational patterns" (p. 317). These unconscious affective interactions "bring to life and consequently alter implicit memories and attachment styles" (p. 317). She further states that such intense manifestations of transference–countertransference entanglements "generate interpersonal as well as internal processes eventually capable of promoting integration and growth" (pp. 317–318).

In a parallel work, Zanocco et al. (2006, p. 145) characterises the critical function of empathic physical sensations in the enactment and their central role in "the foundation of developing psychic structure of a human being". Enactments reflect "processes and dynamics originating in the primitive functioning of the mind", and they involve the analyst accomplishing a way of interacting with those patients who are not able to give representation to their instinctual impulses. These early "primary" activities are expressed in

> an unconscious mental activity which does not follow the rules of conscious activity. There is no verbal language involved. Instead, there is a production of images that do not seem to follow any order, and, even less, any system of logic. (p. 145)

Note the implications to implicit primary process cognition and right brain representations.

It is important to repeat the fact that the relational mechanism of enactments is especially prominent during stressful ruptures of the therapeutic alliance. Enactments occur at the edges of the regulatory boundaries of affect tolerance (Schore, 2009b,c), or what Lyons-Ruth (2005) describes as the "fault lines" of self-experience where "interactive negotiations have failed, goals remain aborted, negative affects are unresolved, and conflict is experienced" (p. 21). However, neuroscientists are describing "neuroplasticity in right hemispheric limbic circuitry in mediating long-lasting changes in negative affect following brief but severe stress" (Adamec et al., 2003, p. 1264). Thus, an enactment can be a turning point in an analysis in which the relationship is characterised by a mode of resistance/counter-resistance (Zanocco et al., 2006), but these moments call for the most complex clinical skills of the therapist.

This is due to the fact that such heightened affective moments induce the most stressful countertransference responses, including the clinician's implicit coping strategies that are formed in his/her own attachment history. Davies (2004) documents,

> It seems to me intrinsic to relational thinking that these "bad object relationships" not only will but must be reenacted in the transference–countertransference experience, that indeed such reenacted aggression, rage, and envy are endemic to psychoanalytic change within the relational perspective. (p. 714)

It is important to note that enactments represent communications of not only stressful conscious affects, but also unconscious affects. Recall the "right hemispheric dominance in processing of unconscious negative emotion" (Sato & Aoki, 2006). Very recent work in interpersonal neurobiology, attachment theory, and traumatology equates unconscious affect with dissociated affect (Schore, 2007, 2009a,b,c, 2010). Bromberg (2006) reports,

> Clinically, the phenomenon of dissociation as a defense against self-destabilization . . . has its greatest relevance during enactments, a mode of clinical engagement that requires an analyst's closest attunement to the unacknowledged affective shifts in his own and the patient's self-states. (p. 5)

On the other hand, Plakun (1999) observes that the therapist's "refusal of the transference", particularly the negative transference, is an early manifestation of an enactment. The therapist's "refusal" is expressed implicitly and spontaneously in non-verbal communications, not explicitly in the verbal narrative. A relational perspective from dynamic system theory clearly applies to the synergistic effects of the therapist's transient or enduring countertransferential "mind-blindness" and the patient's negatively biased transferential expectation in the co-creation of an enactment. Feldman (1997) notes that the fulminating negative state "may evoke forms of projection and enact-ment by the analyst, in an attempt at restoring an internal equilibrium, of which the analyst may initially be unaware" (p. 235).

Making this work even more emotionally challenging, Renik (1993) offers the important observation that countertransference enactments cannot be recognised until one is already in them. Rather, spontaneous activity is expressed by the clinician's right brain, described by Lichtenberg and colleagues (1996, pp. 213–214) as a "disciplined spontaneous engagement". These authors observe that such events occur "at a critical juncture in analysis" and they are usually prompted by some breach or miscommunication that requires "a human response". Although there is a danger of "exchanges degen-erating into mutually traumatizing disruptions" that "recreate patho-genic expectations", the clinician's communications signal a readiness to participate authentically in the immediacy of an enactment. This is spontaneously expressed in the clinician's facial expressions, gestures, and unexpected comments that result from an "unsuppressed emo-tional upsurge". These communications seem more to pop out than to have been planned or edited, and they provide "intense moments that opened the way for examination of the role enactments into which the analyst had fallen unconsciously".

These "communications" are, therefore, right brain primary pro-cess emotional and not left brain rational logical secondary process communications. Thus, explicit, conscious, verbal voluntary responses are inadequate to prevent, facilitate, or metabolise implicit emotional enactments. Bromberg (2006) refers to this in his assertion, "An inter-pretative stance . . . not only is thereby useless during an enactment, but also escalates the enactment and rigidifies the dissociation" (p. 8). Andrade (2005) concludes,

> As a primary factor in psychic change, interpretation is limited in effectiveness in pathologi1.85es arising from the verbal phase, related to explicit memories, with no effect in the pre-verbal phase where implicit memories are to be found. Interpretation—the method used to the exclusion of all others for a century—is only partial; when used in isolation it does not meet the demands of modern broad-based-spec-trum psychoanalysis. (p. 677)

But if not an explicit analytic insight-directed response, then what type of implicit cognition would the therapist use in order to guide him or herself through stressful negative affective states, such as terror, rage, shame, disgust, and so on? What implicit right brain coping strategy could not only autoregulate the intense affect, but, at the same time, allow the clinician to maintain "an attunement to the unacknowledged affective shifts in his own and the patient's self-states"?

Right brain implicit processes and clinical intuition

In my introduction, I proposed that the therapist's moment-to-moment navigation through these heightened affective moments occurs not by explicit verbal secondary process cognition, but, rather, by implicit non-verbal primary process clinical intuition. From a social neuro-science perspective, intuition is now being defined as "the subjective experience associated with the use of knowledge gained through implicit learning" (Lieberman, 2000, p. 109). The description of intu-ition as "direct knowing that seeps into conscious awareness with-out the conscious mediation of logic or rational process" (Boucouvalas, 1997, p. 7), clearly implies a right- and not left-brain function. Bugental (1987) refers to the therapist's "intuitive sensing of what is happening in the patient back of his words and, often, back of his conscious awareness" (p. 11). In his last work, Bowlby (1991) speculated, "Clearly the best therapy is done by the therapist who is naturally intuitive and also guided by the appropriate theory" (p. 16).

In a groundbreaking article, Welling (2005) notes that intuition is associated with preverbal character, affect, sense of relationship, spon-taneity, immediacy, *gestalt* nature, and global view (all functions of the holistic right brain). He further discusses that "there is no cognitive theory about intuition" (p. 20), and, therefore, "what is needed is a model that can describe the underlying formal process that produces intuition phenomena" (pp. 23–24). Developmental psychoanalysis and neuropsychoanalysis can make important contributions to our understanding of the sources and mechanism of not only maternal, but clinical, intuition. With allusions to the right brain, Orlinsky and Howard (1986) contend that the "non-verbal, prerational stream of expression that binds the infant to its parent continues throughout life to be a primary medium of intuitively felt affective–relational communication between persons" (p. 343). There are, thus, direct commonalities between the spontaneous responses of the maternal intuition of a psychobiologically attuned primary carer and the intuitive therapist's sensitive countertransferential responsiveness to the patient's unconscious, non-verbal, affective, bodily based implicit communications.

In the neuroscience literature, Volz and von Cramon (2006) conclude that intuition is related to the unconscious, and is "often reliably accurate" (p. 2084). It is derived from stored non-verbal representations, such as "images, feelings, physical sensations, metaphors" (note the similarity to primary process cognition) (Volz & von Cramon, 2006, p. 2084). Intuition is not expressed in language but, rather, is "embodied" in a "gut feeling" or in an initial guess that subsequently biases our thought and enquiry. "The gist information is realized on the basis of the observer's implicit knowledge rather than being consciously extracted on the basis of the observer's explicit knowledge" (Volz & von Cramon, 2006, p. 2084).

With direct relevance to the concept of somatic countertransference, cognitive neuroscience models of intuition are highlighting the adaptive capacity of "embodied cognition". Allman and colleagues (2005) assert, "We experience the intuitive process at a visceral level. Intuitive decision making enables us to react quickly in situations that involve a high degree of uncertainty; situations which commonly involve social interactions" (p. 370). These researchers demonstrate that right prefrontal insula and anterior cingulate relay a fast intuitive assessment of complex social situations in order to allow the rapid adjustment of behaviour in quickly changing circumstances. This lateralisation is also found in a neuro-imaging study by Bolte and Goschke (2005), who suggest that association areas of the right hemisphere might play a special role in intuitive judgements.

In parallel psychoanalytic work, Marcus (1997) observes, "The analyst, by means of reverie and intuition, listens with the right brain to the analysand's right brain" (p. 238). Other clinicians hypothesise that the intuition of an experienced expert therapist lies fundamentally in a process of unconscious pattern matching (Rosenblatt & Thickstun, 1994), and that this pattern recognition follows a non-verbal path, as verbal activity interferes with achieving insight (Schooler & Melcher, 1995). Even more specifically, Bohart (1999, p. 298) contends that intuition involves the detection of "patterns and rhythms in interaction". But if not verbal stimuli, then which patterns are being intuitively tracked?

Recall, "transference is distinctive in that it depends on early patterns of emotional attachment with caregivers" (Pincus et al., 2007), and that enactments are powerful expressions of "unconscious self-states and relational patterns" (Ginot, 2007). Indeed, updated models of psychotherapy describe the primacy of "making conscious the organizing patterns of affect" (Mohaupt et al., 2006, p. 243). Van Lancker and Cummings (1999) assert, "Simply stated, the left hemisphere specializes in analyzing sequences, while the right hemisphere gives evidence of superiority in processing patterns" (p. 95). Thus, I have suggested that the intuitive psychobiologically attuned therapist, on a moment-to-moment basis, implicitly tracks and resonates with the patterns of rhythmic crescendos/decrescendos of the patient's regulated and dysregulated states of affective arousal. Thus, intuition represents a complex right brain primary process, affectively charged embodied cognition that is adaptive for implicitly processing novelty, including object relational novelty, especially in moments of relational uncertainty.

Welling (2005) offers a phase model, in which the amount of information contained in the intuition increases from one phase to another, resulting in increased levels of complexity. An early "detection phase" related to "functions of arousal and attention" culminates in a "metaphorical solution phase", in which the intuition presents itself in the form of kinaesthetic sensations, feelings, images, metaphors, and words. Here, the solution, which has an emotional quality, is revealed, but in a veiled, non-verbal form. These descriptions reflect the activity of the right hemisphere, which is dominant for attention (Raz, 2004), kinaesthesia (Naito et al., 2005), and the processing of novel metaphors (Mashal et al., 2007).

Phases of intuitive processing are, thus, generated in the therapists's subcortical–cortical vertical axis of the right brain, from the right amygdala to the right orbitofrontal system (see Figure A-2 in Schore, 2003a). The orbital frontolimbic cortex, the highest level of the right brain would act as an "inner compass that accompanies the decoding process of intuition" (Welling, 2005, p. 43). The orbitofrontal system, the "senior executive of the emotional brain" (Joseph, 1996), is specialised to act in contexts of "uncertainty or unpredictability" (Elliott et al., 2000). It functions as a dynamic filter of emotional stimuli (Rule et al., 2002) and provides "a panoramic view of the entire external environment, as well as the internal environment associated with motivational factors" (Barbas, 2007, p. 239). It also formulates a theory of mind, "a kind of affective-decision making" (Happeney et al., 2004, p. 4), and, thereby, is centrally involved in "intuitive decision-making" (Allman et al., 2005, p. 369).

I have suggested that the right orbitofrontal cortex and its sub-cortical and cortical connections represent what Freud described as the preconscious (Schore, 2003a). Alluding to preconscious functions, Welling (2005) describes intuition as

> . . . a factory of pieces of thoughts, images, and vague feelings, where the raw materials seem to float around half formless, a world so often present, though we hardly ever visit it. However, some of these float-ing elements come to stand out, gain strength, or show up repeatedly. When exemplified, they may be easier to recognize and cross the border of consciousness. (p. 33)

Over the course of the treatment, the clinician accesses this precon-scious domain, as does the free associating patient. Rather than the therapist's technical explicit skills, the clinician's intuitive implicit capacities might be responsible for the outcome of an affectively charged enactment, and might dictate the depth of the therapeutic contact, exploration, and change processes.

Right brain implicit process central to change: affect regulation

According to Ginot (2007), "This focus on enactments as communica-tors of affective building blocks also reflects a growing realization that explicit content, verbal interpretations, and the mere act of uncover-ing memories are insufficient venues for curative shifts" (p. 317). This clearly implies that the resolution of œ involves more than the stan-dard Freudian idea of making the unconscious conscious. If not these explicit factors, then what implicit therapeutic experience is essential to the change process, especially in developmentally impaired person-alities who are not psychologically minded? At the base, the implicit change mechanism must certainly include a dysregulating affective experience that is communicated to an empathic other.

But, in addition, the relational context must also afford an oppor-tunity for interactive affect regulation, the core of the attachment process. Ogden and her colleagues (2005) conclude,

> Interactive psychobiological regulation (Schore, 1994) provides the relational context under which the client can safely contact, describe and eventually regulate inner experience . . . [It] is the patient's experience of empowering action in the context of safety provided by a background of the empathic clinician's psychobiologically attuned interactive affect regulation that helps effect . . . change. (p. 22)

It is the regulation of stressful and disorganising high or low levels of affective–autonomic arousal that allows for the repair and reorganisation of the right lateralised implicit self, the biological substrate of the human unconscious.

A cardinal principle of affective science dictates that a deeper understanding of affective processes is closely tied to the problem of the regulation of these processes. Affect regulation, a central mechanism of both development and the change process of psychotherapy, is usually defined as a set of conscious control processes by which we influence, consciously and voluntarily, the conscious emotions we have, and how we experience and express them. In a groundbreaking article in the clinical psychology literature, Greenberg (2007, p. 415) describes a "self-control" form of emotion regulation involving higher levels of cognitive executive function that allows individuals "to change the way they feel by consciously changing the way they think". This explicit form of affect regulation is performed by the verbal left hemisphere, and unconscious bodily based emotion is usually not addressed in this model. Notice this mechanism is at the core of insight, heavily emphasised in therapeutic models of not only classical psychoanalysis, but also cognitive behavioural therapy.

In contrast to this conscious emotion regulation system, Greenberg (2007) describes a second, more fundamental implicit affect regulatory process performed by the right hemisphere. This system rapidly and automatically processes facial expression, vocal quality, and eye contact in a relational context. Therapy attempts not control, but the "acceptance or facilitation of particular emotions", including "previously avoided emotion", in order to allow the patient to tolerate and transform them into "adaptive emotions". Citing my work, he asserts, "It is the building of implicit or automatic emotion regulation capacities that is important for enduring change, especially for highly fragile personality-disordered clients" (Greenberg, 2007, p. 416).

Even more than the patient's late acting rational, analytical, and verbal left mind, the growth-facilitating psychotherapeutic relationship needs to directly access the deeper psychobiological strata of the implicit regulatory structures of both the patient's and the clinician's right minds. Effective psychotherapy of attachment pathologies and severe personality disorders must focus on unconscious affect and the survival defence of pathological dissociation, "a structured separation of mental processes (e.g., thoughts, emotions, conation, memory, and identity) that are ordinarily integrated" (Spiegel & Cardeña, 1991, p. 367). The clinical precept that unregulated overwhelming traumatic feelings cannot be adaptively integrated into the patient's emotional life is the expression of a dysfunction of "the right hemispheric specialization in regulating stress—and emotion-related processes" (Sullivan & Dufresne, 2006). As described earlier, this dissociative deficit specifically results from a lack of integration of the right lateralised limbic–autonomic circuits of the emotional brain (see Figure 4.1).

However, recall Ginot's assertion that enactments "generate interpersonal as well as internal processes eventually capable of promoting integration and growth". Indeed, long-term psychotherapy can positively alter the developmental trajectory of the right brain and facilitate the top-down and bottom-up integration of its cortical and subcortical systems (Schore, 2003a, 2007, 2009b,c, 2010). These enhanced right amygdala–ventral prefrontolimbic (orbitofrontal) connections allow implicit therapeutic "now moments" of lived interactive experience to be integrated into autobiographical memory. Autobiographical memory, an output of the right brain, is the highest memory system that consists of personal events with a clear relation to time, space, and context. In this right brain state of autonoetic consciousness, the experiencing self represents emotionally toned memories, thereby allowing for "subjective time travel" (Kalbe et al., 2008, p. 15). The growth-facilitating expansion of interconnectivity within the unconscious system also promotes an increased complexity of defences, right brain coping strategies for regulating stressful affects that are more flexible and adaptive than pathological dissociation. This therapeutic mechanism supports the possible integration of what Bromberg (2006) calls "not-me" states into the implicit self.

Indeed, these developmental advances of the right lateralised vertical axis facilitate the further maturation of the right brain core of the self and its central involvement in "patterns of affect regulation that integrate a sense of self across state transitions, thereby allowing for a continuity of inner experience" (Schore, 1994, p. 33). These neurobiological reorganisations of the right brain human unconscious underlie Alvarez's (2006) assertion, "Schore points out that at the more severe levels of psychopathology, it is not a question of making the unconscious conscious: rather it is a question of restructuring the unconscious itself" (p. 171).

Earlier, I suggested that the right hemisphere is dominant in the change process of psychotherapy. Neuroscience authors are concluding that although the left hemisphere is specialised for coping with predictable representations and strategies, the right predominates for coping with and assimilating novel situations (Podell et al., 2001) and ensures the formation of a new programme of interaction with a new environment (Ezhov & Krivoschchekov, 2004). Indeed,

> The right brain possesses special capabilities for processing novel stimuli . . . Right-brain problem solving generates a matrix of alternative solutions, as contrasted with the left brain's single solution of best fit. This answer matrix remains active while alternative solutions are explored, a method suitable for the open-ended possibilities inherent in a novel situation. (Schutz, 2005, p. 13)

The functions of the emotional right brain are essential to the self-exploration process of psychotherapy, especially of unconscious affects that can be potentially integrated into a more complex implicit sense of self. At the most essential level, the work of psychotherapy is not defined by what the therapist explicitly, objectively does for the patient, or says to the patient. Rather, the key mechanism is how to implicitly and subjectively be with the patient, especially during affectively stressful moments when the "going-on-being" of the patient's implicit self is disintegrating in real time.

References

Adamec, R. E., Blundell, J., & Burton, P. (2003). Phosphorylated cyclic AMP response element bonding protein expression induced in the periaqueductal gray by predator stress; its relationship to the stress experience, behavior, and limbic neural plasticity. *Progress in Neuro-Pharmacology & Biological Psychiatry*, 27: 1243–1267.

Allman, J. M., Watson, K. K., Tetreault, N. A., & Hakeem, A. Y. (2005). Intuition and autism: a possible role for Von Economo neurons. *Trends in Cognitive Sciences, 9*: 367–373.

Alvarez, A. (2006). Some questions concerning states of fragmentation: unintegration, under-integration, disintegration, and the nature of early integrations. *Journal of Child Psychotherapy, 32*: 158–180.

Andrade, V. M. (2005). Affect and the therapeutic action in psychoanalysis. *International Journal of Psychoanalysis, 86*: 677–697.

Barbas, H. (2007). Flow of information for emotions through temporal and orbitofrontal pathways. *Journal of Anatomy, 211*: 237–249.

Bargh, J. A., & Morsella, E. (2008). The unconscious mind. *Perspectives on Psychological Science, 3*: 73–79.

Benowitz, L. I., Bear, D. M., Rosenthal, R., Mesulam, M. M., Zaidel, E., & Sperry, R. W. (1983). Hemispheric specialization in non-verbal communication. *Cortex, 19*: 5–11.

Blonder, L. X., Bowers, D., & Heilman, K. M. (1991). The role of the right hemisphere in emotional communication. *Brain, 114*(1): 115–127.

Bohart, A. C. (1999). Intuition and creativity in psychotherapy. *Journal of Constructivist Psychology, 12*: 287–311.

Bolte, A., & Goschke, T. (2005). On the speed of intuition: intuitive judgments of semantic coherence under different response deadlines. *Memory & Cognition, 33*: 1248–1255.

Boucouvalas, M. (1997). Intuition: the concept and the experience. In: R. D. Floyd & P. S. Arvidson (Eds.), *Intuition: The Inside Story* (pp. 39–56). New York: Routledge.

Bowlby, J. (1991). The role of the psychotherapist's personal resources in the therapeutic situation. In: *Tavistock Gazette* (Autumn).

Bromberg, P. M. (2006). *Awakening the Dreamer: Clinical Journeys.* Mahweh, NJ: Analytic Press.

Buchanan, T. W., Tranel, D., & Adolphs, R. (2006). Memories for emotional autobiographical events following unilateral damage to medial temporal lobe. *Brain, 129*: 115–127.

Bugental, J. F. (1987). *The Art of the Psychotherapist.* New York: W. W. Norton.

Buklina, S. B. (2005). The corpus callosum, interhemispheric interactions, and the function of the right hemisphere of the brain. *Neuroscience and Behavioral Physiology, 35*: 473–480.

Burgoon, J. K. (1985). Non-verbal signals. In: M. L. Knapp & C. R. Miller (Eds.), *Handbook of Interpersonal Communication* (pp. 344–390). Beverly Hills, CA: Sager.

Carretie, L., Hinojosa, J. A., Mercado, F., & Tapia, M. (2005). Cortical
response to subjectively unconscious danger. NeuroImage, 24: 615–623.
Chused, J. F. (2007). Non-verbal communication in psychoanalysis:
commentary on Harrison and Tronick. Journal of the American Psychoanalytic Association, 55: 875–882.
Cortina, M., & Liotti, G. (2007). New approaches to understanding uncon-
scious processes: implicit and explicit memory systems. International
Forum of Psychoanalysis, 16: 204–212.
Davies, J. M. (2004). Whose bad objects are we anyway? Repetition and
our elusive love affair with evil. Psychoanalytic Dialogues, 14: 711–732.
Devinsky, O. (2000). Right cerebral hemispheric dominance for a sense of
corporeal and emotional self. Epilepsy & Behavior, 1: 60–73.
Dorpat, T. L. (2001). Primary process communication. Psychoanalytic
Inquiry, 3: 448–463.
Elliott, R., Dolan, R. J., & Frith, C. D. (2000). Dissociable functions in the
medial and lateral orbitofrontal cortex: evidence from human neuro-
imaging studies. Cerebral Cortex, 10: 308–317.
Ezhov, S. N., & Krivoschchekov, S. G. (2004). Features of psychomotor
responses and interhemispheric relationships at various stages of
adaptation to a new time zone. Human Physiology, 30: 172–175.
Feldman, M. (1997). Projective identification: the analyst's involvement.
International Journal of Psychoanalysis, 78: 227–241.
Freud, S. (1915e). The unconscious. S. E., 14: 159–205. London: Hogarth.
Freud, S. (1916–1917). Introductory Lectures on Psycho-Analysis. S. E., 16:
241–463. London: Hogarth.
Freud, S. (1950a). Project for a scientific psychology. S. E., 1: 281–397.
London: Hogarth.
Ginot, E. (2007). Intersubjectivity and neuroscience. Understanding enact-
ments and their therapeutic significance within emerging paradigms.
Psychoanalytic Psychology, 24: 317–332.
Grabner, R. H., Fink, A., & Neubauer, A. C. (2007). Brain correlates of self-
related originality of ideas: evidence from event-related power and
phase-locking changes in the EEG. Behavioral Neuroscience, 121: 224–230.
Greenberg, L. S. (2007). Emotion coming of age. Clinical Psychology Science
and Practice, 14: 414–421.
Happaney, K., Zelazo, P. D., & Stuss, D. T. (2004). Development of
orbitofrontal function: current themes and future directions. Brain and
Cognition, 55: 1–10.
Hugdahl, K. (1995). Classical conditioning and implicit learning: the right
hemisphere hypothesis. In: R. J. Davidson & K. Hugdahl (Eds.), Brain
Asymmetry (pp. 235–267). Cambridge, MA: MIT Press.

Hutterer, J., & Liss, M. (2006). Cognitive development, memory, trauma, treatment: an integration of psychoanalytic and behavioural concepts in light of current neuroscience research. *Journal of the American Academy of Psychoanalytic Dynamic Psychiatry, 34*: 287–302.

Joseph, R. (1996). *Neuropsychiatry, Neuropsychology, and Clinical Neuroscience* (2nd edn). Baltimore, MD: Williams & Wilkins.

Kalbe, E., Brand, M., Thiel, A., Kessler, J., & Markowitsch, H. J. (2008). Neuropsychological and neural correlates of autobiographical deficits in a mother who killed her children. *Neurocase, 14*: 15–28.

Lichtenberg, J. D., Lachmann, F. M., & Fosshage, J. L. (1996). *The Clinical Exchange.* Mahwah, NJ: Analytic Press.

Lieberman, M. D. (2000). Intuition: a social neuroscience approach. *Psychological Bulletin, 126*: 109–137.

Lyons-Ruth, K. (2000). 'I sense that you sense that I sense . . .': Sander's recognition process and the emergence of new forms of relational organization. *Infant Mental Health Journal, 21*: 85–98.

Lyons-Ruth, K. (2005). The two-person unconscious: intersubjective dialogue, enactive representation, and the emergence of new forms of relational organization. In: L. Aron & A. Harris (Eds.), *Relational Psychoanalysis, Volume II* (pp. 2–45). Hillsdale, NJ: Analytic Press.

Mancia, M. (2006). Implicit memory and early unrepressed unconscious: their role in the therapeutic process (How the neurosciences can contribute to psychoanalysis). *International Journal of Psychoanalysis, 87*: 83–103.

Marcus, D. M. (1997). On knowing what one knows. *Psychoanalytic Quarterly, 66*: 219–241.

Markowitsch, H. J., Reinkemeier, A., Kessler, J., Koyuncu, A., & Heiss, W. D. (2000). Right amygdalar and temperofrontal activation during autobiographical, but not fictitious memory retrieval. *Behavioral Neurology, 12*: 181–190.

Mashal, N., Faust, M., Hendler, T., & Jung-Beeman, M. (2007). An fMRI investigation of the neural correates underlying the processing of novel metaphoric expressions. *Brain and Language, 100*: 115–126.

McLaughlin, J. T. (1991). Clinical and theoretical aspects of enactment. *Journal of the American Psychoanalytic Association, 39*: 595–614.

Mohaupt, H., Holgersen, H., Binder, P. E., & Nielsen, G. H. (2006). Affect consciousness or mentalization? A comparison of two concepts with regard to affect development and affect regulation. *Scandinavian Journal of Psychology, 47*: 237–244.

Morris, J. S., Ohman, A., & Dolan, R. J. (1998). Conscious and unconscious emotional learning in the human amygdala. *Nature, 393*: 467–470.

Naito, E., Roland, P. E. Grefkes, C., Choi, H. J., Eickhoff, S., Geyer, S., Zilles, K., & Ehrsson, H. H. (2005). Dominance of the right hemisphere and role of Area 2 in human kinesthesia. *Journal of Neurophysiology, 93*: 1020–1034.

Ogden, P., Pain, C., Minton, K., & Fisher, J. (2005). Including the body in mainstream psychotherapy for traumatized individuals. *Psychologist-Psychoanalyst, XXV*(4): 19–24.

Orlinsky, D. E., & Howard, K. I. (1986). Process and outcome in psycho-therapy. In: S. L. Garfield & A. E. Bergin (Eds.), *Handbook of Psycho-therapy and Behavior Change* (3rd edn). New York: Wiley.

Pincus, D., Freeman, W., & Modell, A. (2007). A neurobiological model of perception. Considerations for transference. *Psychoanalytic Psychology,* 24: 623–640.

Plakun, E. M. (1999). Making the alliance and taking the transference in work with suicidal patients. *Journal of Psychotherapy Practice and Research, 10*f: 269–276.

Podell, K., Iovell, M., & Goldberg, E. (2001). Lateralization of frontal lobe functions. In: S. P. Salloway, P. F. Malloy, & J. D. Duffy (Eds.), *The Frontal Lobes and Neuropsychiatric Illness* (pp. 83–89). London: American Psychiatric Publishing.

Raz, A. (2004). Anatomy of attentional networks. *Anatomical Records, 281B*: 21–36.

Renik, O. (1993). Countertransference enactment and the psychoanalytic process. In: M. J. Horowitz, O. F. Kernberg, & E. M. Weinshel (Eds.), *Psychic Structure and Psychic Change: Essays in Honor of Robert S. Wallerstein* (pp. 135–158). Madison, CT: International Universities Press.

Rosenblatt, A. D., & Thickstun, J. T. (1994). Intuition and consciousness. *Psychoanalytic Quarterly, 63*: 696–714.

Rule, R. R., Shimamura, A. P., & Knight, R. T. (2002). Orbitofrontal cortex and dynamic filtering of emotional stimuli. Cognition, affective, & behavioral. *Neuroscience, 2*: 264–270.

Ryan, R. (2007). Motivation and emotion: a new look and approach for two reemerging fields. *Motivation and Emotion, 31*: 1–3.

Sato, W., & Aoki, S. (2006). Right hemisphere dominance in processing unconscious emotion. *Brain and Cognition, 62*: 261–266.

Schooler, J., & Melcher, J. (1995). The ineffability of insight. In: S. T. Smith, T. B. Ward, & R. A. Finke (Eds.), *The Creative Cognition Approach* (pp. 27–51). Cambridge, MA: MIT Press.

Schore, A. N. (1994). *Affect Regulation and the Origin of the Self*. Mahweh, NJ: Lawrence Erlbaum.

Schore, A. N. (1997). A century after Freud's Project: is a rapprochement between psychoanalysis and neurobiology at hand? *Journal of the American Psychoanalytic Association, 45*: 841–867.

Schore, A. N. (2002). The right brain as the neurobiological substratum of Freud's dynamic unconscious. In: D. Scharff (Ed.), *The Psychoanalytic Century: Freud's Legacy for the Future* (pp. 61–88). New York: Other Press.

Schore, A. N. (2003a). *Affect Regulation and the Repair of the Self.* New York: W. W. Norton.

Schore, A. N. (2003b). *Affect Dysregulation and Disorders of the Self.* New York: W. W. Norton.

Schore, A. N. (2005). A neuropsychoanalytic viewpoint. Commentary on paper by Steven H. Knoblauch. *Psychoanalytic Dialogues, 15*: 829–854.

Schore, A. N. (2007). Review of *Awakening the Dreamer: Clinical Journeys* by Philip M. Bromberg. *Psychoanalytic Dialogues, 17*: 753–767.

Schore, A. N. (2009a). Attachment trauma and the developing right brain: origins of pathological dissociation. In: P. F. Dell & J. A. O'Neil (Eds.), *Dissociation and the Dissociative Disorders: DSM-V and Beyond* (pp. 107–141). New York: Routledge.

Schore, A. N. (2009b). Relational trauma and the developing right brain: an interface of psychoanalytic self psychology and neuroscience. *Annals of the New York Academy of Sciences, 1159*: 189–203.

Schore, A. N. (2009c). Right brain affect regulation: an essential mechanism of development, trauma, dissociation, and psychotherapy. In: D. Fosha, M. Solomon, & D. Siegel (Eds.), *The Healing Power of Emotion: Integrating Relationships, Body and Mind. A Dialogue among Scientists and Clinicians* (pp. 112–144). New York: Norton.

Schore, A. N. (2010). Relational trauma and the developing right brain: the neurobiology of broken attachment bonds. In: T. Baradon (Ed.), *Relational Trauma in Infancy* (pp. 19–47). London: Routledge.

Schore, A. N. (2012). *The Science of the Art of Psychotherapy.* New York: W. W. Norton.

Schore, J. R., & Schore, A. N. (2008). Modern attachment theory: the central role of affect regulation in development and treatment. *Clinical Social Work Journal, 36*: 9–20.

Schutz, L. E. (2005). Broad-perspective perceptual disorder of the right hemisphere. *Neuropsychology Review, 15*: 11–27.

Soanes, C., & Hawker, S. (2005). *Compact Oxford Dictionary of Current English.* Oxford: Oxford University Press.

Spiegel, D., & Cardeña, E. (1991). Disintegrated experience: the dissociative disorders revisited. *Journal of Abnormal Psychology, 100*: 366–378.

Stern, D. N. (2005). Intersubjectivity. In: E. S. Person, A. M. Cooper, & G. O. Gabbard (Eds.), *Textbook of Psychoanalysis* (pp. 77–92). Washington, DC: American Psychiatric Publishing.

Stern, D. N., Bruschweiler-Stern, N., Harrison, A. M., Lyons-Ruth, K., Morgan, A. C., Nahum, J. P., Sander, L., & Tronick, E. Z. (1998). The process of therapeutic change involving implicit knowledge: some implications of developmental observations for adult psychotherapy. *Infant Mental Health Journal, 19*: 300–308.

Sullivan, R. M., & Dufresne, M. M. (2006). Mesocortical dopamine and HPA axis regulation: role of laterality and early environment. *Brain Research, 1076*: 49–59.

Uddin, L. Q., Molnar-Szakacs, I., Zaidel, E., & Iacoboni, M. (2006). rTMS to the right inferior parietal lobule disrupts self–other discrimination. *Social Cognitive and Affective Neuroscience, 1*: 65–71.

Van Lancker, D., & Cummings, J. L. (1999). Expletives: neurolingusitic and neurobehavioral perspectives on swearing. *Brain Research Reviews, 31*: 83–104.

Volz, K. G., & von Cramon, D. Y. (2006). What neuroscience can tell about intuitive processes in the context of perceptual discovery. *Journal of Cognitive Neuroscience, 18*: 2077–2087.

Welling, H. (2005). The intuitive process: the case of psychotherapy. *Journal of Psychotherapy Integration, 15*: 19–47.

Zanocco, G., De Marchi, A., & Pozzi, F. (2006). Sensory empathy and enactment. *International Journal of Psychoanalysis, 87*: 145–158.

CHAPTER FIVE

Implicit memory, unrepressed unconscious, and trauma theory: the turn of the screw between contemporary psychoanalysis and neuroscience

Clara Mucci

Where is the unconscious in the brain?
And which unconscious are we talking about?

The question of the relationship between implicit memory and the so-called "unrepressed unconcious" (Mancia, 2006) (as opposed to Freud's repressed content, therefore defined as unconscious, and/or as the mechanism of repression at work in the human psyche, a force contrary to awareness) allows for a rehearsal of the fundamental theoretical and clinical questions in the present debate in contemporary psychoanalysis and neuroscience and lies at the core of both interpersonal neuroscience and relational psychoanalysis.

It also affords an occasion for a re-examination of the efforts Freud made as early as his "Project for a scientific psychology" in 1895 to find fundamentals for a neurobiology of the mind and it enables us in turn, in the third millennium, to evaluate and rewrite his project in contemporary terms, a review that Schore, in his writings, has very thoroughly conducted with his extraordinary interdisciplinary expertise and a task Solms engages with intriguingly within this volume.

I start with a rewriting of Freud's definition of the "unconscious", as it is current today in psychology and neuroscience: that is, as what is not conscious but, none the less, guides most of our mental life, including attitudes, behaviour, and affects.

We now agree that much of what constitutes or describes mental life in humans is unconscious but this very sentence is in need of clarification in the light of the modern concept of unconscious in use here. This unconscious is an implicit nucleus of the self (Schore, 2012, and see Schore, this volume) which was originally created in connection with genetically inherited possibilities by the regulatory movement occurring between the mother's and the child's right brains, which took place primarily in the first year of the child's life, the critical period for attachment. This regulation helps to develop the right brain of the child before the left brain, hinting at a pre-eminence of emotional and affective life over analytic, decisional, and linguistic processes, and it creates a difference in the two systems of memory, implicit and explicit. Allan Schore (2003b, 2012) has proposed a modern view of attachment theory as a form of regulatory process that sets the basis for the creation of a biological substratum for a dynamic unconscious which remains at work during all further social exchanges and relationship formation, including the therapeutic one. As we shall see, this dynamic unconscious is endowed with special potential for reparation.

This implicit self-system encoded in the right brain that evolves in the interaction with a primary carer develops through preverbal and bodily stages and signals of communication; the mother, Schore writes, "is thus a regulator of arousal (van der Kolk & Fisher, 1994) and the transfer of affect between mother and child is thus mediated by right-hemisphere-to right-hemisphere arousal-regulating transactions" (Schore, 2003b, p. 222). During spontaneous right-brain to right-brain visual–facial, auditory–prosodic, and tactile–propriocep-tive emotionally charged attachment communications, a sensitive, psychobiologically attuned carer is capable of regulating, at an implicit level, the infant's states of arousal.

Schore continues,

These events are inscribed in implicit procedural memory in the early developing right hemisphere that is specialized for the processing of visuospatial information (Galin, 1974). But the right cerebral cortex is also dominant for "implicit" learning (Hugdahl, 1995), an adaptive process that underlies all emotional phenomena, including those at the core of the psychotherapeutic relationship. (2003b, p. 222)

It is possible to say, with Schore, that by the end of the first year of life, right lateralised cortical–subcortical circuits have imprinted, in implicit procedural memory, an internal working model of attachment which encodes strategies of affect regulation that unconsciously guide the individual in future interpersonal exchanges.

The orbitofrontal cortex, that is, the central mechanism of affect regulation in the dual hemisphere brain, accesses memory functions by implicit processing (Schore, 2012; Stuss et al., 1982). What Freud would term "preconscious" functioning (Schore, 2003b, p. 272) is directly influenced by this regulatory activity that from the external becomes a form of internal self-regulation. The neural cells, located in the orbitofrontal cortex and in the amygdala, respond to visual and facial expressions and these essential components of active social communications specifically activate these areas in the brain (Brothers, 1997). The orbitofrontal cortex also exerts an essential role in co-ordinating internal states of the organism and the various representational processes that lie at the core of reasoning, motivation, and the creation of emotional meaning (Damasio, 1994; Fuster, 1985; Rolls, 1996).

According to Schore, the limbic system is a three-tiered hierarchical system, with each level (amygdala, anterior cinculate, and insula-orbitofrontal) containing separable state-dependent affective, cognitive, and behavioural functions. Each level contains imprinted, stored representations of early sensory–affectively charged traces, which means that, at different moments, different levels of implicit memory can be activated:

Each of the three levels also manifests itself in different states of consciousness, with the amygdala being the deepest unconscious level, and the orbitofrontal the highest. The primitive amygdala level, farthest from higher cortical operations yet closely adjacent to hypothalamic and autonomic structures, would contain the realm of Freud's (1923) "bodily ego" and Bollas's "unthought known" (1987). (Schore 2003b, p. 234)

From these bodily imprints, the traces of internalised representations of relationship are created, something we can assimilate to the internal working models (IWM) as explained by Bowlby (1969). Because this system develops in stages, if early relational trauma interferes with the experience-dependent maturation of the interconnections of these systems, they might lose the opportunity of integration so that dysregulated somatic states are subsequently created. This is coherent with the present-day description of the development of personality disorders based on dysregulation of affect and related pathologies (Schore, 1994, 2003a,b).

Before the hippocampus develops, between the second and the third year of life, the brain is not capable of properly encoding memories in the sense of episodic memory, or autobiographical memory; it can only retrieve memories encoded in the body in the implicit form, through behavioural, emotional, perceptive, and somato-sensorial cues. If recalled and reactivated, they are not linked to a clear sense of subjectivity but they embody the mental experience of preconscious emotions, behaviours, and perceptions. Early trauma and insecure forms of attachment, including disorganised attachment, are encoded in implicit memory, so that, to quote a famous remark made by van der Kolk (2014), "the body keeps the score" even when the subject "does not know". Implicit memories are formed by the attachment experience, both positive and negative, and by future traumatic experiences. Interestingly, in intergenerational transmission of attachment (and trauma), not only does the parent transmit his/her disorganised modalities to the child, but it works in both directions: that is, disorganised attachment in the child might also reactivate the painful attachment memories in the parent, in a circuit that could become dangerous for the more vulnerable of the two in the relation. In the child, they can be reactivated easily, even after a long time has gone by and the child is, indeed, an adult (Perry et al., 1995). In this chain, the transgenerational experience is transferred automatically, that is, unconsciously, without conscious participation, between parent and child (see Liotti in this volume).

Very similar views were held by neuroscientist and psychoanalyst Mauro Mancia, who, from the 1990s onwards, focused on implicit memory and unrepressed unconscious:

> At birth the infant's experiences—and consequently his or her memory—are purely sensory (*aesthesis*): the mother's odor, her words, how the baby feels contained and watched, all convey affective

messages essential to the organization of these very first representations. These preverbal experiences are filed in the implicit memory.
But the baby may also have occasions to file gross and microscopic
trauma there too: loss of the parents, abandon, neglect, serious frustrations, humiliation, incomprehension, physical mental and even sexual
violence and abuse. These traumas may undermine the baby's attachment system (Bowlby 1969; Fonagy & Target 1997) and endanger the
organization of his or her self (Stern 1985). (Mancia, 2007, p. 43)

Mancia speculates that the repressed unconscious, with the material that has undergone repression as explained by Freud, is located in
the structures of the explicit autobiographic memory. Anderson and
colleagues (2004), to a certain extent, seem to support this view when
they show that purposely forgetting material, comparable to Freudian
repression of material, is accompanied by increased activity in the
prefrontal areas and a parallel reduction in hippocampal activity. This
would be the reverse of what happens in dreams, during REM sleep,
when hippocampal activity increases and there is reactivation of
dorsolateral prefrontal cortex (Braun et al., 1998).

Mancia believes that unrepressed unconscious or implicit memory
is located in the posterior temporo–parieto–occipital associative cortical areas of the right hemisphere. These areas are more active during
REM sleep and, therefore, during dream activity, in comparison to the
left hemisphere. Solms (1995) has also found that patients with lesions
to the posterior associative areas do not dream.

Freud's "unconscious" and "repression" and our present view of the so-called unconscious

Let us have a closer look at Freud's idea of the "unconscious" and how
his views are both accepted and disclaimed by present psychoanalytic
and neuropsychological discourse.

As Drew Westen has thoroughly illustrated in a series of studies in
the 1990s (e.g., Westen, 1997, 1999), a massive body of recent psychological research has demonstrated that, though Freud is repeatedly
pronounced "dead" by other disciplines, he is still in good shape and,
indeed, was right in a number of his tenets: from the fact that many
enduring aspects of personality coalesce in childhood (as infant
research has evidenced), to the fact that mental representations of self

and other do begin to be built up neurologically and psychologically in very early stages of childhood (often becoming a cause for mental pathology), to the conflict that motivations and affects in individuals might undergo simultaneously, so that awareness is a non-linear but complex and multi-dimensional reality, and, first and foremost, his tenet that "most of mental life is unconscious" (Westen, 1999, p. 1062) or that it "operates unconsciously" (Solms & Turnbull, 2002, p. 79). The Freudian image of consciousness as the top of the famous iceberg seems confirmed by current day research in cognitive studies, in so far as it claims that although the largest part of our consciousness is submerged it nonetheless directs or primes our mental life in open or subtle ways (Westen 1999). I will not go through all the details of this discussion because Westen does this magisterially, and so I refer the reader to his work. I would start instead by rephrasing the major questions we are facing in contemporary psychoanalysis and neuro-science when we speak of consciousness and the unconscious, with a consideration of the neurobiological underpinnings.

First of all, what was Freud's unconscious?

A century ago, in "On metapsychology" (1915), in the Preface to the paper on "The unconscious", Freud stated that

> We have learned from psychoanalysis that the essence of the process of repression lies, not in putting an end to, in annihilating, the idea that represents an instinct, but in preventing it from becoming conscious. When this happens we say of the idea that it is in a state of being 'unconscious', and we can produce good evidence *to show that even when it is unconscious it can produce effects,* even including some which finally reach consciousness ... *Everything that is repressed must remain unconscious*; but let us state at the very outset that *the repressed does not cover everything that is unconscious. The unconscious has the wider compass: the repressed is a part of the unconscious.* (Freud, 1915e, p. 166, my emphasis)

In this passage, Freud is clearly stating that the repressed and the unconscious are not one and the same thing: the repressed is only a part of the unconscious (and is precisely what has undergone repression) and a wider area has to be defined as unconscious, meaning, non-conscious, the effects of which are felt in behaviour and attitudes in human beings and can be reconstructed retrospectively or, as Freud says, "translated" back to consciousness.

The modernity of this statement is proved by the distinction we are now capable of making thanks to the differentiation of the two systems of memory, the implicit and the explicit systems, discovered roughly thirty years ago. It would appear, as we have seen in Schore's explanation, that implicit memory, based in the right brain, accounts for what is unconscious (as non-conscious) but not repressed, influencing behaviour and relational attitudes and priming responses and states of mind. Implicit memory points not at what has undergone repression, but at what is not available for immediate retrieval because of the immaturity of the memory system and yet, as is obvious in several situations in which affects and motivations are involved, has an enduring and sometimes uncanny or destructive effect, as appears clearly in traumatic memories influencing pathological beliefs and future destructive behaviour, or a tendency to revictimisation.

Repression, in contrast, as Freud had already stated, has to do with an active removal from consciousness of material or contents that have undergone a process of repression by a subject, almost by intentional defence, or, at least, a defence initiated by intentional movement and subsequently being forgotten as such.

It would, therefore, seem that only within the explicit and episodic memory, or autobiographical memory, where an "I" has been modulated and the structure of the brain and the functions pertaining to memory are more mature, is it possible to have the kind of defence that subtracts those contents from the mass of conscious information, and represses them. As processes controlled by the left brain, they deal with contents that have been consciously learnt and maintained (following the second or third year of development of the brain); they must have undergone repression only in a later moment and subsequently might become retrievable under certain circumstances (linked to a collaboration of both implicit and explicit systems and through language).

The right brain, as the site of implicit memory, becomes the psychobiological base of the unconscious in its most comprehensive meaning in terms of "what is not conscious" and, none the less, leads relevant aspects of our life. In doing so, it is the basis of our motivational and affective life, in the three-tiered levels described; implicit affective processes become distinguished from explicit cognitive and learning processes. This results in a solution to the misunderstandings between cognitivists and psychoanalysts in so far as cognitivism has, by now, accepted the fact that memory, cognition, learning, and decisional processes cannot be understood without the contribution of affection and motivation, while psychoanalysis is accepting the reality that affects and motivation are embodied and better understood in a mind–body connection summarised by the brain itself as the site where both mental (mostly cultural) and biological (mostly natural) elements intersect. The importance of a mind–body connection situated precisely in the brain (as has been shown by all the research on mirror neurons and other bodily interpersonal aspects rooted in the brain) explains why the body in the mind is so pre-eminent in neuroscientific studies nowadays (Ammaniti & Gallese, 2014). The recent development of epigenetics is a further case in point.

Also, the concept of the drive, bodily rooted for Freud, needs to be understood within this wider interrelational and intersubjective frame of bodily rooted processes mediated intersubjectively throughout the entire life of a person and developmentally constituted by two minds (and two bodies) in relation. It also calls to mind, as Damasio has pointed out, Decartes's error, (Damasio, 1994), which we are now capable of avoiding through a number of interdisciplinary connections.

In this way, not only does the field of discussion opened by the recognition of the existence of the two systems of implicit and explicit memory shed light on the functioning of unconscious processes of which Freud was well aware and relentlessly exposed in his work from the end of the nineteenth to the middle of the twentieth century,[1] but it also aims at sustaining the debate about what is unconscious as repressed (by the subject) and what is unconscious as belonging to implicit memory and, therefore, recorded in the body and capable of retrieval through tactile, olfactory, vocal, and in general non-verbal cues. It would seem that repression is linked to a system that suggests, so to speak, a one-person psychoanalytic model *vs.* a two-person (relational, intersubjective) psychoanalytic model that would lead to an interpersonal and intersubjective debate, as opposed to psychoanalysis, which is mainly drive based, libido centred, and rooted in one subject only. It is in the field of trauma that the debate was born (which means, of course, that it has been going on since the very beginning of psychoanalytic theory and practice) and this debate has generated a variety of different positions, with the pre-eminence, in

Freudian psychoanalysis, of fantasy over reality (Bohleber, 2010; Mucci, 2008, 2013).

Freud, with his rejection of the seduction theory in 1897, radicalised a view that made drive, fantasy, and intrapsychic reality the bulwarks of his idea of psychoanalytic theory and practice, leaving aside another path, that of dissociation as the response to a real, overwhelming encounter between a young and too fragile subject incapable of sustaining such an attack and an uncaring adult. In so doing, he rejected the possibility that psychoanalysis, born out of an active act of listening between two subjects, could, in effect, be founded on an intersubjective practice. This refusal of early overwhelming trauma also explains why he needed a theory of *nachtraglichkeit*, to say that the original traumatic blow to a younger subject becomes traumatic and causes pathology only afterwards, or belatedly.

This other path left open to Freud's contemporaries (that of early real trauma and subsequent dissociation, encoded implicitly in the body) would be the course taken by Pierre Janet's theorisation, on one hand, and Sandor Ferenczi's theory and practice, on the other (Lingiardi & Mucci, 2014).

Yet, in several places in *Studies on Hysteria*, the existence of dissociation is posited and described and only later, through an active form of disavowal, does Freud erase dissociation as the early response of an overwhelmed, too young subject (a response encoded in implicit memory) to a voluntary form of repression implying an older, more mature subject (what would be, in our contemporary language) encoded and subsequently rejected by explicit memory).

The discovery of what is inscribed in implicit memory (unconscious but organising what the subject experiences and directing future social exchanges and even personality development) shows that experience is not encoded by a Self in the sense of an autonomous, intentional subject as agent, but a Self that is, none the less, capable of encoding in the body a personal piece of experience. In other words, it points at the reality of some kind of utter experience not registered verbally, nor encoded semantically (episodic and autobiographical memory, explicit system) but, none the less, existing, directing and influencing the subject in his/her life and often creating suffering.

In "Abstracts for the preliminary communication", written right before *Studies on Hysteria*, Freud argues (in point 3) that the memory creating the content of hysterical attacks is an unconscious memory, or belongs to the "second state of consciousness". It is absent from the memory of the patient, but if he/she succeeds in carrying this memory through to consciousness the capacity to evoke an attack ceases.

In point 4, he also adds that the problem of the origin of the content of the memory in hysterical attacks coincides with the question of what the normal conditions are under which an event (representation, intention) is admitted into the "second state of consciousness". If the event is deliberately forgotten, this physical activity is transformed into a hysterical attack.

In "On the psychical mechanism of hysterical phenomena: preliminary communication" (1893a) by Freud and Breuer, we read,

> each individual hysterical symptom immediately and permanently disappeared when we had succeeded in bringing clearly to light the memory of the event by which it was provoked and in arousing its accompanying affect, and when the patient had described that event in the greatest possible detail and had put the affect into words. (Freud, 1893a, p. 6, original emphasis)

Again, the "intentional aspect" is explained as follows: "because it was a question of things which the patient wished to forget, and *therefore intentionally repressed*, from his conscious thought and inhibited and suppressed" (p. 10, my emphasis). And the authors go on: "The second group of conditions are determined not *by the physical states in which the patient received the experiences* in question" (p. 10, my emphasis).

It would seem that the distinction between a state where the subject intentionally represses an idea or content and a state in which the subject undergoes the traumatic process that leads to symptoms instead of memories is already there: the two ways of reacting to a traumatic event, repression, with intentional processes implying the subject's effort, and dissociation, implying implicit memory encoding and an overwhelming bodily reaction, are something Freud considers, but decides to leave aside.

The road towards repression becomes the way of explaining the pathogenesis of hysteria and neuropsychosis, while dissociative responses have not been considered by Freud as a reaction to trauma.

Repression vs. dissociation: the road that Freud (and psychoanalysis) could have taken and contemporary developments

Recent studies on early relational trauma and disorganised attachment by Schore, van der Kolk (2014; van der Kolk & Fisher, 1994), Liotti (2000), and Farina, among others, and on maltreatment, neglect, and abuse or incest, by Perry and colleagues (1995), Briere (1992), Courtois (1996), Herman and colleagues (1989), and many other authors, stress how trauma results in a cancellation of memory, or an implicit response, leading, in the presence of a vulnerability, to dissociation.

Very clearly, Freud himself talks of dissociation and of a "splitting in consciousness" in the case of Miss Lucy in *Studies on Hysteria*, but for him what causes the split in consciousness (originating hysterical symptoms) is an "intentional act":

> The actual traumatic moment, then, is the one at which the incompatibility forces itself upon the ego and at which the latter decides on the repudiation of the incompatible idea. That idea is not annihilated by a repudiation of this kind, but merely repressed into the unconscious. When this process occurs for the first time, there comes into being a nucleus and centre of crystallization for the formation of a psychical group divorced from the ego – a group around which everything would imply an acceptance of the incompatible idea subsequently collects. *The splitting of consciousness in these cases of acquired hysteria is accordingly a deliberate and intentional one.* At least one is often introduced by an act of volition; for the actual outcome is something different from what the subject intended. What he wanted was to do away with an idea, as though it had never appeared, but all he succeeds in doing is to isolate it psychically. (Freud, 1895d, p. 123, my emphasis)

Here, Freud is hinting at a splitting in consciousness, a reaction to trauma that he has, in his theory and practice, historically disavowed, in the moment that he posits an intentional desire to erase the disturbing idea that, as a consequence, has become repressed and has created a symptom in its turn; in place of a memory that is repressed, a symptom is created, something embedded in the body. In contrast, the path of splitting, or actually of dissociation or of fragmentation, would have been the pathological reaction described by Janet as a response to the traumatic shock, or by Ferenczi when, in his theoretical and clinical reflections (1932), he talks about fragmentation in personality.

Here is Ferenczi, with the famous entry on "Fragmentation" in his *Clinical Diary* (1988[1932]), on 21 February 1932:

> A child is the victim of overwhelming aggression, which results in "giving up the ghost" . . . with the firm conviction that this self-abandonment (fainting) means death. However, it is precisely this complete relaxation induced by self-abandonment that may create more favorable conditions for him to endure the violence. . . . Therefore someone who has "given up the ghost" survives this death physically and with a part of his energy begins to live again; he even succeeds in reestablishing unity with the pre-traumatic personality, although this is usually accompanied by memory lapses and retroactive amnesia of varying duration. But this amnesic piece is actually a part of the person, who is still "dead", or exists permanently in the agony of anxiety. The task of the analysis is to remove this split. (Ferenczi, 1988, p. 39)

The extraordinary accuracy of this description of the dissociative traumatic reaction which might even result in a fainting of the body, a freezing response, has been confirmed by neurophysiological findings, as in the research by Stephen Porges (2011), or the vagal response leading to blunting and analgesia (compatible with the "shrinking of conscious experience" as described by Janet, 1899). More than a defence, and certainly not an intentional or even partially intentional defence, the neurophysiology of trauma describes a collapse of mental and psychical resources as a response to the external overwhelming experience, more than the intrapsychic defence at work.

This has also been described by Schore as follows:

> The dissociative metabolic shutdown state is a primary regulatory process, used throughout the life-span, in which the stressed individual passively disengages in order to conserve energies, foster survival by the risky posture of "feigning death", and allow the restitution of depleted resources by immobility. In this passive hypometabolic state heart rate, blood pressure, and respiration are decreased, while pain numbing and blunting endogenous opiates are elevated. It is this energy-conserving parasympathetic (vagal) mechanism that mediates the "profound detachment" of dissociation. (Schore, 2011, p. xvii)

In another revealing passage, extremely relevant for developments in psychoanalytic theory and in practice, on 25 March 1932 ("Psychic bandage"), Ferenczi describes how the overwhelming experience leaves a permanent mark, and results in a splitting in the personality, and, ultimately, in a change in the victim's behavior:

> From the moment when bitter experience teaches us to lose faith in the benevolence of the environment, *a permanent split in the personality occurs.* . . . . Actual trauma is experienced by children in situations where no immediate remedy is provided and where adaptation, that is, a change in their own behavior, is forced on them—*the first step towards establishing the differentiation between inner and outer world, subject and object. From then on, neither subjective nor objective experience alone will be perceived as an integral emotional unit* . . . (Ferenczi, 1988, p. 69, my emphasis)

As a consequence of trauma, the child adapts his/her behaviour to the environment and in this way a permanent cognitive distortion and a twist in personality is initiated. For Ferenczi, trauma also bears the traces of an external, overwhelming interpersonal experience that has become internalised, intrapsychic, but maintains an interpersonal force in so far as the relationship with the external world is concerned (a sort of IWM, in Bowlby's terms, or a representation, a system similar to Bucci's symbolic sub-symbolic communications (Bucci, 1997). Moreover, what Ferenczi stresses in his trauma theory and clinical implications is that the child will very probably internalise the aggressiveness and the dissociated sense of guilt of the persecutor (which are also extremely important elements for future pathology).

Similarly to Ferenczi's traumatic and dissociative model, Janet had privileged the idea that at the basis of pathological hysteria lay a *désaggrégation psychologique* that was the contrary of that synthetic and integrated superior function in which higher levels of consciousness rested (Janet, 1899). For Janet, an environmental trauma, not necessarily a sexual trauma, had arrested the cognitive and affective development of the subject and caused the "shrinking of the field of consciousness" so typical of the traumatic effect (Lingiardi & Mucci, 2014, p. 43). Several studies by Janet stressed the relevance of environmental conditions, or primary relations, as we would call them today. As Giovanni Liotti has clearly underlined in a recent reconsideration of the critique of Janet to Freud's assumptions,

Janet's idea that the pathological response to psychological trauma, once the above mentioned vulnerability has been posited, is the passive consequence of the overwhelming emotion over the superior forces of consciousness (namely, that it is a functional deficit induced by the traumatic memory) is clearly opposed to Freud's idea that pathology depends on an active defence on behalf of the ego aiming at excluding uncanny emotions and representations from consciousness. (Liotti, 2014, p. 32, translated for this edition)

Both Janet and Ferenczi privilege the bodily reaction and the absence of consciousness, and of subjectivity, in traumatic states, leaving space to a traumatised subject that is literally in a place of estrangement and erasure of superior, cortical strategies, and might be present only through somatic, non-verbal olfactory and sensorimotor cues, a *lieu* where subjectivity (and consciousness) are, by definition, deleted, erased; where trauma is, only the body is present with its peculiar language and the experience can be recalled as if it belonged to someone else, since subjectivity and consciousness are not there.

In privileging the deliberate and intentional defence of repression of an idea (and a memory) that creates, in turn, a symptom rooted in the compromise formation between the repressed idea and the pain of the unacceptability of the idea to consciousness, Freud has opened the road to a psychoanalysis (as opposed to Janet's "psychological analysis") in which fantasmatic reaction is privileged over the collapse of a body that is the only witness left there without awareness, a dissociated and divided body. In Freud's theorisation, the libido system and the drive were to prevail over the relational, intersubjective, environmentally determined quality of the mind–body system (all elements that subsequent interdisciplinary studies on how the subject is born have proved, as is evident from such studies in infant research, attachment studies, and interpersonal neurobiology or regulation theory).

In addition, in describing a system that privileges the way the ego responds with defensive strategies as a way to protect itself, Freud privileges a top-down system that modern neuroscience seems to have replaced with a bottom-up model, as in Porges's findings: the response goes from the bottom—from the stem—to the cortex, that is rather deprived in its response (Liotti, 2014, p. 35; Porges, 2011).

As a consequence of this Freudian attitude, the pathology that Freud analysed and treated was more likely to be of a neurotic and less severe range than the severely traumatised patients Ferenczi and

Janet were willing to treat. This is also why the dissociative road to pathology is more in line with present day severe borderline pathologies or severe somatisations, in contrast with the neuropsychosis treated by Freud.

As Schore cogently highlighted over ten years ago,

> current neurobiology suggests that repression is a developmentally more advanced left brain defense against affects like anxiety that are represented at the cortical level of the right brain, but the earlier-appearing and more primitive dissociation is a defense against traumatic affects like terror that are stored subcortically in the right brain. *This neurobiological conceptualization indicates that Freud's idea about trauma must be reassessed* (van der Kolk, Weisaeth, & van der Hart, 1996) *and that the concept of dissociation must be reincorporated into theoretical and clinical psychoanalysis.* It is now clear that dissociation represents the most primitive defense against traumatic affective states and that it must be addressed in the treatment of severe psychopathologies. (Schore, 2003b, p. 246, my emphasis)

For Schore, and I could not agree more, the consequence of this is that the treatment must match the developmental level of the patient, and, therefore, *"with early forming severe right-brain pathologies, the clinician's primary function is as an affect regulator for the patient's primitive, traumatic states, including those affective states that are walled off by dissociation"* (Schore, 2003b, p. 246, my emphasis).

We shall deal further with these important implications for treatment in the last paragraph of our essay on treatment.

Selflessness and trauma: or where trauma is, there is no subject (just the body)

The traumatic terrain is also the place of another fundamental twist in the theory of self and selflessness, or unconscious state: it has to do with the fact that in order for episodic memory to be active, there needs to be a subject capable of narrating the experience (which can be done also retrospectively, as a consequence of the therapeutic process). In other words, where trauma is, the subject has been deleted, together with the capacity to remember in a left-brain kind of explicit narration, involving linguistic awareness and representation.

As Laub and Auerhahn have cogently written,

> Freud labels "hysterical fantasies" what we would now understand as re-enactment of childhood trauma in dissociative states . . . It is the nature of trauma to elude our knowledge, because of both defence and deficit. During massive trauma . . . this blurring of boundaries between reality and fantasy conjures up affects so violent that it exceeds the ego's capacity of regulation. (1993, p. 288)

Laub and Auerhahn define the specific status of traumatic subjectivity as a paradoxical status of "knowing and not knowing", a place outside temporal and spatial framing for the subject. In other words, where trauma is, there is no subject (or consciousness). For the subject to exist, there needs to be a retrieval of the experience through verbal and episodic memory, therefore there is consciousness (but that state is not the traumatic state).

As Solms and Turnbull write (2002, p. 160):

> When we say "I remember . . . [anything]" we are speaking of an episodic memory. According to Schacter (1996), the episodic memory system "allows *explicitly* to recall the personal incidents that *uniquely* define our lives". (p. 17)

The authors continue,

> In other worlds, states of the SELF might be intrinsically conscious (One cannot say the "I" in "I remember . . ." without simultaneously being it). The sense of self (of "I was there . . ."; "it happened to me . . .") appears to be necessarily conscious. This implies that although external events can be encoded unconsciously in the brain (as semantic, perceptual, or procedural traces), the episodic living of those events apparently cannot. Experiences are not mere traces of past stimuli. Experiences have to be lived. It is the reliving of an event as experience ("I remember . . ." that necessarily renders it conscious. And it is the sense of self (of "being there") that combines the traces into an experience. This is another way of saying what we said in chapter 3 in relation to consciousness in general: it is the SELF that binds our fragmented representations of the world into unified, lived experiences. The link in a self-world coupling is therefore the SELF itself. (2002, p. 161)

This is exactly what is not possible in the traumatic experience, characterised by a collapse of a sense of self, and so the "cure" aims to retrieve a Self for that experience. Here are Laub and Auerhahn (1993):

> In this form of traumatic memory, the center of experience is no longer in the experiencing "I". Events happen somewhere, but are no longer connected with the conscious subject. The self is fragmented into a "me" and a "not-me" and any connection between the two has been severed. What the survivor manifests is a painful state of concurrent awareness of a depleted self and of an intense experience that is disconnected and "forgotten", but nevertheless affectively permeates and compromises life strategies of adaptation and defense. This double state of knowing and not knowing leaves the survivor in grief not only for his dead loved ones but also for his lost memories. That lack of knowledge prevents the revival of despair that would accompany mourning, but leaves the survivor alone and unknown to himself. (1993, p. 291).

Very appropriately, Laub and Lee (2003) find the presence of a total death instinct and a withdrawal of cathexis at work in severe states of traumatic experience (another point Janet criticised in Freud: death is not the other side of a libido-erotic or life force within the subject; death has to do with annihilation because of an extremely negative relational experience, it is not an intrapsychic force originating from within) (see also Liotti, 2014; Mucci, 2013):

> The withdrawal of cathexis or the failure of the empathic connection at the time of traumatization is the strongest characteristic of massive psychic trauma. Traumatic loss of the internal good object and of libidinal ties seems to release the hitherto libidinally neutralized forces of the death instinct and to intensify the clinical manifestations of their derivatives in the aftermath of massive trauma. (Laub & Lee, 2003, p. 404)

The loss of the internal object and the decathexis lead to a failure in representation and verbalisation, therefore a collapse of explicit memory, an inability to say and, therefore, to remember, even when the subject is more mature, or is an adult:

> the victim, to ward off the horrors of objectlessness, internalises and identifies with the only object available to him: the perpetrator, a bad object . . . Failure of the empathic connection and the consequent loss

of the internal good object produce feelings of absence and of rupture, a loss of representation, an inability to grasp and remember trauma, and a loss of coherence. Libidinal binding to associative links, to meaning and to words, as well as to the internal object and to oneself, becomes at least temporarily suspended. There is a profound sense that structure and representation—the ability to tell one's story to oneself and to another—are missing from the survivor's experience. (Laub & Lee, 2003, p. 441)

In other words, the survivor's experience remains mute, encoded in the body and in implicit memory, and cannot be possessed and expressed by explicit memory and the self.

This erasure and this annihilation of the resources of the self in traumatic experience are much more similar to what Janet, on the one hand, and Ferenczi, on the other, had described, in contrast to Freud's intentional repression by the subject.

If trauma means the rupture of the "empathic dyad" (Laub & Auerhahn, 1989), it is only in a relational process that vital trust can be recovered: this is why, before giving testimony, or before the therapeutic work, the subject does not necessarily know his entire story. Here is Laub again (Laub, 2005):

To begin with, the survivor does not fully know what he or she knows. It is only as the testimony emerges that the survivor comes to know his or her full story and the impact it has had on his or her life. Even then, parts that are beyond the imaginable will remain left out or retained as frozen, encapsulated, and split-off foreign images. These are the parts of the story that are not to be told. Off-limits, abysmally cold and empty, while at the same time also threateningly violent, tumultuous, and dangerous, they have no form. These parts of the survivor's story, and thus a piece of human history, are lost to silence. I have earlier searched for a word for this muting or loss—and I have come to call it *an erasure*. (p. 257)

Erasure is this blank in place of experience, something that leaves no memory trace and no words except in the body and in the right brain. It is a *mànque à être* of the subject, it cannot be the intentional attempt of the subject to erase memory. Erasure is the missing part in lieu of experience, that for which there are no words because in that place or position there is no subject and consciousness is split, divided, dissociated, while repression comes afterwards, at a later time, somehow voluntarily enforced by the ego through the dynamics of the explicit self, and, therefore, implies a subject and a consciousness.

This is confirmed by Solms and Turnbull when they write, "Thus we seem to have rediscovered, from a neuroscientific standpoint, the obvious fact that what we feel about our experience is what renders them susceptible to "repression" (Solms & Turnbull, 2002, p. 162).

At the same time, this testifies to the fact that until a memory becomes an episodic memory, reactivated by a current self, usually in the therapeutic process, it is just an unconscious memory, or an as-if memory; "for a memory to be expressed in semantic memory and become autobiographical, episodic memory there needs to be a subject" (Solms & Turnbull, 2002, p. 162).

What therapy, when successful, can do is to reactivate those memories in the current self, and at that point they (as such) exist (Solms & Turnbull, 2002).

What contemporary trauma theory and practice has taught us is that the "knowing" of the traumatic experience emerges, or can be recuperated, as a piece of reality and truth (belonging not only the individual, but also to society and history) only within a relationship. As in the practice of testimony, the retrieval of the memory requires an apt listener who becomes, in turn, a witness; as Dori Laub has frequently affirmed, for the witness to become a witness, there needs to be a companion, an apt companion: "a totally present listener who creates the holding space for them to do it" (Laub, in Caruth 2015, p. 48). Testimony does not come and cannot be verbalised in a void; there needs to be an other, that internal–external other who, by definition, has been destroyed in the traumatic experience (the break of the empathic dyad, the lack of the presence of an internal, maternal good object, in Laub's definition). Testimony is

a healing way to put fragments together. But to get it out in the interpersonal space there has to be a companion. Basically I think it's the necessity for an internal companion, because the process of symbolization and the formation of narrative only happens within an internal dialogue, that addressee . . .

There has to be a certain amount of ego structure, a certain amount of object relationship, a certain connectedness, and appropriate others in order to speak. (Laub, in Caruth, 2015, pp. 48–49)

This is how psychoanalysis, from being simply a theory and a clinical practice may become, in my mind, a form of testimony (Mucci, 2013). It is also in coherence with Ferenczi's realisation that the attitude of the therapist is of primary importance if the patient is to accept and "believe" what has happened, that is, the reality of his traumatic past: "It appears that patients cannot believe that an event took place, or cannot fully believe it, if the analyst, as the sole witness of the events persists in his cool, unemotional and . . . purely intellectual attitude" (Ferenczi, 1988[1932], p. 24). And he concludes, in opposition to Freud, that "an abreaction of quantities of trauma is not enough; the situation must be different from the actually traumatic one in order to make possible a different, positive outcome" (p. 108). What is needed is a totally committed, benevolent (Ferenczi, 1988[1932], p. 24) therapist capable of rewriting a different story within the therapeutic relationship, even at the level of implicit memory and IWM.

The consequences of this discourse on repression vs. dissociation on contemporary psychopathology and psychotherapy

The last realm in which dissociation *vs.* repression opens a divide is that of psychopathology. Pathologies that have repression at their root are typical of neurotic structure, while pathologies based on dissociation are of more severe, mostly borderline nature. Here is how Bromberg, working mostly on dissociation with traumatised patients, defines the two "defences":

> Repression as a defense is responsive to anxiety—a negative but regulable affect that signals the potential emergence into consciousness of mental contents that may create unpleasant, but bearable intrapsychic conflict. Dissociation as a defense is responsive to trauma—the chaotic, convulsive flooding by unregulatable affect that takes over the mind, threatening the stability of selfhood and sometimes sanity. (Bromberg, 2011, p. 49)

The traumatic aetiopathology of borderline disorders is not easy to define and several authors do indeed not accept current attempts at a definition.

None the less, many authors and an extensive body of research seems to prove that

1. Disorganised attachment, in the presence of factors of vulnerability and no reparatory elements, predisposes to the instabilities and the dysregulation that characterise borderline disorders. (Fonagy, 2000; Lyons-Ruth & Jacobvitz, 1999; Patrick et al., 1994).

2. Abuse and especially sexual abuse and incest have been identified as a cause for the kind of dysfunctional response to images of self and other and destructiveness and impulsivity in several areas which seem to be one of the major dimensions of the painful condition of borderline disorders.

Gabbard (2014), Paris (2010), and Zanarini and colleagues (1989) all testify to the high percentage of abuse (especially sexual abuse) in patients who have been diagnosed as borderline. Otto Kernberg as well has acknowledged "the prevalence of physical and sexual abuse in the history of patients with severe personality disorders" (Carkim et al., 1999, p. 245); van der Kolk (2014) and Pat Ogden and colleagues (2006) identify in affective dysregulation and in dissociation the major cause of the pathology.

In Schore's explanation,

> Importantly, due to the later maturation of the parasympathetic nervous system and the resultant cognitive advances of the late practising period, the child's attempts to defensively cope with the stress inducing mother are more complex. With the additional maturation of the ANS, the child can now lock in to two distinct, nonoverlapping dissociated psychobiological states of existence. According to Kernberg (1975), a major structural characteristic of the borderline condition is the utilization of the splitting defenses that allow for the presence of mutually dissociated or split off states. It is now thought that the cognitive preconditions for defensive splitting become established by the time the infant is between 12 to 18 months old (Gergely, 1992). Its function may be to avoid external stimuli that could precipitate an unregulated or hypoaroused state. (1994, p. 420)

Lack of emotional regulation, with dissociation, projective identification, and primitive defences, combines with the internal impossibility of a soothing object to which to return when they are imbalanced and overwhelmed, because of very poor attachment experiences or even neglect, maltreatment, and abuse protracted over a long time. Self-regulating strategies are not capable of preventing the subjects from going from hyperactivity to extreme hypoactivity of the orbitofrontal cortex and of the amygdala, so that an internal void is accompanied by internal chaos and constant turmoil. Right parietal and frontal regions reveal deficits in these patients.

As several authors have proved in their research, the right hemisphere is dominant not only for regulating affect, but also for maintaining a coherent sense of one's body (Tsakiris et al., 2008), for attention (Raz, 2004), and for pain processing (Symonds et al., 2006), and so the right-brain strategy of dissociation represents the ultimate defence for blocking emotional, bodily-based pain (Schore, 2011, p. xxix)

On the link between disorganised attachment and the development of a borderline disorder, several authors underline how the personality of an individual is the result of the continuous interactions between genetically inherited traits and the relational intersubjective experience from his/her environment (Bouchard, 1994; Calkins & Fox, 1994; Kagan, 1997; Kendler & Eaves, 1986; Rothbart & Ahadi, 1994; Thomas & Chess, 1997).

From attachment relationships to following social exchanges, neural connections and synapses can be reinforced, reduced, or modified even in adult circumstances; while traumatic relational experiences have a toxic effect especially on the child: cortisol and other hormones affect cortical and limbic processes that regulate emotions.

Disorganisation in attachment has been identified by Lyons-Ruth and Jacobvitz (1999), by John Gunderson (1996), by Fonagy and colleagues (2004) as a deviant developmental pattern that, when present, might be an identifiable risk factor for the later development of BPD. Also, disorganised attachment has been seen as the possible basis for a further dissociative disorder. In general, borderline personality disorders, in so far as they imply a disturbance in the integrated and stable representation of self and other, with dysregulation (or impulsivity and dysregulation) as its basis, can be understood as a particular right-brain disorder (Schore, 2012) that requires a particular right-brain therapy (van der Kolk, in Caruth, 2015, p. 165).

Borderline disorders might or might not imply high levels of dissociation.

Even if dissociative responses might not have been activated by the self in the borderline patient, they have, none the less, permanently caused a split in the organisation of self and other representations. Splitting is not dissociation, but it still implies the presence of opposite views of the object, both internal and external (this is, according to Kernberg, the core of the pathology, which is expressed in the session through dyadic, opposite elements rehearsing an internal contradictory, or even torturing, emotional and cognitive process, so that, at the same moment, different levels of self are available).

On abuse as aetiopathogenesis of borderline disorders, very cogently Schore writes,

> It is now well established that early childhood abuse specifically alters lateralised limbic system maturation, producing neurobiological alterations that act as a biological substrate for a variety of psychiatric consequences, including affective instability, inefficient stress tolerance, memory impairment, and dissociative disturbances. (Schore, 2011, p. xx)

Herman and van der Kolk, in their 1987 research, found that borderline patients had suffered severe trauma, with physical and sexual violence before the age of six; only a minority of patients did not refer to traumatic events, but they suffered from severe amnesia; similar data emerge from the study of Ogata (1990) and from Zanarini and colleagues (1989).

As Schore (2012) writes about attachment trauma patients (whom he defines as personality disorder patients),

> The patient brings into treatment an enduring imprint of attachment trauma: an impaired capacity to regulate stressful affect and an over-reliance on the affect-deadening defense of pathological dissociation [and many others]. Under relational stress this affect disregulation deficit is characterologically expressed in a tendency toward low-threshold, high-intensity, emotional reactions followed by slow return to baseline. Highs and lows are too extreme, too prolonged, or too rapidly cycled and unpredictable. Patients with histories of attachment trauma (i.e. personality disorders) thus contain unconscious insecure working models that automatically trigger right brain stress responses at low thresholds of ruptures of the therapeutic alliance. In addition to their hypersensitivity to even low levels of interpersonal threat (narcissistic injuries), they also frequently experience enduring states of high-intensity negative affect and defensively dissociate at lower levels of stressful arousal. (2012, p. 164)

Interestingly, and in connection with Schore's findings, van der Kolk has observed a strong lateralisation of the activity of the right brain when traumatic memories are reactivated, in addition to a striking reduction of activity of the Broca area in the left hemisphere, the area known to be implicated in language and verbalisation of meaningful experiences. The possibility of attributing new meaning to the traumatic events restructures the brain activity, making it more balanced, and deactivates the excessive response of the limbic system, while augmenting the possibility of cortical awareness and explicit verbalisation.

Ruth Lanius and colleagues (2005) have shown, in functional magnetic resonance, a predominant right-hemispheric activation in post traumatic stress disorder (PTSD) patients, while they are dissociating: patients dissociate in order to escape the overwhelming emotions for which they have no words.

Implicit traumatic memories thus encoded and encysted in the right brain, in connection with amygdala activation more than cortical awareness, have to find a path towards explicit consciousness and verbal expression, which in turn means that a self with wider awareness has been restored to reality. This is the route of psychotherapy. A psychotherapy that is fine-tuned between patient and therapist through the right brain, in any case, is particularly useful for this kind of (traumatised, right-brain lateralised) patient. Narrational processes seem to be able to perform the neuronal integration that is missing or poor in traumatised minds.

Psychotherapy will work on the implicit, bodily imprints, the traces of internalised representations of past relationships, starting from attachment traces. As Siegel (1999) confirms, when implicit memory is retrieved, the neural net profiles that are reactivated involve circuits on the brain that are a fundamental part of our everyday experience of life: behaviours, emotions, and images that are encoded in non-verbal operational models of the mind are there in the here and now of the session. Destructive patterns are there repeated and enacted in moments of one-to-one exchanges in which both participants in the dialogue rehearse a right-brain-implicit model that has been interiorised (but the therapist can make use of left-brain strategies through language and interpretation, too). Especially severe patients, such as the borderline ones, prone as they are to a mass of unregulated emotions and massive primitive defences, will enact a flood of unstable and violent affects that is mostly unconscious in the sense that they cannot be cortically controlled and balanced. Any occasion in the limits of the setting of the therapy will re-enhance and reactivate the emotional *Sturm und Drang* they are subject to: the continuous storm of enactments will, on the one hand, enable the repetition of what has not been dominated and understood consciously; on the other hand will be the object of the exploration and the exchange with the ongoing dialogic mental and bodily process of the therapeutic encounter: it is the process that guides the content, this is why content *per se* and interpretation *per se* will not affect the process. Moreover, as Laub has argued, language has to be understood and will be understood within a relational process in which Freudian abreaction is not enough (as Ferenczi stated as early as 1932) and a real change in the implicit interiorised representation of experience has to be reinscribed.

As Laub and Auerhahn argue in "Failed empathy" (1989, p. 392), "since the traumatic state cannot be represented it cannot be modified by interpretation . . . and what is initially requested by the therapy is not the elucidation of the conflict but the restructuring of a new relationship and a new connection between self and other".

I totally agree with Lyons-Ruth and colleagues of the Boston Change Process Study Group (2001, pp. 13–17, in particular p. 17) when they affirm that:

> If clinical process is affect-guided rather than cognition guided, [then] therapeutic change is a process that leads to the emergence of new forms of relational organization. New experiences emerge but they are not created by the therapist for the benefit of the patient. Instead, they emerge somewhat unpredictably from the mutual searching of patient and therapist for new forms of recognition, or new forms of fitting together of initiatives in the interaction between them. (Dell & O'Neil, 2009, p. 647)

In other words, the content of the interaction needs to be "embedded" in relational experience that embodies what they call "implicit relational knowing"—an ongoing process that is itself part of the content.

Enactments are fundamental moments in the therapy with these patients, both because they are prone to act out their stressful affects and because enactments are unmediated by the left hemisphere.

As "affectively driven repetition of converging emotional scenarios from the patient's and the analyst's lives" (Maroda, 1998, p. 520) and right-brain patterns of interaction based on their own implicit and unconscious representations, enactments are fundamental tools in the therapeutic process; they are not only repetitions, but active rein-scriptions of different models of relationships that provide "a new opportunity for awareness and integration" (Maroda, 1998, p. 520).

The therapeutic movement is from unconscious cognition to unconscious emotion and self-regulatory processes. Affect regulation therapy is linked to intersubjectivity and implicit–procedural processes. In Schore's (2012) terms, enactments are right brain to right brain transference–countertransference communications, interactions occurring between the patient's relational unconscious and the thera-pist's relational unconscious.

From Freud's univocal and intrapsychic perception (corresponding to a neutral, one-sided, and, according to Ferenczi, hypocritical and cold therapeutic process) we have, therefore, arrived at an inter-subjective, relational unconscious that is right-brain based. To con-clude with Schore, "enactments, common in psychotherapy with borderline patients, potentially allow for the reorganization of cortical (orbitofrontal)–subcortical (amygdala) connectivity" (2012, p. 175).

Note

1.   I refer, of course, to Freud's theorisation that much mental life is unconscious, and within this reality some mental life is characterised by repression as an active force, established to subtract certain elements from consciousness, elements that would be unacceptable to consciousness and censorship.

References

Ammaniti, M., & Gallese, V. (2014). *The Birth of Intersubjectivity. Psychodynamics, Neurobiology and the Self.* New York: Norton.

Anderson, M. C., Ochsner, K. N., Kuhl, B., Cooper, J., Robertson, E., Gabrieli, S. W., Glover, G. H., & Gabrieli, J. D. E. (2004). Neural systems underlying the suppression of unwanted memories. *Science, 3*(5655): 232–237.

Bohleber, W. (2010). *Destructiveness, Intersubjectivity and Trauma: The Identity Crisis of Modern Psychoanalysis.* London: Karnac.

Bouchard, T. J. (1994). Genes, environment, and personality. *Science, 264:* 1700–1701.

Bowlby, J. (1969). *Attachment and Loss.* London: Hogarth.

Braun, A. R., Balkin, T. J., Wesensten, N. J., Gwadry, F., Carson, R. E., Varga, M., Baldwin, P., Belenky, G., & Herscovitch, P. (1998). Dissociated pattern of activity in visual cortices and their projection during human rapid eye movement sleep. *Science, 279*: 91–95.

Briere, J. N. (1992). *Child Abuse Trauma: Theory and Treatment of the Lasting Effects.* London: Sage.

Bromberg, P. M. (2011). *The Shadow of the Tsunami and the Growth of the Relational Mind.* New York: Routledge.

Brothers, L. (1997). *Friday's Footprint: How Society Shapes the Human Mind.* New York: Oxford University Press.

Bucci, W. (1997). *Psychoanalysis and Cognitive Science: A Multiple Code Theory.* New York: Guilford Press.

Calkins, S. D., & Fox, N. A. (1994). Individual differences in the biological aspects of temperament. In: J. E. Bates & N. A. Fox (Eds.), *Temperament: Individual Differences at the Interface of Biology and Behavior* (pp. 199–217). Washington, DC: American Psychological Association.

Carkim, J., Yeomans, F., & Kernberg, O. (1999). *Psychotherapy of Borderline Personality.* New York: Wiley.

Caruth, C. (Ed.) (2015). *Listening to Trauma. Conversations with Leaders in the Theory & Treatment of Catastrophic Experience.* Baltimore, MD: Johns Hopkins University Press.

Courtois, C. A. (1996). *Healing the Incest Wound: Adult Survivors in Therapy.* New York: Norton.

Damasio, A. (1994). *Decartes' Error: Emotion, Reason and the Human Brain.* New York: Putnam.

Dell, P. F., & O'Neil, J. A. (Eds.) (2009). *Dissociation and Dissociative Disorders: DSM-V and Beyond.* New York: Taylor and Francis Group.

Ferenczi, S. (1932). *The Clinical Diary of Sandor Ferenczi,* E. Dupont (Ed.). Cambridge, MA: Harvard University Press, 1988.

Fonagy, P. (2000). Attachment and borderline personality disorder. *Journal of the American Psychoanalytic Association, 48*(4): 1129–1145.

Fonagy, P., & Target, M. (1997). Attachment and reflective function: their role of self-organization. *Development and Psychopathology, 9*: 679–700.

Fonagy, P., Gergely, G., Jurist, E. L., & Target, M. (2004). *Affect Regulation, Mentalization, and the Development of the Self.* London: Karnac.

Freud, S. (with Breuer, J.) (1893a). On the psychical mechanism of hysterical phenomena. *S. E., 2*: 3–17. London: Hogarth.

Freud, S. (with Breuer, J.) (1895d). *Studies on Hysteria. S. E., 2.* London: Hogarth.

Freud, S. (1915e). The unconscious. *S E., 14*: 161–215. London: Hogarth.

Fuster, J. M. (1985). *The Prefrontal Cortex: Anatomy, Physiology, and the Neuropsychology of the Frontal Lobe*. New York: Raven Press.

Gabbard, G. (2014). *Psychodynamic Psychiatry in Clinical Practice*. Washington, DC: American Psychiatric Publishing.

Galin, D. (1974). Implications for psychiatry of left and right cerebral specialization: a neuropsychological context for unconscious processes. *Archives of General Psychiatry, 31*: 572–583.

Gunderson, J. G. (1996). *Borderline Personality Disorder. A Clinical Guide*. Arlington, VA: American Psychiatric Publishing.

Herman, J. J., & van der Kolk, B. A. (1987). Traumatic antecedents of borderline personality disorder. In: B. A. Van der Kolk (Ed.), *Psychological Trauma* (pp. 111–126). Washington, DC: American Psychiatric Press.

Herman, J. J., Perry, J. C., & van der Kolk, B. A. (1989). Childhood trauma in borderline personality disorder. *American Journal of Psychiatry, 146*: 490–495.

Hugdahl, K. (1995). Classical conditioning and implicit learning: the right hemisphere hypothesis. In: R. J. Davidson & K. Hugdahl (Eds.), *Brain Asymmetry* (pp. 235–267). Cambridge, MA: MIT Press.

Janet, P. (1899). *L'automatisme psychologique*. Paris: L'Harmattan, 2005.

Kagan, J. (1997). Conceptualising psychopathology. The importance of developmental profiles. *Development and Psychopathology, 9*: 321–334.

Kendler, K. S., & Eaves, L. S. (1986). Models for the joint effect of genotype of environment on liability to psychiatric illness. *American Journal of Psychiatry, 143*: 279–289.

Lanius, R. A., Williamson, P. C., Bluhm, R. L., Densmore, M., Boksman, K., Neufeld, R. W., Gati, J. S., & Menon, R. S. (2005). Functional connectivity of dissociative responses in post traumatic stress disorder: a functional magnetic resonance imaging investigation. *Biological Psychiatry, 57*: 873–884.

Laub, D. (2005). Traumatic shutdown of narrative and symbolization: a death instinct derivative? *Contemporary Psychoanalysis, 41*(2): 307–326.

Laub, D., & Auerhahn, N. (1989). Failed empathy: a central theme in the survivor's Holocaust experience. *Psychoanalytic Psychology, 6*: 377–400.

Laub, D., & Auerhahn, N. C. (1993). Knowing and not knowing massive psychic trauma: forms of traumatic memory. *International Journal of Psychoanalysis, 74*: 287–302.

Laub, D., & Lee, S. (2003). Thanatos and massive psychic trauma: the impact of the death instinct on knowing, remembering, and forgetting. *Journal of the American Psychoanalytic Association, 51*(2): 433–463.

Lingiardi, V., & Mucci, C. (2014). Da Janet a Bromberg passando per Ferenczi. *Psichiatria e Psicoterapia, XXXIII*(1): 41–62.

Liotti, G. (2000). Disorganized attachment, models of borderline states, and evolutionary psychotherapy. In: P. Gilbet & K. Bailey (Eds.), *Genes of the Couch: Essays in Evolutionary Psychotherapy* (pp. 232–256). Hove: Psychology Press.

Liotti, G. (2014). Le critiche di Pierre Janet alla teoria di Sigmund Freud: corrispondenze nella psicotraumatologia contemporanea. *Psichiatria & Psicoterapia, XXXIII*(1): 31–40.

Lyons-Ruth, K., & Jakobvitz, D. (1999). Attachment disorganization: Unresolved loss, relational violence and lapses in behavioral and attention strategies. In: J. Cassidy & P. R. Shaver (Eds.), *Handbook of Attachment* (pp. 520–554). New York: Guilford Press.

Mancia, M. (2006). Implicit memory and early unrepressed unconscious: their role in the therapeutic process (how the neurosciences can contribute to psychoanalysis. *International Journal of Psychoanalysis, 87*(1): 83–103.

Mancia, M. (2007). *Feeling the Words. Neuropsychoanalytic Understanding of Memory and the Unconscious.* London: Routledge.

Maroda, K. J. (1998). Enactment: when the patient's and the analyst's past converge. *Psychoanalytic Psychology, 15*: 517–535.

Mucci, C. (2008). *Il dolore estremo. Il trauma da Freud alla Shoah.* Rome: Borla.

Mucci, C. (2013). *Beyond Individual and Collective Trauma. Intergenerational Transmission, Psychoanalytic Treatment, and the Dynamics of Forgiveness.* London: Karnac.

Ogata, S. N. (1990). Childhood and sexual abuse in adult patients with borderline personality disorder. *American Journal of Psychiatry, 147*(8): 1008–1013.

Ogden, P., Minton, K., & Pain, C. (2006). *Trauma and the Body: A Sensorimotor Approach to Psychotherapy.* New York: W. W. Norton.

Paris, J. (2010). *Treatment of Borderline Personality Disorder.* New York: Guilford Press.

Patrick, M., Hobson, P., Castle, D., Howard, R., & Maughan, B. (1994). Personality disorder and the mental representation of early social experience. *Development and Psychopathology, 6*(2): 375–388.

Perry, B. D., Pollard, R. A., Blakeley, T. L. Baker, W. L., & Vigilante, D. (1995). Childhood trauma, the neurobiology of adaptation, and use-dependent development of the brain: how states become traits. *Infant Mental Health Journal, 16*: 271–291.

Porges, S. W. (2011). *The Polyvagal Theory.* New York: Norton.

Raz, A. (2004). The anatomical record Part B. *The New Anatomist, 281B*(1): 21–36.

Rolls, E. T. (1996). The orbitofrontal cortex. *Philosophical Transactions of the Royal Society of London: Series B. Biological Sciences, 351*: 1433–1444.

Rothbart, M. K., & Ahadi, S. A. (1994). Temperament and the development of personality. *Journal of Abnormal Psychology, 103*: 55–66.

Schore, A. N. (1994). *Affect Regulation and the Origin of the Self. The Neurobiology of Emotional Development.* Hillsdale, NJ: Lawrence Erlbaum.

Schore, A. N. (2003a). *Affect Disregulation and the Disorders of the Self.* New York: Norton.

Schore, A. N. (2003b). *Affect Regulation and the Repair of the Self.* New York: Norton.

Schore, A. N. (2011). Foreword. In: Bromberg, P. M., *The Shadow of the Tsunami and the Growth of the Relational Mind* (pp. ix–xxxvii). New York: Taylor and Francis.

Schore, A. N. (2012). *The Science of the Art of Psychotherapy.* New York: Norton.

Siegel, D. (1999). *The Developing Mind: How Relationships and the Brain Interact to Shape Who We Are.* New York: The Guilford Press.

Solms, M. (1995). New findings on the neurological organization of dreaming: implications for psychoanalysis. *Psychoanalytic Quarterly, 64*: 43–67.

Solms, M., & Turnbull, O. (2002). *The Brain and the Inner World. An Introduction to the Neuroscience of Subjective Experience.* London: Karnac.

Stern, D. N. (1985). *The Interpersonal World of the Infant.* New York: Basic Books.

Stuss, D. T., Kaplan, E. F., Benson, D. F., Qwir, W. S., Chiulli, S., & Sarazin, F. F. (1982). Evidence for the involvement of orbitofrontal cortex in memory function: an interference effect. *Journal of Comparative Physiological Psychology, 96*: 913–925.

Symonds, L. L., Gordon, N. S., Bixby, J. C., & Mande, M. M. (2006). Right-lateralized pain processing in the human cortex: an fMRI study. *Journal of Neurophysiology, 95*(6): 3823–3830.

Thomas, A., & Chess, S. (1997). *Temperament and Development.* New York: Brunner/Mazel.

Tsakiris, M., Hesse, M. D., Boy, C., Haggard, P., & Fink, G. (2007). Neural signatures of body ownership: a sensory network for bodily self-consciousness. *Cerebral Cortex, 17*: 2235–2244.

Van der Kolk, B. A. (2014). *The Body Keeps the Score.* London: Penguin Books.

Van der Kolk, B. A., & Fisher, R. E. (1994). Childhood abuse and neglect and loss of self-regulation. *Bulletin of the Menninger Clinic, 58*: 145–168.

Westen, D. (1997). Towards a clinically and empirically sound theory of motivation. *International Journal of Psychoanalysis, 78*: 521–548.

Westen, D. (1999). Scientific status of unconscious process: is Freud really dead? *Journal of the American Psychoanalytical Association, 47*: 1061–1106.

Zanarini, M. C., Gunderson, J. G., Marino, M. F., Schwartz, E. O., & Frankenburg, F. R. (1989). Childhood experiences of borderline patients, *Comprehensive Psychiatry, 30*: 18–25.

CHAPTER SIX

The role of unrepressed and repressed unconsciousness in clinical work

Giuseppe Craparo

M y purpose in this chapter is to address two different relational processes (transference–countertransference and enactment) and their respective connections to the repressed and the unrepressed unconscious.

The repressed unconscious

The repressed unconscious remains to this day a key concept in defining the work of the psychoanalyst. The innovative aspect in Freud's conceptualisation of the unconscious was not so much the hypothesis that the functioning of the psyche is influenced by conscious and unconscious content (indeed, mankind had been familiar with this idea from time immemorial) but, rather, the suggestion that the subject might repress things he prefers to know nothing about: truths, that is, that are so painful that, unless they were removed to an area outside of his awareness, might provoke an unmanageable pain. The so-called unconscious formations (e.g., neurotic symptoms), Freud tells us, are quite simply *psychic representations* of repressed contents that, thanks to defensive strategies employing condensation or displacement, are allowed to emerge to the level of consciousness. In an earlier work (Craparo, 2013), I used the notion of "un-said" in order to describe neurotic symptoms. In my perspective, a neurotic symptom consists in the negation (un/non) of unacceptable mental contents slipped out of voluntary control, and is, at the same time, an inability to speak the repressed: that is, that which is "this side" (the patient's past) and "on the other side" (a disposition towards the future) of any conscious conceptualisation. The hyphen between "un" and "said" represents the relationship, as well as the (distressing) "gap", between that which is simultaneously negated and affirmed, taking the form of a compromise (as in slips, humour, dreams, etc.).

As I see it, the un-said opens up a space through which unconscious truth can break into the analytical relationship by means of a word that points to the presence of unconscious, symbolised, emotional content (unconscious feelings) that the patient seems to prefer to remain unaware of because of the anxiety they would generate, but which, none the less, manifest themselves through constant and often embarrassing slip-ups.

One of my patients told me about a dream she had: she was at the seaside with her boyfriend when suddenly her sister's ex-fiancé appeared. She woke up covered with sweat, and as she remembered this in our session she used the word "wet". Of course, the word was meant to refer to her being sweaty, though in common usage the term also has a clear sexual connotation. When I pointed this out to my patient, she was herself surprised that she had used that word, but then also added that she had awoken from her dream in a mixed feeling of fear and arousal. Later on in the session, it emerged that the arousal was linked to an interest she had had in her sister's fiancé, an interest that had always remained unspoken because of the relationship of the man with my patient's sister. The fear was caused by her concern that those very feelings she had managed to conceal so well might be discovered by her sister, or even by the sister's boyfriend. This psychic conflict had been unconsciously resolved by my patient through experiencing a sense of guilt that led her to be completely servile and passive in relation to her sister, and also resulted in her being servile in other situations, including analysis. Clearly, in order to make these kinds of "mistakes" (such as using the word "wet" to point to what had remained un-said), mistakes that are so useful for the analytic work, the patient has to speak in a way that says more than she believes she knows.

It is against this background of analytic listening that the patient can experience her own singularity, the singularity of her own desires for which she must in time take, rather than deny, responsibility. In the case of my patient, even though "saying" the word "wet" did not allow the unconscious content to emerge into her own conscious level (though a substitute might have been extracted from content deposited in her declarative memory), it did, in fact, communicate the presence of this content to the other (i.e., myself, in this case). It is precisely within the area opened up by the ambiguity and the misunderstanding of a word that the "mistake" reveals the presence of an unconscious truth (Lacan, 1975): a word that finds its co-constructed meaning in "the act of listening on the part of the Other" (Recalcati, 2012, p. 59, translated for this edition).

In this crucial re-evaluation of the role of the symbolic, as well as of language and words, in our description of the nature of the repressed unconscious, it is paramount to always consider the importance of emotion.

In fact, also when working with neurotic patients, the analyst must always remember that it is not simply the meaning of a word but also, and sometimes above all, the *way* in which the word is pronounced that is important. Indeed, the analyst should keep this in mind even when he assesses the implications of the words he himself says.

As Mancia (2006) has argued, attention to the intonation and rhythm of the patient's voice is a useful tool for entering into empathic contact with those feelings towards which the neurotic patient displays a resistance. I still remember what an orthodox colleague once said to me in this regard: he maintained that emotion is an epiphenomenon which eliminates the chance for a patient to articulate in words something that has been repressed from consciousness because it was too distressing. "A patient", he went on to explain, "when in the grip of an emotion, may withhold the very words that would be useful for our work and would betray, if he pronounced them, an unconscious intention. This means that we must not allow emotional content to enter the scene, and that we must instead give space to the spoken word." What my colleague seemed to have overlooked, however, is that emotion is, in fact, the very *foundation of speech*. This basic idea leads us to a number of further considerations on the intersection of transference, speech, and emotion.

Transference and countertransference

Analysis is an emotional and relational experience in which the past and present of the patient are inevitably intertwined with the past and present of the analyst. Unconscious contents come to be part of the analytic process through language (both what is left *unsaid* and what is *un-said*) and its relationship with the world of emotions. Those emotions that have entered the symbolic order (feelings) are destined to be either consciously named or else, when they are a source of conflict, to be repressed, silenced, or condensed in a psychic act such as transference.

Clinical experience suggests that transference involves the patient's past and its re-evocation under the form of a psychic acting out in the relation with the analyst. It is an accepted fact that a patient's transference can be activated and may assume its expressive form in relation to the real characteristics (physical traits or emotional behaviour) of the analyst. A patient of mine, for example, became aware of a momentary distraction on my part and reacted by becoming aggressive and accusing me of not being interested in what he was saying at that moment. "I may as well stop coming, considering that I even have to pay you," he remarked vehemently. I felt unjustly accused, since my distraction was due to my attempt, before he made his remark, to understand why I felt so distant from what he was saying. I admitted that I had been distracted; however, I also added that my sense was that his angry reaction had to do with the feeling that he was repeating a scene that was familiar to him: the scene of being involved with an emotionally distant parent. At first the patient was silent, and then said that it was true, that he had never felt that his mother was close to him because she was more interested in her social life and in having a good time. As Racker (1968) would say, I had experienced, as a result of my distraction, a complementary countertransference: I had found myself cast in the role and acting the part of the patient's mother.

In the early years of psychoanalysis, countertransference was judged dismissively as an unresolved childhood conflict which impaired the analyst's capacity to listen, but it has since been re-evaluated and is now considered a precious tool that can help the analyst understand aspects of the patient's internal world as they are transferred to the scene of the analysis.

As an experience necessary for achieving empathy (Bolognini, 2001), countertransference is essentially the ideational–affective answer to the patient's transference, whereby conflictual contents in the analyst's unconscious produce a *temporary* loss of his capacity for reflection and insight. The temporary nature and the analyst's subsequent awareness of this loss are key elements in the analytical process, since, without them, the analyst would be led to collude with the patient's *mise en scène* (acting out). When this occurs, it should be understood as an indication that the analyst has failed to resolve some conflicts in his unconscious psychic life, which might impair his ability to listen.

To imagine that an analyst does not have limitations, or that he might be able to remain constantly focused on what the patient is saying, is clearly unrealistic since, as a human being, he inevitably brings his past, his personal story, his weaknesses and emotions with him into the analytic session.

> The patient evokes certain responses in the therapist, but it is the therapist's own conflicts and internal self- and object representations that determine the final shape of the countertransference response. In other words, the process requires a "hook" in the recipient of the projection to make it stick. Some projections constitute a better fit with the recipient than do others. (Gabbard, 2014, p. 48)

Acting out

We have now reached the point where it is necessary to discuss a controversial term that has been given different meanings throughout the years. Acting out is sometimes defined as having an essentially motor-impulsive nature aimed exclusively at discharging emotional tension; at other times it is defined as the externalisation of an act related to the transference outside of the clinical setting, in contrast with the acts that take place "within" the analysis (*acting in*). It is also considered by some authors as some kind of a theatrical representation (to act a part). Finally, for other analytic writers, acting out and enactment are the same thing. In my opinion, what underlies the latter interpretation is a fundamental confusion between acts that reveal contents that are related to unconscious intentions and other acts that, on the contrary, are characterised by dissociative mechanisms related to unsymbolised emotional contents: the unspeakable (traumatic emotions) that emerges from the unrepressed unconscious of traumatised subjects.

However, let us proceed in order. When acting out first emerges in the clinical situation, the analyst immediately realises that the patient is behaving in a very unusual way, or also that the patient's behavior is characterised by a certain type of resistance that limits the effectiveness of the analyst's interpretative intervention. A specific example of this would be when the patient repeats, rather than remembers, significant events in his past.

The patient does not say that he remembers that he used to be defiant towards, and critical of, his parents' authority; instead, he behaves that way to the doctor. He does not remember how he came to a helpless and hopeless deadlock in his infantile sexual researches, but he produces a mass of confused dreams and associations, complains that he cannot succeed in anything, and asserts that he is fated never to carry through what he undertakes. He does not remember having been intensely ashamed of certain sexual activities and afraid of their being found out; but he makes it clear that he is ashamed of the treatment on which he is now embarked and tries to keep it secret from everybody (Freud, 1914g, p. 150).

Unbeknown to him, the patient *is performing* his memories through a metonymic operation involving the displacement of unconscious contents from the past to the present. The close connection between transference and acting out was clear to Freud, who, not coincidentally, wrote that the patient

> does not remember anything of what he has forgotten and repressed, but acts it out. He reproduces it not as a memory but as an action; he repeats it, without, of course, knowing that he is repeating it . . . As long as he is in the treatment he cannot escape from this compulsion to repeat; and in the end we understand that is his way of remembering. (Freud, 1914g, p. 150)

It is clear from the way that acting out emerges in the clinical setting that, unlike enactment, it is directed towards another person (the analyst) who is called upon to decipher what the patient is trying to communicate. The analyst becomes aware that, through action, the patient is actually performing a truth that is too painful to bear, revealing at the same time that there are spoken words that are attempting to help that truth emerge into consciousness.

Acting out, then, has to do with repressed contents and with the return of what has been repressed in the analytic relationship. In acting out, the action is not a mere motor activity, but the expression of an unconscious intention. The intentionality to which Freud refers, however, can be understood as a kind of directionality towards an unconscious object: in other words, what Freud talks about is the tension present in affects and emotions that can find their space in the patient's awareness through a psychic act rooted in the symbolic discourse.

In its function of communication with the other, an action is, therefore, a psychic act which replaces repressed unconscious feelings. This contrasts with enactment, where the subject experiences emotional content that has remained primitive because of a lack in symbolisation contents against which he defends himself through evacuation (i.e., projective identification).

What the patient acts out are fantasies, representations associated with past feelings that he would prefer to know nothing about but which, nevertheless, come to be acted out in the analytic relation. Acting out, then, is a psychic mechanism around which the dual relation of transference and countertransference is organised, but it is also a privileged channel for the therapist to understand the unconscious dynamics that are at the root of the patient's symptoms. What I mean to say here is that symptoms, acting out, and transference are all closely intertwined. Still, in other words, acting out and transference are useful tools for getting to know about the unconscious feelings that cause the patient's symptoms. The particular characteristics of enactment make it quite different from acting out and require a separate treatment, as detailed in the following paragraphs.

The unrepressed unconscious

A ccording to Mauro Mancia (2006), the unrepressed unconscious has

its foundations in the sensory experiences the infant has with his mother (including hearing her voice, which recalls the infant prosodic experiences in the womb). It is through these sensory experiences that the mother sends to the infant messages of affectivity, emotionality, reliability, happiness and dedication. But she can also send messages that the infant can experience as traumatic, terrifying, threatening, non-reassuring or strongly frustrating ... They cannot be repressed because the structures which concern the explicit memory, indispensable for repression, are lacking. They will organize, instead, an early unrepressed unconscious nucleus of the self. (p. 88)

Franco De Masi (2015), returning to Bion's (1959, 1962) theory of the emotional–receptive unconscious (composed of the proto-emotions), described the traits of this unconscious, from which, in adequate environments, a mind may develop that is able to repress intolerable emotional contents in the dynamic unconscious. However, De Masi clearly states that this is not what happens in the case of severe pathologies. In this respect, De Masi writes,

it is my belief that at the base of the most complex psychopathologies lies the deterioration of the unconscious functions, particularly those of emotional understanding. If neurosis is the result of an inharmonious functioning of the dynamic unconscious, borderline or psychotic structures are fed by a change in the emotional–receptive unconscious, or the mental system able to symbolize emotions and use the emotional function of intrapsychic and relational communication. (2015, p. 99)

In the next paragraph, I focus on a specific mental process related to these unsymbolised emotions connected with the unrepressed unconscious.

Enactment

Described for the first time by Theodore Jacobs (1986), enactment consists in the re-actualisation of already experienced, unsymbolised unconscious emotions occurring in the relationship between patient and therapist. To be more precise, Jacobs speaks of countertransference enactment, emphasising the ways in which the analyst's personality traits, affective spectrum, representations, and conflicts affect the patient as well as the analytic relationship more generally.

Frank (1999) in turn highlights the relational nature of enactment, arguing that it consists of a "pattern of automatic preconscious interaction, that involves the individual psychodynamic systems of each participant in the therapy as well as the intersection of those two systems" (cited in Albasi, 2006, p. 213).

Above and beyond the various descriptions of its characteristics as a process, enactment should be understood as an unconscious communication of emotional content that occurs within the analytic couple. More specifically, it concerns "pre-verbal, gestural, and procedural components" (McLaughlin, 1991, cited in Filippini & Ponsi, 1993, p. 505).

For Maroda (1998), enactment occurs at the juncture of the lived emotions of the patient and the analyst. This description highlights the notion of analysis as a setting in which the analyst acts and reacts, feels emotions and takes an active part in what is happening in the here and now of his relation with the patient.

While it is true to say that the analytic relationship is constituted by two psychic worlds that meet, two stories that interact, it is important to remember that this interaction is in its essence asymmetrical. And it is precisely this asymmetry that in the first place led the patient to consult an expert whom he *supposes will know* how to help him and will understand the causes of his illness. This asymmetry is also what allows the analyst to understand *a posteriori* his own lived emotions and those of the patient, as well as how both occur in the analytic relation.

For Owen Renik (2006), enactment "is an interaction between analyst and patient in which the unconscious motivations of one or the other are expressed—an interaction in which an unconscious fantasy of the analyst's or of the patient's is realized" (p. 88). Further on, the author proposes that enactment and acting out may actually overlap, a hypothesis with which I do not agree:

> this view of enactment involves the very same thinking that has always applied to acting out. The older term *acting out* is directly linked to Freud's early, obsolete model of the mind. The newer term *enactment* leaves behind that embarrassing theoretical connection; therefore, analysts are more comfortable with it. But there is no substantial difference between the concepts of acting out and enactment, and their implications for technique are the same. (Renik, 2006, p. 88)

Thus, for Renik, there is no difference between acting out and enactment because, in his theory of the mind, these two mental processes are both related to the unrepressed unconscious. In my opinion, a distinction between the two types of unconscious (unrepressed and repressed) is necessary in order to distinguish acting out and enactment. While acting out, in accordance with Freud's drive theory, is the repetition of fantasies related to the symbolic–linguistic unconscious in the transference, enactment involves the analytic couple in acts (not actions) that are aimed at regulating primitive emotional states (traumatic emotions) that have been deposited in the unrepressed unconscious.

Following Maria Ponsi (2013), we should consider acting out and enactment as describing "situations that remain distinct under clinical observation" (p. 173).

In this regard, in his recent volume entitled *The Science of the Art of Psychotherapy*, Allan Schore wrote that

> enactment contains expressions of not only conscious but also *unconsciously strong affect*. This seminal observation clearly indicates that the clinical phenomenon of the heightened affective moment of an enactment cannot be understood without a theory of unconscious processes. (2012, p. 156)

More specifically, Schore proposes a neurobiological interpretation of enactment as an unconscious communication of affect that involves the right brain of both protagonists (patient and analyst): "enactments are dialogically re-created in right brain-to-right brain transference-countertransference communications, interactions occurring between the patient's relational unconscious and the therapist's relational unconscious" (2012, p. 158). In accordance with the developmentally focused model of psychopathology, for Schore enactments are common in psychopathologies related to early traumatic experiences.

On the relationship between enactment and trauma, Philip Bromberg (2011) maintains that enactment is a dyadic dissociative process characterised by sub-symbolic communications of "not-me" states

> that reflects those areas of the patient's self-experience where trauma (whether developmental or adult-onset) has to one degree or another compromised the capacity for affect regulation in a relational context

and thus compromised self-development at the level of symbolic processing by thought and language. (p. 16)

In other words, enactment is an unconscious communication where a patient with a history of relational trauma pushes the analyst to become attuned to those areas of himself that have been compromised by developmental trauma. For the author, trauma is caused "by 'the shock of strangeness' in an interpersonal field on which security of selfhood depends and is relative to the developmental threshold at which a person can accommodate the "strangeness" at that point in time" (Bromberg, 2003, p. 690). In relation to the activation of traumatic memories, enactment, thus, takes on the characteristics of a dyadic dissociative process of which the patient makes use, through his relationship with the analyst, in his attempt to control aspects of the self that are inaccessible to reflective functioning. Bromberg offers an evocative description of enactment by comparing it to a dissociative affective experience that is communicated within a shared "not-me" cocoon. Certainly—Bromberg argues—this cocoon exists outside of analytical relations and even before the patient gets to know the analyst, but it is in the analytical relationship that it finally becomes possible to use it in a new way. It is the only way for the analyst to come into contact with the remaining affects of the subject's evolution to a primitive presymbolic state.

Agreeing with Bromberg, Donnel Stern (2003) considers enactment as the expression of a mutual pathological dissociation on the part of both patient and analyst—a dissociation involving experiences which, to the extent that they are unsymbolised, are also untranslatable into words. More specifically, the patient "plays out" unformulated experiences that he cannot tolerate experiencing directly (2004, p. 210). Stern summarises the main characteristics of enactment in the following list (2004, p. 213):

1. Enacted experience, and, thus, dissociated states as well, cannot be symbolised and, therefore, do not exist in any other explicit form than enactment itself. Enacted experience is unformulated experience.
2. Dissociated states, because they are unsymbolised, do not and cannot bear a conflictual relationship to the states of mind safe enough for us to identify as "me" and inhabit in a consciously appreciable way.

3. Enactment is the interpersonalisation of dissociation: the conflict that cannot be experienced within one mind is experienced between or across two minds. The state dissociated by the patient is explicitly experienced by the analyst, and the state explicitly experienced by the patient is dissociated in the analyst's mind. Each participant therefore has only a partial appreciation of what is transpiring.
4. Enactment, then, is not the expression of internal conflict. Enactment is the *absence* of internal conflict—though the external conflict, the conflict between the two people in the enactment, may be intense.
5. Enactment ends in the achievement of internal conflict, which occurs when the two dissociated states, one belonging to each participant in the enactment, can be formulated inside the consciousness of one or the other of the two psychoanalytic participants.

According to Cesare Albasi (2006), enactment consists

in a "dramatization" of internal working models and dissociated internal working models of both members of the therapeutic dyad (in their implicit relational dimension) through which authentic participation is accomplished and subjectively experienced by the therapist in interaction with the patient: this is the only way in which dissociated internal working models can reveal themselves. (p. 219, translated for this edition)

In addition:

When enactments take place in the clinical relation they might hinder the ability to listen to the patient. The spontaneity of the narrative is blocked because the content of the enactments cannot be narrated. A symbolic understanding of the unformulated may, at times, be reached only at a later moment, when the dialogic narrative is reactivated. The development of mental functioning, and therefore the possibility for new versions of the Self, can be generated in the "here and now" through the use of simple expedients, a careful attention to detail, a preservation of "the secret for discovering the paintings that are hidden within other paintings"—paintings which emerge in the therapeutic process, shifting the interactive experience and giving it a new spontaneity, expanding and transforming the enactment, generating the potential for new dialogic accounts with the witness–interlocutor–therapist. (Albasi & Ferrero, 2013, p. 349, translated for this edition)

These last three authors restate the direct relation between enactment, traumatic experiences, the feelings connected with them, and dissociation.

At this point in the discussion, some clarifications are called for concerning the relation between enactment, traumatic emotions, dissociation, and the psychic mechanism that facilitates the sharing of traumatic memories: projective identification.

Enactment and traumatic emotions

I have already described traumatic emotions (Craparo, 2013) as raw, particularly intense, and concretely experienced by the subject through the body; more specifically, I have defined them as the physiologically provoked experience of unbearably painful feelings.

These are emotional contents that cannot be symbolised because they were not originally symbolised in the relationship with caring figures, often due to psychological problems in the carers (in some cases, I have observed maternal postpartum depression), who were unable to provide adequate support and mirror the emotional requests of the child: we can, thus, define these emotional contents as traumatic emotions. They are: (a) *non-symbolic*, since they are defined by their lack of mental representation; (b) *physiological*, due to the absence of reflective processes. Their activation produces stereotypical, rigid and frequently out-of-control reactions; (c) *painful*, due to their failure in identification and modulation, which produces an increase in the perceived intensity, partly resulting from an unbearable hyperarousal; (d) *disorganising*, because they activate mechanisms of disconnection in the state of the self as a response to stressful conditions experienced by the individual as a source of threat to his/her own identity.

In my opinion, there is a connection between such emotions and evolving trauma, and, more specifically, the experience of rejection and lack of emotional responsiveness on the part of the carer felt by the child in the first two years of life. I also observed that for those emotions to become truly traumatic, the period of neglect has to extend beyond the first two years of life. The intensity of those emotions is related to their disorganising power, as can be seen, for example, in cases of psychosis and borderline personality disorder; the power is such that it determines a condition of bio-psychological dissociation. The idea of an emotional origin of trauma and of dissociation recalls the theories of Pierre Janet, who recognised that violent emotions derived from traumatic events were at the root of a decomposition of consciousness, responsible for the emergence of the automatic mental states frequently observed in hysterical patients. "Emotion", writes Janet,

> exerts a disintegrative action on the mind, it diminishes its synthetic function and places it, if only temporarily, in a disrupted state. Emotions, particularly depressive ones like fear, disrupt mental synthesis; their actions are, so to speak, analytic as opposed to those of the will, attention, and perception which, in contrast, are synthetic. (Janet, 1889, p. 457, translated for this edition)

In a fashion similar to this description of violent emotions, traumatic emotions form the basis not only of mental disorganisation, but also of symbolisation deficit, mentalization, and deregulation. Traumatic emotions are, thus, at the root of a biological and psychological disaggregation of personality that can result in a secondary dissociation, a defensive response adopted in order to stop the advancement of those emotions. The consequence of this secondary dissociative reaction, which should not be confused with disaggregation, is the profound sense of emptiness that is often described to us by our seriously ill patients. But, as I have already affirmed, a more in-depth consideration leads us to see that this sense of emptiness is actually an imaginary representation of the condition of being too full of raw, sensory contents (the traumatic emotions) of which the subject can have only somatic, as opposed to episodic, memory. It is the black hole of traumatic emotion, and is comparable to the *presence of absence* or the presence of a *no-thing* (Bion, 1970) about which there can be no thought. In this regard, Bromberg (2006) speaks of dissociative emptiness, a mental condition not accessible to reflective thought, experienced by people as a "sensation of the absence rather than the presence of something" (p. 10) and as the expression of self-states that are not integrated but are distinct from each other. For Bromberg, the opposite of the sense of emptiness is the sense of *me-ness* (Bromberg, 2003). He remarked (Bromberg, 1993) that "health is the ability to stand in the spaces between realities without losing any of them—the capacity to feel like one self while being many" (p. 166). According to Bromberg's theorisation, dissociation

> is a healthy, adaptive function of the human mind. It is a basic process that allows individual self-states to function optimally (not simply defensively) when full immersion in a single reality, a single strong affect, and a suspension of one's self-reflective capacity is exactly what is called for or wished for . . . In other words, dissociation is primarily a means through which a human being maintains personal continuity, coherence, and integrity of the sense of self. (2012, p. 273)

In line with what I have argued with reference to traumatic emotions, I think that enactment has to do with conscious experience, one that results from a patient's defensive reaction to being confronted with traumatic emotions—with something, that is, which resides beyond the boundaries of any linguistic, symbolic, or reflective determination.

The activation of traumatic emotions during a session can cause the patient to react with actions aimed at creating an emotional atmosphere that might lead the analyst to experience temporary states of blackout in his reflective capacity; at any rate, this is the condition in which we can truly speak of enactment and not simply of a sort of emotional contagion. It might happen, for example, that, at a certain point, the analyst experiences emotional dulling, a sense of estrangement from his surroundings, or a perceptual alteration. Enactment, thus, marks a specific moment in the analysis in which the patient enacts traumatic emotional experiences from his past, unsymbolised emotional contents coming from his unrepressed unconscious.

The reference to the unrepressed unconscious better emphasises the clinical importance of a distinction which, if not made, might, in my opinion, lead one to make the same mistake as Renik (2006) when he likened acting out to enactment. In doing so, Renik acknowledges the existence of only one unconscious, the repressed unconscious, and he fails to consider the effects on psychic and somatic equilibrium brought about by those emotions that are located on a pre-symbolic level: that is, in the unrepressed unconscious.

The relationship between enactment
and projective identification

At this point, we need to understand which psychic mechanism the analyst can use to come into contact with the lived emotions involved in enactment. It is my belief that enactment is based on projective identification, the psychic mechanism through which the traumatic emotions present in the patient's (disorganised) unrepressed unconscious are conveyed to the analyst's (organised) unrepressed unconscious.

For Glen Gabbard (2004), the concept of enactment has gradually taken on a meaning not dissimilar to that of projective identification. He writes,

> Enactments can be a form of acting in on the part of the patient but the American Ego psychologists have underlined that there can also be a corresponding acting in on the part of the therapist. The idea of countertransference as a jointly created phenomenon is sustained by both constructs, protective identification and countertransferencial enactment: the therapist's behavior influences the transference of the patient, while the patient's behavior influences the countertransference of the therapist. (p. 158)

Formulated for the first time by Melanie Klein (1946), projective identification is described as a particular defensive mechanism aimed at controlling primitive affective states that are usually negative. In her paper entitled "Notes on some schizoid mechanisms", Klein describes projective identification (p. 102) as follows:

> Together with these harmful excrements, expelled in hatred, split off parts of the ego are also projected on to the mother or, as I would rather call it, into the mother. These excrements and bad parts of the self are meant not only to injure the object but also to control it and take possession of it. Insofar as the mother comes to contain the bad parts of the self, she is not felt to be a separate individual but is felt to be the bad self.
>
> Much of the hatred against parts of the self is now directed towards the mother. This leads to a particular kind of identification which establishes the prototype of an aggressive object relation.
>
> Also, since the projection derives from the infant's impulse to harm or control the mother he feels her to be a persecutor . . .

It is, however, not only the bad parts of the self which are expelled and projected, but also good parts of the self. Excrements then have the significance of gifts . . .

Over the years, this construct has become a sort of umbrella concept, thus maintained by Hanna Segal (1973) in the following description:

> In projective identification, a part of the patient's ego is in phantasy projected into the object, controlling it, using it, and projecting into it his own characteristics. Projective identification illustrates perhaps most clearly the connection between instincts, phantasy, and mechanisms of defense. It is a phantasy that is usually very elaborate and detailed; it is an expression of instincts in that both libidinal and aggressive desires are felt to be omnipotently satisfied by the phantasy; it is, however, also a mechanism of defense in the same way in which projection is—it rids the self of unwanted parts. It may also be used as a defense, for instance, against separation anxiety . . . Often a transference situation can only be understood in terms of projective identification, a situation, for instance, in which the patient is silent and withdrawn, inducing in the analyst a feeling of helplessness, rejection, and lack of understanding, because the patient has projected into the analyst the child part of himself with all its feelings. (pp. 11–12)

In the course of its evolution, the concept has been given a variety of formulations. It has been seen as: a pathological defense mechanism; a precocious form of empathy and the basis for symbol formation (Segal, 1973); an emotional communication in the framework of the relationship of parental reverie (Bion, 1962); or, as suggested by Malin and Grotstein (2012), as a specific way of entering into relations with others. Notably, the latter two authors hypothesised that projective identification is a normal process

> that exists from birth. It is one of the most important mechanisms responsible for growth and development through object relations. This mechanism can be described as a situation in which objects and the affects associated with them come to be re-experienced at a new level of integration so that a further synthesis and another level of development of the ego are achieved. (2012, p. 271)

Modell (1993) interpreted projective identification as a defensive measure that is useful in regulating the affects associated with traumatic memories.

According to Sands (1997), projective identification allows the therapist to come into contact with unsymbolised affects that pertain to a preverbal period of life.

From a neurobiological point of view, Schore (2012) maintains that projective identification is an unconscious communication involving the right hemispheres of both the person who projects (the patient) and the person who identifies (the therapist). The main function of this mechanism, according to Schore, is the regulation of preverbal emotions (p. 170).

Despite the broad and somewhat disorganised amount of formulations on projective identification, there is general consensus in acknowledging the primary role of the unconscious. The problem that arises at this point is which unconscious is being referred to here. Is it the repressed or the unrepressed unconscious?

In line with the theoretical–clinical perspective adopted in the preceding paragraphs, I hypothesise that projective identification has to do with the unrepressed unconscious.

In order to avoid misunderstandings, I would like to stress here that in *normal* psychic development the unrepressed unconscious plays an important role in terms of reception and projection towards higher levels of emotional communication—both functions that are carried out by the unrepressed unconscious in synergy with the repressed unconscious.

In agreement with De Masi (2015), I maintain that the unrepressed unconscious (which he calls the emotive–receptive unconscious) is an essential part of a bottom–up process whereby external stimuli are initially recognised by the emotive–receptive unconscious and subsequently passed over to the activity of the dynamic unconscious, becoming objects of reflective knowledge. According to De Masi:

> . . . The dynamic unconscious (repressed) and the emotive–receptive unconscious work in parallel. Indeed, before it can be repressed, an emotion must be intercepted and registered by a psychic receiver. In other words, the dynamic unconscious can repress affects that are incompatible only after they have been intercepted by the emotional receptors. First the subject unknowingly registers the emotions and then he makes them unconscious if they are felt to be incompatible. (2015, p. 98)

In difficult patients, for example, such as those with borderline personality disorders, what we observe is, in contrast, a psychic deficit whereby the unrepressed unconscious is disorganised to such an extent that it hinders the development of the repressed unconscious, as well as of secondary psychic functions. The responsibility for this disorganisation, as I have mentioned, is to be ascribed to the sedimentation of traumatic emotions whose unbridled force thwarts the normal development of the secondary functions of reflective knowledge, and the cognitive and meta cognitive competencies involved in social relations, affect regulation, and the management of impulses.

To return to the example of the black hole, the wider its circumference, the greater the explosive force of traumatic emotions and, consequently, the more serious the level of psychic disorganisation. In analytic relationships, it sometimes happens that in situations of stress, for example, just after an interpretation, the patient tends to enact (*mise en acte*) and unconsciously communicate, through projective identification, the traumatic emotions that have been activated in the session. A connection between both the patient's and the analyst's unrepressed unconscious is created in the analytic dyad, and the sensation experienced by the latter will be that of being enveloped in a particular emotional atmosphere in which body and sense perceptions acquire a predominant role. I remember a session when, at a certain point, my perception of the patient became altered. My vision began to blur slightly and I had the feeling that the patient had physically distanced himself from me—a feeling which, of course, did not correspond to reality. This alteration of my sensorial perception prevented me from listening to what the patient was saying. I tried to understand what was happening to me and asked my patient how he was feeling at that precise moment. He answered that he felt distant, as if he were suspended. Exploring this further, I understood that I had identified with traumatic emotions the patient had projected and which were circulating in the analytic field. I recognised that the psychosomatic reaction I had was an experience of enactment that had begun with the sharing of an unformulated sensory experience.

Like transference and countertransference, enactment is always recognised by the analyst—or, in other words, it is the analyst who *becomes aware* of the patient's enactment of his unsymbolised or pre-symbolic emotional states. In short, enactment is the result of the analyst's recovery from a temporary state of blackout of awareness which permits him to *feel together with* the patient and then *think about* what is happening in the here and now of the analytic relationship.

Essentially, then, enactment can be a favourable condition for sharing and empathising with particularly painful emotional contents. On the distinction between sharing and empathy, Bolognini has written,

> . . . from my point of view, when things go particularly well, the latter comes about as the mature and well-integrated result of a process of understanding. It occurs when feeling and thought become harmoniously shared, and organized together—and this is a process where sharing is the unrefined, necessary premise but not at all the final product, and even less a guarantee. (2001, p. 118)

I would like to conclude this section by restating the difference between the transference–countertransference relationship, which involves the repressed unconscious of the two participants, and enactment, which instead results from the experience of the analyst (equipped with an integrated unrepressed unconscious) of the traumatic emotions externalised by the patient from his disorganised or non-integrated unrepressed unconscious.

Language of the enactment

As we know, the analytic work consists in *listening* to the symptoms (to the extent that they are narratives) so that they can then be scrutinised for what they reveal about the emotional complexes implicit in them. A symptom must then be understood as an act (psychic or somatic) that inevitably has to do with the body, and so it follows that, more than focusing on the act itself, the analyst should *listen* to what the patient is saying through a particular gesture, facial expression, or tone in his voice. It is in this perspective, I believe, that the idea of psychoanalysis as a talking cure must be understood. Psychoanalytic practice is not limited to a simple deciphering of unconscious content after it has been externalised, as is believed by many inexperienced practitioners as well as by the detractors of the profession. Quite the contrary, it consists in articulating that externalised content (meaning) in a dimension of meaning-making structured around a relational field (the analytic field) where the patient addresses the other (the therapist) within the boundaries of the setting. It is important for the analyst to create a relational space which is not saturated with his own knowledge: indeed, although that knowledge can, in some ways, be reassuring, it would invariably end up limiting the patient's opportunities for emotional growth. In other words, if the analytic space is saturated, it is not possible for the analyst and the patient to meet in a space where their two psychic worlds can interact and produce a knowledge that will encourage and not block the emergence of truth. This individual truth that emerges in the analytic field is a desire-based truth that continuously and dialectically includes the other of desire, the other of language, and the other of the word. In this context, the word has a causative function. For Muriel Dimen (1998), words do not just say, they do. Language uses words to express not only a more or less refined meaning (depending on the sophistication of one's vocabulary), but also to express emotional states. This means that we can understand what is said as *a word act*. It is up to the analyst to understand the essential nature of that act.

In so far as they are acts (albeit acts with different natures), both transference and enactment speak to the other and to the self. In the case of enactment, because there is a relationship with the reality of traumatic emotions, the patient quite literally "puts into act", articulating with his body, that which "is beyond language and cannot be assimilated by symbolization" (Evans, 1996, pp. 159–60). Through its relation with the *unsaid*, enactment then talks about what the patient is unable to consciously articulate, using a language that takes its meaning from the intertwining of sounds, rhythms, voices, and gestures.

References

Albasi, C. (2006). *Attaccamenti traumatici. I modelli operativi interni dissociati.* Turin: Utet.

Albasi, C., & Ferrero, V. (2013). Racconto dialogico e testimonianza terapeutica: Dimensioni narrative del trattamento, trauma e dissociazione in una prospettiva psicoanalitica relazionale. *Psichiatria e Psicoterapia*, 32: 339–359.

Bion, W. R. (1959). Attacks on linking. *International Journal of Psychoanalysis*, 40: 308–315.

Bion, W. R. (1962). *Learning from Experience.* New York: Basic Books.

Bion, W. R. (1970). *Attention and Interpretation.* London: Tavistock.

Bolognini, S. (2001). Empathy and the unconscious. *Psychoanalytic Quarterly*, 70: 447–473.

Bromberg, P. M. (1993). Shadow and substance: a relational perspective on clinical process. *Psychoanalytic Psychology*, 10: 147–168.

Bromberg, P. M. (2003). One need not be a house to be haunted. *Psychoanalytic Dialogues*, 13: 689–709.

Bromberg, P. M. (2006). *Awakening the Dreamer: Clinical Journeys*. Mahwah, NJ: The Analytic Press.

Bromberg, P. M. (2011). *The Shadow of the Tsunami*. New York: Routledge.

Bromberg, P. M. (2012). *The Shadow of the Tsunami and the Growth of the Relational Mind*. New York: Routledge.

Craparo, G. (2013). Addiction, dissociazione e inconscio non rimosso. Un contributo teorico secondo la prospettiva evolutivo-relazionale. *Ricerca psicoanalitica*, 24: 73–84.

De Masi, F. (2015). *Working with Difficult Patients*. London: Karnac.

Dimen, M. (1998). Polyglot bodies: thinking through the relational. In: A. Lewis & F. S. Anderson (Eds.), *Relational Perspectives on the Body* (pp. 65–93). New York: Routledge.

Evans, D. (1996). *An Introductory Dictionary of Lacanian Psychoanalysis*. New York: Routledge.

Filippini, S., & Ponsi, M. (1993). Enactment. *Rivista di Psicoanalisi*, 39: 501–516.

Freud, S. (1914g). Remembering, repeating, and working-through. *S. E.*, 12, 147–156. London: Hogarth.

Gabbard, G. O. (2004). *Long-term Psychodynamic Psychotherapy: A Basic Text*. Washington, DC: American Psychiatric Publishing.

Gabbard, G. O. (2014). *Psychodynamic Psychiatry in Clinical Practice* (5th edn). Washington, DC: American Psychiatric Publishing.

Jacobs, T. J. (1986). On countertransference enactments. *Journal of the American Psychoanalytic Association*, 34: 289–307.

Janet, P. (1889). *L'automatisme psychologique*. Paris: Alcan.

Klein, M. (1946). Notes on some schizoid mechanisms. *International Journal of Psychoanalysis*, 27: 99–110.

Lacan, J. (1975). *Le séminaire de Jacques Lacan. Livre I. Les écrits technique de Freud*. Paris: Seuil.

Malin, A., & Grotstein, J. S. (2012). Projective identification in the therapeutic process. In: E. Spillius & E. O'Shaughnessy (Eds.), *Projective Identification. The Fate of a Concept* (pp. 264–274). New York: Routledge.

Mancia, M. (2006). Implicit memory and early unrepressed unconscious: their role in the therapeutic process. *International Journal of Psychoanalysis*, 87: 83–103.

Maroda, K. J. (1998). Enactment. When the patient's and analyst's pasts converge. *Psychoanalytic Psychology*, 15: 517–535.

Modell, A. H. (1993). *The Private Self*. Cambridge, MA: Harvard University Press.

Ponsi, M. (2013). Development of psychoanalytic thought: acting, acting out, enactment. *The Italian Psychoanalytic Annual*, 7: 161–176.

Racker, H. (1968). *Transference and Countertransference*. New York: International Universities Press.

Recalcati, M. (2012). *Jacques Lacan. Desiderio, godimento e soggettivazione*. Milan: Raffaello Cortina.

Renik, O. (2006). *Practical Psychoanalysis for Therapists and Patients*. New York: Other Press.

Sands, S. (1997). Self psychology and projective identification-whither shall they meet? A reply to the editors (1995). *Psychoanalytic Dialogue*, 7: 651–668.

Schore, A. (2012). *The Science of the Art of Psychotherapy*. New York: W. W. Norton.

Segal, H. (1973). *A Kleinian Approach to Clinical Practice*. London: Jason Aronson.

Stern, D. B. (2003). The fusion of horizons. *Psychoanalytic Dialogues*, 13: 843–873.

Stern, D. B. (2004). The eye sees itself. *Contemporary Psychoanalysis*, 40: 197–237.

The psychoanalytic clinical unconscious: a guide for the perplexed?

Howard B. Levine

"Our problem . . . is, how are we to see, observe . . . these things which are not visible?"

(Bion, 2005a, p. 38)

Apologia

It is hard to imagine a concept that is more central to psychoanalysis than that of the unconscious. Indeed, Freud (1923a, p. 247) believed that affirming the existence of unconscious mental processes was one of the required "corner-stones of psycho-analytic theory."

> The assumption that there are unconscious mental processes, the recognition of the theory of resistance and repression, the appreciation of the importance of sexuality and of the Oedipus Complex – these constitute the principle subject matter of psycho-analysis and the foundations of its theory. (Freud, 1923a, p. 247)

While few, if any, in a psychoanalytic audience would doubt or question that assumption, after more than a century of analytic practice, we find ourselves still struggling to fully operationalise and define the limits of this core foundational term, as we continue to debate and disagree about its very nature and structure.

One strategy for attempting to refine our understanding of what we mean by the unconscious, a strategy favoured by many of the contributors to this volume, has been to re-examine classical analytic formulations in the light of discoveries in related fields, such as neuroscience, cognitive psychology, parent–infant interaction, and developmental psychology. This strategy is clearly of interest in an intellectual sense and, when it leads to a verification of psychoanalytic propositions, it may also prove supportive for analysts who are concerned about the status of psychoanalysis as a science or medical sub-speciality. However, as Roussillon (2011) points out, if the encounter between psychoanalysis and the facts and theories derived from adjacent or related disciplines is to prove to be truly constructive, any adumbration of psychoanalytic theory so derived must "prove its generative potentiality with regard to interpretation or free association" (p. 222). That is, the "proof of the pudding" will be in what the newly proposed additions do or do not add to the core of the analytic *clinical* process.

Analysts who look to neuroscience often do so with an eye to demonstrating that "Freud was right" by showing that there is congruence within, and support from, allied fields for basic psychoanalytic propositions. Such congruence could also prove useful for the field as a whole in the competing marketplace of government and insurance regulations, public relations, etc. The crucial question I wish to raise following Roussillon, however, is *whether—or to what extent— this or any other strategy opens new ways of thinking about analytic process, therapeutic action, psychic functioning, and emotional development.* If it does, then we and our patients will reap the benefits; if not, then we run the risk of merely proposing new, more "fashionable" labels for already existing concepts and formulations; that is, pouring old wine into new bottles.

It is my belief that we now have sufficient clinical experience and maturation of our science as to put to rest questions of psychoanalysis's "usefulness" or "validity". (Unfortunately, *viability*, which is an economic and political question, may be another matter.) Thus, psychoanalytic propositions should not be judged on the basis of their congruence with facts or formulations that reside in related disciplines. Psychoanalysis is a unique and singularly individual practice and field of study and so the most important measure of any reformulation of the definition, limits, or structure and content of such a central term as the unconscious will be its implications and relevance for our clinical work with patients. Without this crucial, pragmatic *clinical* touchstone and anchor, investigations into related fields and the debates and disagreements that those investigations can produce might yield results that are at best interesting from an historical, factual, or biological vertex and, at worst, might prove to be yet another bout of infighting, politics, and polemics in our continuing intra- and extra-territorial turf battles and culture wars.

The view that I am advancing rests squarely on the assertion that, as a clinical praxis, psychoanalysis is not simply a derivative or component of psychiatry, general psychology, or biology, but is, and deserves to be seen as, a unique and significant domain of human endeavour. Bion (1970) made a similar point when he contrasted psychoanalysis to the study of physical medicine:

> Most people think of psycho-analysis, as Freud did, as a method of treatment for a complaint. The complaint was regarded as similar to a physical ailment, which, when you know what it is, has to be treated in accordance with the rules of medicine. The parallel with medicine was, and still is, useful. But as psycho-analysis has grown so it has been seen to differ from physical medicine until the gap between them has passed from the obvious to the unbridgeable. (p. 6)

Bion (1970) also noted that if an analyst maintains a consistent psychoanalytic perspective and method (e.g., attempting to encounter each patient in each session without memory and desire) then "the experience the analyst gains bears little resemblance to the files and case histories with which psychiatry is familiar" (p. 49). One could whimsically—but still quite seriously—assert that while medicine concerns itself with the biology of the body, psychoanalysis, as the Greek origin of the work, *psyche*, implies, is a *praxis of the soul*.

Thus, my contention that the "validity" of psychoanalysis, as a unique and separate domain, will not depend upon its congruence with discoveries or established views of related fields, but on its efficacy in facilitating a certain kind of therapeutic change. I say "a certain kind", because I believe that, at its best and most powerful, analytic therapy holds out the promise of a distinctive form of therapeutic action and change that includes, but goes beyond, improved adaptation. The latter, which is the provenance of many different kinds of psychotherapy and is also a by-product of successful psychoanalysis, is significant and worthwhile as a therapeutic aim in its own right. Yet, the aims and potential rewards of psychoanalysis are qualitatively different and go beyond the strengthening of defences and better adaptation to the circumstances of one's life. The therapeutic action and change that is possible in psychoanalysis is what analysts refer to when they speak about psychic growth and the *expansion* of the unconscious. (See, also, Bion's 1970 assertion that psychoanalysis is an investigation that expands the very field it seeks to explore.)[1]

Psychoanalytic discourse in its unique and peculiar psychoanalytic setting (Bleger, 2013)—for the psychoanalytic setting is truly that; a thing unto itself—seems to concentrate and focalise a potential in human interaction and relationships that stimulates emotional growth and development and is inherently therapeutic. When it works—and to the extent that it works—in any given individual instance, it deepens one's emotional contact with one's self and others, liberates and enriches one's mind, and fosters emotional growth and development. It is not that we do not sometimes "get better" as a result of our more ordinary familial and social relationships and interactions, or that we do not benefit from other kinds of therapy. It is that the power of whatever it is that catalyses and produces those "getting better" forces in the course of human relationships can be magnified and intensified in the analytic relationship and setting, igniting and focalising the unique and qualitatively different curative power of psychoanalysis.

Readers of this book will immediately note that this view, of the independence of psychoanalysis as a clinical field, may be in stark contrast to, and an abrupt departure from, that of the other contributors, with their emphasis on trying to affirm and amend psychoanalytic thinking by integrating it with contemporary discoveries in neuroscience, cognitive psychology, and attachment theory. Of course, the latter are each worthwhile areas of study in their own right and, as Roussillon (2011) has said, if their findings can contribute something to psychoanalysis, so much the better. But, as I have implied, I believe that the power and relevance of these disciplines might principally belong to domains that are more directly biological, psychological, and developmental than psychoanalytic. In addition to the pragmatic question of what implication any given finding in these fields may have for analytic clinicians, I would argue that these other disciplines occupy a different conceptual, epistemological realm than does psychoanalysis.[2] They are closer to *factual reality*, while psychoanalysis occupies a unique position in the realm of what we have come to call *psychic reality*.

I make this assertion with some trepidation, aware that I may be creating a self-serving fiction built on an axiomatic base that has no justification or possibility for "proof" or disproof in the factual world of external reality. But, as readers might see if they continue, this is exactly the point and the problem.

In his Tavistock Seminars, Bion (2005b) put the matter this way:

> When we are at a loss we invent something to fill the gap of our ignorance . . . The more frightening the gap . . . the more we are pressed from outside and inside to fill the gap . . . [I]n a situation where you feel completely lost . . . you are thankful to clutch hold of any system, anything whatever that is available on which to build a kind of structure. So from this point of view it seems to me that we could argue that the whole of psychoanalysis fills a long-felt want by being a vast Dionysiac system; since we don't know what is there, we invent these theories and build this glorious structure that has no foundation in fact—or the only fact in which it has any foundation is our complete ignorance, our lack of capacity. (p. 2)

The saving grace is that this is not always and inevitably the case:

> However, we hope . . . that psychoanalytic theories [and interpretations] would remind you of real life at some point in the same way as a good novel or a good play would remind you how human beings behave. (Bion, 2005b, p. 2)

Thus, while some propositions in psychoanalysis and its metapsychology might turn out to be demonstrable in "real world" terms or may be verified or supported by the findings of other disciplines, psychoanalysis as a clinical praxis might, at certain points and perhaps even in large measure, have to rest upon a theory of psychic functioning and therapeutic action that, in "reminding us how human beings behave", may answer only to the question: "Is it clinically useful to make this assumption?" and not "Can it be proved to be true in the so-called 'real world' of neurobiology, neuroscience, and developmental psychology?"

It is for this reason that I am asserting that the validity of psycho-analysis is best demonstrated by its clinical successes, which, although difficult to come by, hard to describe, and nearly impossible to predict ahead of time, none the less are powerful and do exist. Demonstrating the "validity" of psychoanalysis is akin to the old quip in response to the question, "Is sex dirty?" . . . "Only if you do it right!" So, even if to some, or even large, extent psychoanalysis rests upon assumptions and propositions that are not veridically true as measured in objective terms as stated in related disciplines, if they are pragmatically useful in the analytic clinical setting, then this in itself is sufficient testimo-nial to their "validity" and will justify their existence and use.

My position, of course, is also very different from one side of Freud, who, from all accounts, remained a Helmholtzian biologist at heart. He believed that there existed a discoverable, neuro-anatomical basis for psychoanalytic formulations and used quasi-anatomical spatial models to describe the psychic apparatus and its modes of functioning. In retrospect, when looked at from a historical perspective, I believe that Freud's grounding in neurology and the neuroscience and biology of his day offered him a rich and evocative set of metaphors, which helped shape his creativity and thinking and which he used to formu-late and develop a powerful and rather ingenious system of concepts that have become the foundational basis of our field. Even though he described his metapsychology as the scaffolding that can be discarded as we gain experience and accumulate new and more specific know-ledge and findings, I have found his meta-theories to be of continuing use in helping to generate new clinical concepts and formulations, even as I remain aware that these might be useful only as "mythic" assumptions with which to operate in the clinical field and may never turn out to be demonstrably "true" in real world terms.

A statement of the problem

Inevitably, we live and function in a world of psychoanalytic plural-ism. As Green (2005) aptly noted, the clinical experiences that led Freud (1923b) to reformulate his first topography produced a

> dispersion, or even fragmentation of psychoanalytic thought into many opposing theories (ego psychological, Kleinian, Lacanian,

Bionian, Winnicottian, Kohutian, etc) . . . all [of which could] be interpreted as attempts to propose a solution to the limitations of the
results of classical treatment. (p. 47)

In addition, *the domain of psychic reality is the realm of the ineffable.* There
are major epistemological differences between psychic reality and
consensually validatable social or "commonsense" reality and these
spill over into our psychoanalytic usage and understanding of what
we mean by "the unconscious" and extend to related ideas, such as
our conceptualisations of "memory", "thought", and "perception".

Bion (1970) addressed an important dimension of this epistemological divide in *Attention and Interpretation*, when he said that psychoanalytic enquiry is dependent upon the recognition and exploration of
a kind of experience that is not of the senses. While a physician may
observe (see) a patient's jaundice, feel (touch) their irregular pulse, or
recoil at the stench (smell) of an infected wound, "the realizations
with which a psycho-analyst deals cannot be seen or touched; anxiety
has no shape or colour, smell or sound" (p. 7).

Of course, anxiety may produce physiological changes that are
observable, such as rapid pulse or respirations, sweating, etc. However, Bion considered these to be secondary to the thing-in-itself, the
psychic state. While they might lead one to infer its presence, that
inference or indication is not assumed to be the same as observing the
psychic state.

If Bion is correct, then he is in a sense—or in some instances—
questioning the value of empirical observation as a fundamental tool
for psychoanalysis. Thus, he proposed "to use the term 'intuit' as a
parallel in the psychoanalyst's domain to the physician's use of 'see,'
'touch,' 'smell,' and 'hear'" (Bion, 1970, p. 7). In elevating the analyst's
intuition to a place analogous to that of empirical observation in physical medicine, Bion was implicitly indicating that the realm of psychic
reality is the ultimate subject of psychoanalytic investigation and
concern and preparing the way for valorising a theory of unconscious
communication based upon the communicative dimension of projective identification and the processes of container–contained. He was
also responding—and perhaps also inadvertently contributing—to
what Kirsner (2000) called the "epistemic anxiety" inherent to our
field. That is, bringing to the fore the uncertainty attending the questions "What do we know and how do we come to know it?" and

underlining the necessity of our sitting for long periods of time with patients in relative states of confusion and ignorance (what Bion (1970), following the poet, Keats, called "negative capability").

The psychoanalytic unconscious

In regard to the nature of the unconscious, I have argued elsewhere (Levine, 2013, pp. 42–43) that:

> When Freud (1900a, 1901b) first demonstrated that unconscious thoughts and feelings could be both legible and comprehensible, his discovery was so powerful that it may have obscured the fact that he only claimed that *some part* of the unconscious can be known by the symbolic traces it leaves on our conscious, waking lives. Freud (1915) delineated this portion when he noted that some unconscious instinctual impulses are "highly organized, free from self-contradiction" (Freud, 1915e, p. 190), relatively indistinguishable in structure from those which are conscious or pre-conscious and yet "they are unconscious and incapable of becoming conscious". (Freud, 1915e, pp. 190–191)

> He continued, "*qualitatively* they belong to the system *Pcs.* but *factually* to the *Ucs*" (Freud, 1915e, pp. 190–191, original italics).

> The distinction that Freud was making was between the organised, articulatable subset of the unconscious that we call the repressed, or dynamic, unconscious and the much larger, perhaps infinite, formless, not yet organised, and not yet articulated or articulatable subset of "pre-" or "proto-psychic" elements that we might call the unstructured or unformulated unconscious. How small a part the repressed unconscious is of all that is unconscious and of the totality of what can ever come to be known about the psyche or about one's own, raw existential unconscious Experience is often overlooked.

In the passage above, I have capitalised the word, Experience, to indicate raw, existential Experience in contrast to the more ordinary "experience" with a small e, which refers to that which is potentially knowable and amenable to self-perception and self-reflection. While aspects of "small e experience" are sometimes unconscious, they are organised psychic elements that are potentially knowable, articulatable, and contained within the psyche. In contrast, Experience with a capital E, like Bion's (1970) O, can never, in its unmodified form, be fully known or contained within the mind as thought or perception and is most usefully thought of as pre-psychic or proto-psychic.

I further assume, following Bion (1970), that "Experience" is inherently—or potentially—traumatic, unless and until it can be transformed into something containable within the mind, that is, into "experience". So, for example, the capacity to use what we colloquially would call "a traumatic event" and turn it into a work of art would, according to this formulation, be an example of Experience (the raw, unmodulated happening) being transformed into experience (the perceived and articulatable version of that Experience) and then the latter being further transformed into the work of art.

The problem, then, in trying to come in contact with and discern what is unconscious in the other or in our selves, is that we are in pursuit of something which is not directly available to our senses, may be emergent rather than fully formed and hidden, is part of a domain of psyche that is always expanding, can never be completely contained within the mental apparatus, and, therefore, can never be fully known. In contrast to the more limited view of classical analysis, which taught us to rely upon observation and inference as we search for or await the emergence of something organised but *hidden* in the minds of our patients, contemporary formulations remind us that since it is the very capacity to think that is at issue, what we are after might not yet have achieved a level of specificity and organisation as to be discernible and hidden; might not yet be embedded in a network of associated meanings; might not yet have achieved a specific form, and so might "exist" only as a spectrum of possibilities that have yet to come into existence.

Another way of framing the problem—or possibility—of the emergent unconscious is to ask if our theories assume that all Experience, internal and external, somatic (e.g., drive) based or perceptual, is registered as psychic *ab initio* or else, as in Freud's description of the drives as a "frontier concept" between soma and psyche, requires some form of "work" to be performed upon it in order to become psychic. That is, is there experience, perhaps deriving from the soma, the preverbal period of infancy, or from traumatic states, that is inscribed—somewhere, somehow—but not yet *psychically* represented? If so, how do we understand such inscriptions and speak about their impact? What kinds of theories are available to us to do so? Do we hold a theory that assumes that all registrations of drive derivatives and perceptions, internal and external, are psychic in some sense and so there is no "frontier" in need of crossing? Or do we believe that some registrations are pre- or proto-psychic, not yet organised, and a theory of frontier crossing, perhaps from soma to psyche, is necessary? Most important of all, what are the clinical implications and opportunities afforded by the adoption of such a theory?

The ego psychology and conflict theory that I grew up with seemed to make the tacit assumption that all experience, internal and external, was psychically represented, even if unrecoverable or too deeply defended against to ever become conscious. Similarly, the usual reading of Kleinian theory implies that all internal experience is organised and stored as "unconscious phantasy" somewhere in the mind and so, by definition, is both psychic and represented.

In contrast, the theories of André Green (following Winnicott's 1971) description of de-cathexis) and the Paris Psychosomatic School allow that traumatic disruptions of psychic organisation can produce areas of psychic void, de-cathexis or discontinuity in psychic organisation and functioning; what Green (2005) called "tears in the fabric of the psyche". These, in turn, can lead to, or are associated with, weakness, loss, or failure of representation that clinically manifests itself as "overload phenomena", such as impulsive discharges, affect storms, somatic illnesses, structural failures of the capacity for thought, and symptoms associated with massive economic imbalances and breakdowns.

The term representation (*Vorstellung*) is one that has roots in Freud's metapsychology and that we confuse with similar terms from neuroscience or child development at our conceptual peril. Representation in the Freudian, psychoanalytic sense is the culmination of a process through which drive (often manifest in the conscious mind as an aspect of affect), object, ideational content, and unconscious or disguised phantasies must all be linked. It is also the prerequisite for the creation of symbols, the linkage of associational chains, and the production of night-time and waking dreams.

It is important to emphasise that references to representational "weakness" or absence do not necessarily imply a complete lack of "registration" or "inscription" in the psyche or soma, but to different levels or gradients of registration or inscription, with representation being among the most highly organised and advanced.³ Such references, however, present epistemological problems, as they shift the ground on which psychoanalytic technique must stand from that of the discovery or recovery of veridical and objective historical truth towards the phenomenological ambiguity of the *creation* of psychic reality, the necessity of co-construction and beyond, towards the *actual* and the truly ineffable.⁴

If these not-yet-emerged potential elements are to achieve any form at all (become saturated and associatively connected to other psychic elements—memories, thoughts, feelings, desires), that form will only be shaped as a result of our analytic efforts. These efforts have been described by various authors using many different names, such as construction or co-construction, alpha function, working as a similar other, figurability, etc. What they have in common, however, is the expansion of mind and the development and strengthening of mental processes and the capacity for thought, rather than the retrieval or recollection of past forgotten memories.

The necessity—indeed, the inevitability—of the analyst's participation in the catalysis of the emergence and creation of these newly created psychic elements underlines the problems of suggestion, compliance, and the analyst's authority in the construction of truth in the analytic setting. When new forms are created—or co-created—rather than uncovered and new meanings are established, how are we to distinguish the "spontaneous gesture" that marks the creation, acceptance, or appearance of the patient's true self (Winnicott) from the imposition of an alien, false (analytic) self upon the Other? This might prove to be an insoluble problem for psychoanalysis, but one that we must struggle and live with, none the less.

While one might interrogate the emergent unconscious and the processes that lead to its creation from the cognitive psychological perspective of implicit and explicit memory, I think the reader can see that that interrogation might not necessarily add to the clinical implications or importance of similar phenomena seen from the more interior psychoanalytic perspective of Green, Bion, Winnicott, and others' adumbrations of Freud's theory of psychic representation. (For a more extensive immersion in the latter, I would refer readers to Levine et al., 2013 as a starting point and introduction to an extensive and rapidly developing literature.)

Coda

As a final thought, I would like to re-emphasise that any advances in the clinical understanding of the unconscious and the expansions of analytic listening and technique that may follow are welcome and necessary additions to our praxis. But the kind of addition to our understanding of the unconscious that I favour comes most urgently from a deeper experience of analytic clinical experience than from adjacent fields of interest.

Bion teaches us that facts by themselves are of limited use. They must be worked upon by the mind, "dreamt", to achieve personal meaning, just as dreams must be interpreted in order to be more truly understood. This is as true of our theoretical investigations and excursions as it is in the clinical setting. The shift in analytic focus from neurotic organisations and states to pathologies of narcissism, identity formation, and subjectivisation has been accompanied by a change in analytic aim from the recovery of repressed memories to the development and strengthening of the mind and creation of the capacity to think. This has led analysts further and further into the exploration and formulation of the realm of non-verbal "languages" and forms of communication: "memories in feeling" (Klein, 1957, p. 180), proto-emotions (Bion, 1962), and the "languages" of the body and the act, all of which are, in the words of Roussillon (2011),

> fundamentally ambiguous. They bear a potential, virtual meaning, but one that depends upon the meaning that the object, to which it is directed, gives to it. It is a language which, more than any other, must be "interpreted". It is but the potential for meaning, the bearer of potential: it is meaning that has not yet been finished (Freud would say that it is incomplete). It seeks a respondent, it does not exhaust its meaning in a single expression, and the reaction or the response of the object is necessary for its signifying integration. (pp. 203–204)

As I have tried to indicate, this is the domain of the pre-verbal, the traumatic, and what Freud called the id; of the unrepresented and weakly represented in search of transformation and emergence and in process of becoming. The means through which such transformational processes are helped to occur is provided by the unconscious, inter-subjective relationship. I believe that rather than turning to other disciplines, psychoanalysis is best served in its growth and evolution by the addition of an understanding of the emergent and unstructured unconscious to our well-developed understanding of the repressed or dynamic unconscious. The appreciation of the clinical implications and opportunities that this addition provides will give analysts the opportunity to more comfortably think and operate *analytically* in their clinical encounters with the more primordial, archaic, and traumatically organised and derived parts of their patients' personalities.

Notes

1. The domain of personality is so extensive that it cannot be investigated with thoroughness. . . . The more nearly thorough the investigation, the clearer it becomes that however prolonged a psycho-analysis may be it represents only the start of an investigation. It stimulates growth of the domain it investigates. (Bion, 1970, p. 69).

2. Roussillon (2011) offers a similar view:

    The issue of research in psychoanalysis—or, better, that of the relationship between psychoanalysis and research—cannot be dealt with straightaway as if . . . it was sufficiently clearly defined to be worked upon without any epistemological preamble. The manner in which the question is usually approached does, indeed, seem . . . to be marked by a series of confusions that *ab initio* make the whole matter more obscure. (p. 211)

3. The presumed "location" of non-representational registrations or inscriptions will depend on the particular theory one holds.
4. I believe that this was, in part, what Bion (1970) had in mind when he said that psychoanalytic enquiry is dependent upon the recognition and exploration of a kind of experience that is not of the senses: "the realizations with which a psycho-analyst deals cannot be seen or touched; anxiety has no shape or colour, smell or sound" (p. 7).

References

Bion, W. R. (1962). *Learning From Experience*. London: Heinemann
Bion, W. R. (1970). *Attention and Interpretation*. New York: Basic Books.

Bion, W. R. (2005a). *The Italian Seminars*. London: Karnac.

Bion, W. R. (2005b). *The Tavistock Seminars*. London: Karnac.

Bleger, J. (2013). *Symbiosis and Ambiguity*. Hove: Routledge.

Freud, S. (1900a). *The Interpretation of Dreams*. S. E., 4–5. London: Hogarth.

Freud, S. (1901b). *The Psychopathology of Everyday Life*. S. E., 6: 1–310. London: Hogarth.

Freud, S. (1915e). The unconscious. S. E., 14: 159–216. London: Hogarth.

Freud, S. (1923a). Two encyclopedia articles. S. E., 18: 233–259. London: Hogarth.

Freud, S. (1923b). *The Ego and the Id. S. E., 19*: 109–124. London: Hogarth.

Green, A. (2005). *Key Ideas For A Contemporary Psychoanalysis. Misrecognition and Recognition of the Unconscious*, A. Weller (Trans.). London: Routledge.

Kirsner, D. (2000). *Unfree Associations*. London: Process Press.

Klein, M. (1957). Envy and gratitude. In: *Envy and Gratitude and Other Works* (pp. 176–235). New York: Delacorte Press.

Levine, H. B. (2013). The colourless canvas: representation, therapeutic action, and the creation of mind. In: H. B. Levine, G. S. Reed, & D. Scarfone (Eds.), *Unrepresented States and the Construction of Meaning: Clinical and Theoretical Contributions* (pp. 42–71). London: Karnac.

Levine, H. B., Reed, G., & Scarfone, D. (Eds.) (2013). *Unrepresented States and the Creation of Meaning: Clinical and Theoretical Contributions*. London: Karnac.

Roussillon, R. (2011). *Primitive Agony and Symbolization*. London: Karnac.

Winnicott, D. W. (1971). *Playing and Reality*. London: Tavistock.

INDEX